MW01595073

CONSIDER A CHRISTIAN COLLEGE

A Guide to 78 Private Liberal Arts
Colleges and Universities Combining
Academic Excellence and Enduring
Spiritual Values

Second Edition

Christian College Coalition

Peterson's Guides
Princeton, New Jersey

Library of Congress Cataloging-in-Publication Data

Consider a Christian college : a guide to 78 private lib-
    eral arts colleges and universities combining aca-
    demic excellence and enduring spiritual values /
    Christian College Coalition. — 2nd ed.
        p. cm.
    Includes index.
    ISBN 1-56079-019-9
        1.   Church colleges—United States—Directories.
    I. Christian College Coalition (U.S.)
    L901.C828   1990
    378.73—dc20

                                                        90-38504
                                                        CIP

Composition and design by Peterson's Guides

Cover design by Laurie Lohne

Printed in the United States of America

10 9 8 7 6 5 4 3 2 1

CONTENTS

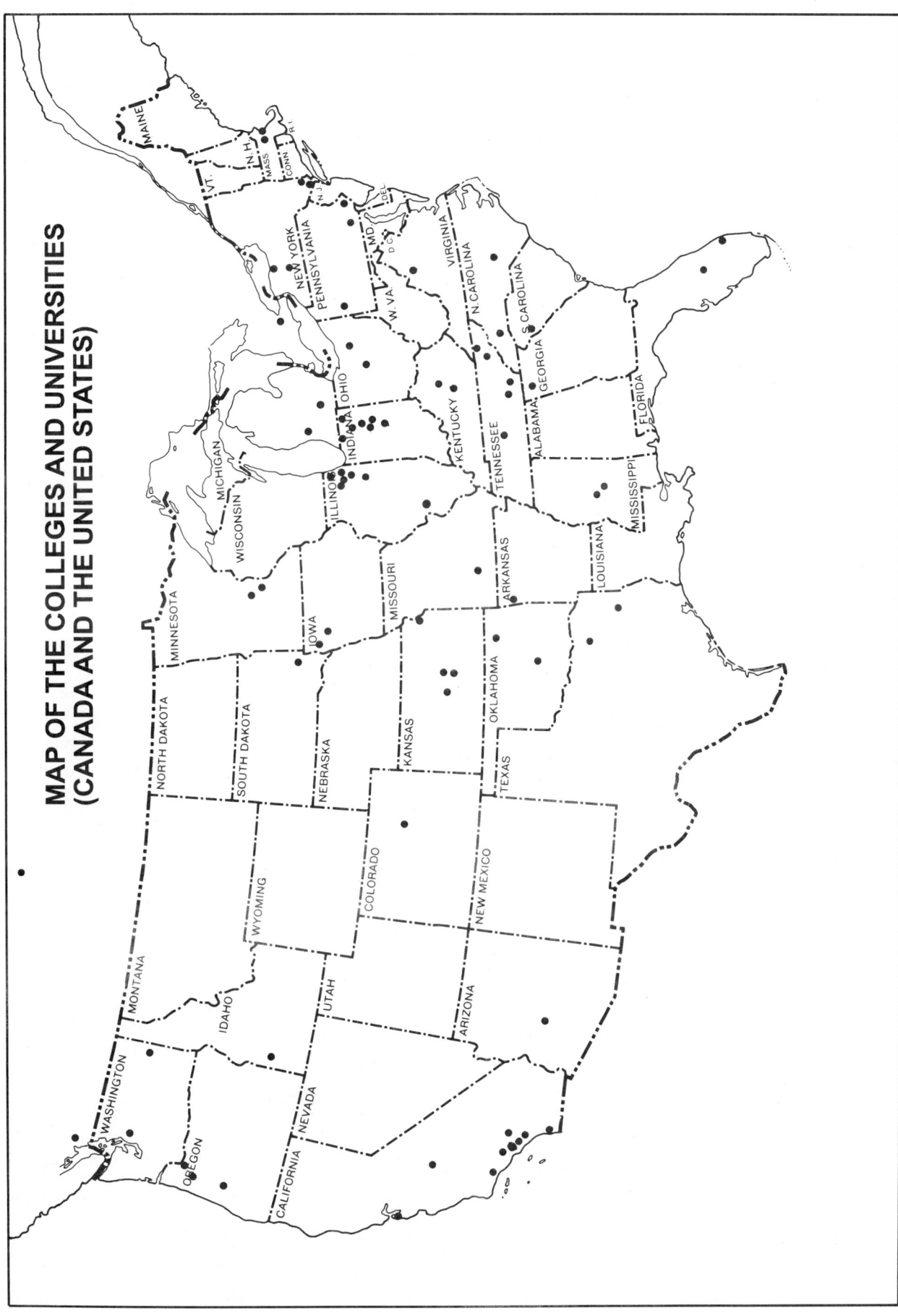

MAP OF THE COLLEGES AND UNIVERSITIES (CANADA AND THE UNITED STATES)

▼ *Whitworth College*

WHY CONSIDER A CHRISTIAN COLLEGE?

Do you want a college education that will prepare you for a job, teach you how to learn, and open the door to deep and lasting friendships? Are you seeking a college where people are valued and values are paramount? Do you believe that a complete education is one that addresses every aspect of our humanity and treats each student as a magnificently unique gift to the world? If so, then consider a Christian college or university.

We're absolutely convinced that a Christian liberal arts college education is "right" for tens of thousands of young people. *Consider a Christian College* is designed to give you a sense of the flavor and philosophy of Christian colleges today. Read. Reflect. Consider. Consider a Christian liberal arts college.

THE CHRISTIAN COLLEGE DIFFERENCE

What sets Christian colleges apart from other institutions—more than size or academic offerings or denominational ties—is the educational environment: the culture of living and learning, sharing and caring.

At Christian colleges, students—and faculty—struggle with basic human questions. For example, "How can I square my Christian beliefs with being successful in today's materialistic world?" "What is 'success' for a Christian?" "How can I live in harmony alongside others whose beliefs differ from mine?" "How can I really be 'my brother's keeper'?" and "Who is my brother?"

At Christian liberal arts colleges, the integration of faith and learning is an ongoing quest. It is not a matter of teaching "Christian biology," "Christian music," or "Christian political science." It is a matter of viewing the facts and theories of various disciplines from a Christian perspective. For, indeed, as we go out into the world to do our chosen work—be it as a biologist, a musician, or a political scientist— we cannot leave our faith back home. We take our values and mindsets and ethical barometers with us wherever we go. The Christian college environment helps students integrate faith and learning and pre-

Anderson University ▼

pares students to live out their faith in all areas of life.

The faculty members at Christian colleges play a major role in determining the nature of the educational environment. They have chosen to teach at Christian colleges because they are Christian and because they love teaching. As fellow Christians in the quest for truth, faculty members are actively engaged in asking questions as well as dispensing information. In the process of being the best that they can be as teachers, they challenge students to be the best that they can be as students of God's Word and world. They challenge, prod, provoke, and constructively criticize as well as support and encourage their students. They're willing to reveal their own imperfections as humans and uncertainties as Christians, thereby freeing up students to ask the "stupid" question or take the courageous "leap of faith." For many students, faculty members become much more than teachers; they are role models and mentors who become lifelong friends.

YOU WILL DEAL WITH TODAY'S REALITIES

Some people harbor the mistaken assumption that Christian colleges are somehow removed from the world. The fact is, Christian colleges are very much in the world today. And, in truth, American society and the world at large have never been in greater need of people who have been educated with *a values orientation*. Pick up any major newspaper or tune in to any evening news show. Or look around your house, your school, your neighborhood. You will discover example after example of people who have made "bad" decisions, "good" decisions, or, from the standpoint of values, "no" decision in the course of their day-to-day working or personal lives. Each hour of every day we encounter other people who also are struggling with matters of morality and ethics. These are the painful, challenging realities of being human in an imperfect world, of being fellow travelers in the struggle to inhabit, in a concerned way, and to preserve the planet God made for us.

▼ *California Baptist College*

Northwest Nazarene College ▼

▼ *Northwestern College (IA)*

King's College (AB) ▼

▼ *Azusa Pacific University*

Evangel College ▼

▼ *Northwestern College (IA)*

▼ *Belhaven College*

PUTTING CHRISTIAN COLLEGES IN PERSPECTIVE

Just what is a Christian college? And how many are there in the United States? Good questions. Let's take the second one first. There are about 3,300 colleges in the United States. Of these, only 600 or 700 retain some tie to a specific Christian denomination. About 125 of these are "Christ-centered" liberal arts colleges, meaning that they remain committed to really helping students think about how their Christian faith relates to every area of life—in the classroom, in extracurricular activities, on the playing fields, in human relationships, and in service opportunities around the world. And 78 of these Christian colleges are members of the Christian College Coalition (CCC), the sponsor of this guide.

WHAT IS A CHRISTIAN COLLEGE?

Just as no two people are alike, so are no two Christian colleges alike. They differ in size, location, tradition, denominational tie, academic offerings, religious requirements, and social expectations. That is as it should be. Indeed, the diversity among the Christian College Coalition members represents a strength for faculty seeking the best environment in which to teach and for students seeking the best college at which to form and pursue their life goals. Diversity will be discussed later in this introduction and will be apparent in reading and comparing the descriptions of the individual colleges starting on page 19 of this guide. Despite their diversity, the Christian liberal arts colleges described in this guide do share several solid beliefs. Call them the beliefs that bind.

Northwestern College (IA) ▼

Basically, faculty and administrators at these Christian colleges believe:

- That we live in a world created by God.

- That God is love.

- That Jesus Christ is the son of God, the "author and finisher of our faith," our eternal role model.

- That a truly complete education must deal with matters of the heart as well as of the mind.

- That a college education should be much more than simply a stepping-stone for getting a job. Rather, it should provide a solid foundation for living an active, meaningful, concerned, contributing life in God's world.

- That faculty members should serve as active, questioning role models, not as mere dispensers of knowledge or publishers of scholarly works.

- That the ultimate value of a college education derives not simply from taking classes or passing exams but from the ongoing, loving, painful, growth-inducing human interactions that take place on campus at all hours of the day and night, throughout the academic year.

- That students should graduate not just with a degree, sharpened skills, and a bag of right answers but with an enhanced sense of wholeness and the courage to ask the right questions.

- That while every college is to an extent an ivory tower, a place of retreat and reflection, no college experience, if it is to be whole and valuable, can long ignore the problems of our society or the major issues of our world. Indeed, colleges must give students the chance to address the concerns beyond their campuses; their ivory towers must have windows to the world.

- That a liberal arts education provides the best foundation for living a good life as well as for earning a good livelihood.

WHAT ACADEMIC PROGRAMS DO CHRISTIAN COLLEGES OFFER?

Each of the members of the Christian College Coalition is, at heart, a "Christ-centered liberal arts college." We have discussed what it means to participate in a "Christ-centered" educational experience. But what about the "liberal arts"?

Jay Kesler, a Coalition college president and past president of Youth for Christ, states well the case for the liberal arts college in today's world:

In a society where pluralism is replacing the melting pot, it is imperative that young people under-

LeTourneau College ▼

stand and appreciate the variety, complexity, and unique contributions of those with whom we must live on this crowded planet. North America cannot be viewed by its citizens as a large protected island with unending independent resources that ensure affluence and unimpeded growth while our neighbors scratch out mere existence. Others who have struggled for centuries without the blessing of this fertile land and democratic government have much to teach us. Arrogance based on ignorance and disregard of others is a dangerous ingredient in a nuclear world. Students should develop knowledge of self, of the natural world, of human cultures, and of human relationships to God. . . . Students must be taught to evaluate critically, to reason logically, and to communicate effectively while developing a sensitivity to personal and social relationships, moral responsibilities, and spiritual needs.

Our capacity to live above function is related directly to our understanding and appreciation of the aesthetic, the beautiful, and the musical.

The spring is silent not only when the birds die of the overuse of pesticides. It is also silent when that which sparks the creative, the artistic, and the melodic die in the human spirit. The liberal arts college is a place to cultivate and nurture the creative expressions of humanity.

Graduates must be able to make a living, but, beyond that, they must find the living they make worth the effort. The wisest of all once said, "Man cannot live by bread alone" and also that "only by losing our lives can we save them." The most satisfying examples in each of our lives bear out these truths. Our families, friends, and students, those we have learned to serve, provide the deepest of all satisfactions. The extension of this principle to a life of service through the application of knowledge to technology, statecraft, business, education, medicine, and, indeed, the whole range of human experience must be the goal of our efforts.

As a student at a Christian college you will "cul-

▼ *Messiah College*

▼ *John Brown University*

Spring Arbor College ▼

LeTourneau College ▼

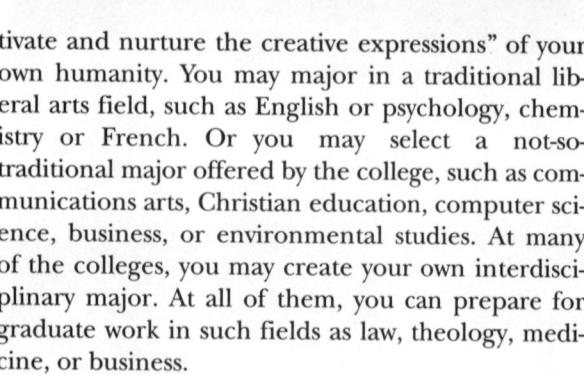

tivate and nurture the creative expressions" of your own humanity. You may major in a traditional liberal arts field, such as English or psychology, chemistry or French. Or you may select a not-so-traditional major offered by the college, such as communications arts, Christian education, computer science, business, or environmental studies. At many of the colleges, you may create your own interdisciplinary major. At all of them, you can prepare for graduate work in such fields as law, theology, medicine, or business.

ESTABLISHING LIFELONG FRIENDSHIPS

Students at Christian liberal arts colleges also develop what become lifelong friendships with their fellow students. Friendships emerge for the typical reasons: sharing a room or a major or an extracurricular interest. They emerge, too, for deeper reasons. Students find that an environment that examines faith, tests values, and encourages risk-taking leads to close and meaningful relationships. In such an environment, students do not end up thinking alike; indeed, the diversity of opinion students encounter on campus helps them to sharpen and strengthen their own faith and sense of self-awareness. At the same time, they grow in their respect for the faith and integrity of others. They develop

Bethel College (MN) ▼

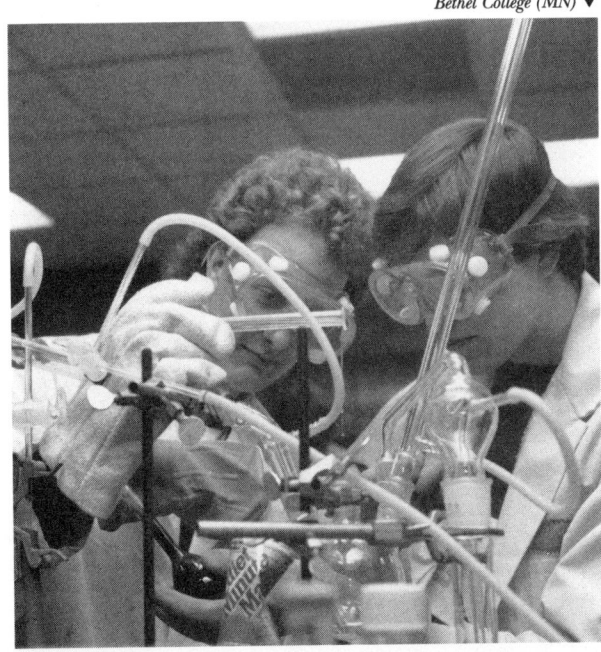

lifelong friendships with their fellow travelers who have shared in the process of self-discovery.

LAUGHS ALONG THE WAY

Do students at Christian colleges enjoy their educational experience? Do they have fun along the way? One visit to any campus, on any day of the academic year, will give you the answer: Yes! Students at Christian colleges are, well, students. They play on soccer teams, act in plays, sing in choirs, and edit newspapers. They make music and listen to it. They argue in Bible study groups and make peace over pizza. They cheer for their teams to win on the playing field or their roommates to "win" in the classrooms. They have snowball fights—on our northern campuses—and have popcorn parties everywhere. They encounter the day-to-day tensions present with any group of people living together, but they do so in an atmosphere of compassion and caring, of teamwork and trust.

Northwestern College (IA) ▼

▼ *Spring Arbor College*

▼ *Spring Arbor College*

PUTTING CONVICTION INTO ACTION

To be a Christ-centered student at a Christian college is to do more than take classes, attend chapel talks or convocations, participate in extracurricular activities, and engage in mind-stretching, value-testing discussions. To be a Christian involves acting in a Christ-like manner. Often, inevitably, that means reaching out, taking risks, making a difference in the lives of others.

Christian college students do just that through their participation in social service groups and Christian organizations and through individual endeavors. They tutor the young and read to the old. They march for hunger and speak out on social issues. They give blood to the Red Cross and time to Big Brothers. They teach Sunday School and advise Young Life groups. They speak with their time and their actions as well as their words and their prayers.

A GLOBAL CLASSROOM

Israel . . . England . . . People's Republic of China . . . Mexico . . . Greece . . . Africa . . . Japan . . .

Australia . . . Germany . . . France . . . Costa Rica . . . Spain. This is just a partial listing of the locations of the off-campus study programs available to students of Coalition colleges.

Students often cite "off-campus" or "foreign-study" programs as among the most valuable chapters in their college lives. By living and learning in countries beyond the borders of North America, they learn about their homeland. By talking with Christians from other cultures, they come to appreciate that the inherent principles of Christianity transcend matters of nationality, race, language, or socioeconomic structure.

The Christian College Coalition, headquartered in Washington, D.C., sponsors three exciting off-campus programs: the American Studies Program in Washington, D.C.; the Latin American Studies Program in San José, Costa Rica; and the Los Angeles Film Studies Center in Los Angeles, California. A fourth unique off-campus study opportunity is the Au Sable Institute of Environmental Studies in Michigan's Lower Peninsula. These programs are described on pages 99–102. A listing of other foreign-study op-

Covenant College ▼

portunities provided by CCC colleges can be found on page 123. Specifics on the full range of off-campus and foreign study programs available to students at Coalition colleges may be obtained by contacting the colleges directly.

WILL I GET A JOB WHEN I GRADUATE?

Yes, if history is a teacher. The graduates of the CCC colleges have compiled an excellent record upon graduation—either in getting accepted to graduate or professional schools or in landing their first job.

It is not an easy task, the business of finding the right niche after graduation. Recognizing the competitive forces at work, the CCC member institutions offer a tremendous range of resources to help students get from where they are to where they want to be: academic advisers, personal counselors, career counseling and placement officers, career-related

seminars and workshops throughout the academic year, and alumni—a traditionally powerful network at all Christian colleges.

Notable alumni who have graduated from Christian colleges include Evangelist Billy Graham; U.S. Senate Chaplain Richard Halverson; leaders in the world of Christian music, such as Gloria Gaither and Sandi Patti; the president of the American Red Cross, Richard Schubert; Dr. Roger Heyns, president of the William and Flora Hewlett Foundation; and the chairman of the board of The ServiceMaster Company, Kenneth Wessner.

As important as the "name" alumni who have gained national and international recognition are the thousands of alumni who are leading equally successful, if less newsworthy, personal and professional lives around the world. Their collective faith-centered efforts in dealing with life's major issues as

▼ *Dordt College*

Eastern College ▼

▼ *Campbellsville College*

Bethel College (KS) ▼

Taylor University ▼

▼ *Southern California College*

▼ *Campbell University*

well as everyday concerns stand as the best living testimony to the inherent value and impact of a Christian college education.

THE SPECIAL ACADEMIC QUALITY OF CHRISTIAN COLLEGES

"Academic quality" is one of those elusive, ephemeral terms. Everyone is looking for it. Few can agree what determines it. We believe that the CCC member colleges, individually and collectively, offer an education of outstanding academic quality—"academic character" may be a better term—for students seeking an environment characterized by small classes; challenging, caring professors; a wide range of traditional and nontraditional academic majors; strong preprofessional programs; an orientation to the development of the whole person; access to internships and off-campus and study-abroad programs; an emphasis on both academic and personal advising; and a record of successful alumni.

The academic quality of a Christian college is rooted in the strength of its professors and its students. Professors care about teaching, believe in the Scriptures, and open their homes and their hearts to students. The students care about learning, are active, and strive to learn and be the best that they can be. The base of a Christian education rests on Christian commitment and academic excellence. Students develop into well-rounded, well-educated Christians prepared to live in an ever-changing world.

In the final analysis, the best way to get a feel for an institution's academic quality is to visit the campus, attend classes, talk with students and faculty, wander around the library, and talk with some alumni. By taking these steps, you will get a sense of how the college in question measures up to *your* expectations in terms of academic quality.

YOU CAN AFFORD A CHRISTIAN COLLEGE

In all likelihood you can afford a Christian college regardless of your family's financial circumstances.

▼ *Eastern Mennonite College*

Westmont College ▼

▼ *Sterling College*

Bethel College (MN) ▼

First of all, because of the support of sponsoring denominations and donors, Christian colleges are often more affordable than private secular colleges of comparable quality. Second, Christian colleges are committed to attracting students from a wide range of socioeconomic backgrounds. That commitment is backed up by significant resources allocated to financial aid. Indeed, at many of the CCC member colleges, well over half the student body receives some form of institutional financial aid. The message is clear: investigate the financial aid possibilities before deciding you can't afford to attend a Christian college. It is the job of the financial aid office to structure a financial aid package that allows you to attend the college of your choice. Explore the options for grants, scholarships, loans, and work-study opportunities—after subtracting the amount of available financial support. Then compare the cost with other private colleges or public institutions. If

you're like students who have faced this issue in recent years, you may be pleasantly surprised, especially when you consider the great value of a long-term investment in your future.

FINAL WORD: NARROWING THE CHOICE

On the preceding pages, we have stated the case for a Christian college. We have tried to describe those threads that are woven throughout the fabric of each of the members of the Christian College Coalition. But despite the common threads, each of these colleges has a distinctive style, character, educational environment, course listing, mission statement, denominational affiliation, location, and slate of academic and extracurricular offerings. In truth, you will probably only seriously consider a few colleges, and, barring unforeseen circumstances, you will attend only one.

▼ *John Brown University*

We hope the one you attend is the college that is right for you, be it a Christian college or a secular institution. We wish you God's leading and wisdom as you continue your search.

COLLEGE PROFILES

This section presents data for each college in a standard format for easy comparison. All college information presented was supplied to Peterson's by the colleges themselves. The special notes, which appear at the end of the profiles, were written by the colleges to supplement the data with information on such areas as campus life, the college's mission, and special programs.

The material that follows will help clarify terms and abbreviations found in the listings that may be unfamiliar to students.

Profile Highlights

Abbreviations that occur include UG—undergraduate, N/R—not reported, N/App—not applicable, and N/Avail—not available.

General Information

Degrees awarded: A—associate degree, B—bachelor's degree, M—master's degree, and D—doctoral and professional degrees.

Primary accreditation: Full accreditation or candidate for accreditation status granted either to the college as a whole by one of the six regional associations of schools and colleges and/or by other recognized institutional accrediting bodies or for programs in a particular field by a recognized specialized accrediting body. The following accrediting body is listed in the profiles by its initials: AABC—American Association of Bible Colleges.

Barrier-free denotes that the institution meets federal standards for access to facilities by handicapped students.

Freshman Admissions

Admissions policies and options include the following:

Open admissions: Virtually all applicants are accepted without regard to standardized test scores, grade average, or class rank.

Early entrance: Highly qualified students may matriculate before graduating from high school.

Early decision: Students apply early, are notified of acceptance or rejection well in advance of the usual notification date, and agree to accept an offer of admission.

Early action: The same as early decision except that applicants are not obligated to accept an offer of admission.

Deferred entrance: An accepted student may postpone entrance in order to travel, work, or study elsewhere for a specified period.

Standardized tests: PSAT—Preliminary Scholastic Aptitude Test, SAT—Scholastic Aptitude Test, ACT—American College Testing Program's ACT Assessment, TOEFL—Test of English as a Foreign Language, and WPCT—Washington Pre-College Test.

Entrance difficulty level:

Very difficult: More than 50% of the freshmen were in the top 10% of their high school class and scored over 1150 on the SAT or over 26 on the ACT; about 60% or fewer of the applicants were accepted.

Moderately difficult: More than 75% of the freshmen were in the top half of their high school class and scored over 900 on the SAT or over 18 on the ACT; about 85% or fewer of the applicants were accepted.

Minimally difficult: Most freshmen were not in the top half of their high school class and scored somewhat below 900 on the SAT or below 19 on the ACT; up to 95% of the applicants were accepted.

Noncompetitive: Virtually all applicants were accepted regardless of high school rank or test scores.

Financial Aid

Types of college-administered aid include the following:

SEOG: Supplemental Educational Opportunity Grants, a federally funded need-based award program administered by colleges.

College Work-Study: A federal program that enables students to earn money by working on or off campus in public or private nonprofit organizations.

Part-time jobs: On-campus work provided by the college apart from College Work-Study.

Supporting data students may have to provide:

AFSA/SAR: The federal government's Application for Federal Student Aid/Student Aid Report.

FAF: Financial Aid Form of the College Scholarship Service.

FFS: Family Financial Statement of the American College Testing Program.

Financial aid transcript: A record of aid previously received for college study, required of transfer applicants.

Institutional form: A college's own financial aid application form.

IRS: Federal income tax form 1040.

Athletics

Membership organizations: NCAA—National Collegiate Athletic Association, NAIA—National Association of Intercollegiate Athletics, NJCAA—National Junior College Athletic Association, and NLCAA—National Little College Athletic Association.

Individual sports: M—for men, W—for women, (s)—scholarship offered, and (c)—club sport. A roman numeral following an M or W indicates that the college competes in that NCAA division in that sport.

ANDERSON UNIVERSITY
Anderson, Indiana

Total enrollment: 2,115

UG enrollment: 2,015 (53% W)

Application deadline: 9/1

Tuition & fees: $7330

Room & board: $2610

Entrance: moderately difficult

SAT ≥ 500: 20% V, 37% M

ACT ≥ 21: N/R

Denominational affiliation: Church of God

GENERAL INFORMATION Independent comprehensive coed institution. Founded 1917. Awards A (college transfer and terminal), B, M. Primary accreditation: regional. City setting, with easy access to Indianapolis; 100-acre campus. Total enrollment: 2,115. Faculty: 194 (98 full-time, 96 part-time); 42% of full-time faculty have doctoral degrees; graduate assistants teach no undergraduate courses. Library holdings: 152,368 bound volumes, 10,828 titles on microform, 829 periodical subscriptions, 2,817 records/tapes. Computer terminals/PCs available for student use: 125, located in computer center, instructional materials center.

UNDERGRADUATE PROFILE Fall 1989: 2,015 undergraduates (581 freshmen) from 43 states and territories and 12 foreign countries; 14% part-time; 98% state residents; 6% transfers; 85% financial aid recipients; 53% women; 47% men; 4% blacks; 1% Native Americans; 0% Hispanics; 0% Asian Americans; 2% international students.

1989 FRESHMAN DATA 1,247 students applied for fall 1989 admission; 79% were accepted; 59% of those accepted enrolled. 24% of freshmen were in top 10% of secondary school class, 42% were in top 25%, 84% were in top half.

ENROLLMENT PATTERNS 80% of fall 1988 freshmen returned for fall 1989 term.

FRESHMAN ADMISSIONS Options: early entrance, early decision, deferred entrance. Required: high school transcript, 2 recommendations, SAT or ACT. Recommended: 3 years of high school math and science, 1 year of high school foreign language. Test scores used for counseling/placement. Application deadlines: 9/1, 12/1 for early decision. Notification dates: continuous until 9/6, continuous until 1/15 for early decision. College's own assessment of entrance difficulty level: moderately difficult.

TRANSFER ADMISSIONS Required: high school transcript, 2 recommendations, college transcript, minimum 2.0 grade point average. Application deadline: 9/1. College's own assessment of entrance difficulty level: moderately difficult.

EXPENSES (1990–91) Comprehensive fee of $9940 includes full-time tuition ($7330) and college room and board ($2610). College room only: $1390. Part-time tuition: $305 per semester hour.

FINANCIAL AID Fall 1989 full-time freshmen: 81% applied for aid, 89% of those were judged to have need, 100% of those were aided; the average aided freshman received an aid package worth $4800 (50% scholarships/grants, 50% self-help) meeting 100% of need. College-administered aid for all 1989–90 undergraduates: 1,200 need-based scholarships (average $1055); 117 non-need scholarships (average $2560); low-interest long-term loans from college funds (average $2500), from external sources; SEOG; College Work-Study; 450 part-time jobs. Supporting data: institutional form required; FFS, FAF, AFSA/SAR acceptable. Priority application deadline: 3/1.

CAMPUS LIFE/STUDENT SERVICES Mandatory chapel; drama/theater group; student-run newspaper and radio station. Institution provides health clinic, personal/psychological counseling. Social organizations: 11 social clubs.

ATHLETICS Member NAIA. Intercollegiate sports: baseball/softball M, W; basketball M, W; cross-country running M, W; equestrian sports M, W; football M; golf M; soccer M; tennis M, W; track and field M, W; volleyball W. Intramural sports: baseball/softball, basketball, bowling, football, soccer, swimming and diving, volleyball.

MAJORS Accounting B; American studies B; art education B; art/fine arts B; biblical studies B; biology/biological sciences B; broadcasting B; business administration/commerce/management B; business education B; chemistry B; child care/child and family studies B; communication B; computer science B; criminal justice A, B; (pre)dentistry sequence B; early childhood education A; ecology/environmental studies B; economics B; education B; elementary education B; (pre)engineering sequence A; English B; environmental sciences B; French B; German B; graphic arts B; history B; journalism B; (pre)law sequence B; marketing/retailing/merchandising B; mathematics B; medical technology B; (pre)medicine sequence B; museum studies B; music B; music education B; nursing A, B; philosophy B; physical education B; physics B; piano/organ B; political science/government B; psychology B; public affairs and policy studies B; public relations B; recreation and leisure services B; religious studies B; sacred music B; secondary education B; secretarial studies/office management A; social work B; sociology B; Spanish B; speech/rhetoric/public address/debate B; sports medicine B; theater arts/drama B; (pre)veterinary medicine sequence B; voice B. Majors with highest enrollment: business administration/commerce/management, education, music.

SPECIAL NOTE FROM THE COLLEGE Anderson University is a community of Christian higher education where high-quality learning and Christian service come alive. Believing that scholarship and scholars should serve a purpose, Anderson University is a mission-minded school that offers students a strong liberal arts foundation on which to build career credentials. Business, computer science, education, music, religious studies, social work, and sociology are among the most popular of the 60 majors and programs offered. The Tri-S program (study, serve, and share) is probably most representative of the spirit of the University. Through this program, more than 500 students volunteer each year for 50 different cross-cultural work projects throughout the world. Bill and Gloria Gaither and Sandi Patti are a few of the nearly 25,000 loyal alumni who make up the University's international alumni association and whose strength is not only in their numbers but also in their belief.

CONTACT Mr. Phil M. Fair, Director of Admissions, Anderson University, Anderson, IN 46012, 317-641-4080 or toll-free 800-421-3014 (in-state), 800-428-6414 (out-of-state).

ASBURY COLLEGE
Wilmore, Kentucky

Total enrollment: 1,082 (all UG)

Women: 52%

Application deadline: rolling

Tuition & fees: $6734

Room & board: $2271

Entrance: moderately difficult

SAT ≥ 500: 31% V, 45% M

ACT ≥ 21: 55%

Denominational affiliation: nondenominational

GENERAL INFORMATION Independent 4-year coed college. Founded 1890. Awards B. Primary accreditation: regional. Small-town setting; 500-acre campus. Total enrollment: 1,082. Faculty: 97 (65 full-time, 32 part-time). Library holdings: 132,925 bound volumes, 383 titles on microform, 560 periodical subscriptions, 6,309 records/tapes. Computer terminals/PCs available for student use: 40, located in computer center.

UNDERGRADUATE PROFILE Fall 1989: 1,082 undergraduates (306 freshmen) from 46 states and territories and 17 foreign countries; 3% part-time; 20% state residents; 22% transfers; 89% financial aid recipients; 52% women; 48% men; 1% blacks; 1% Hispanics; 1% Asian Americans; 2% international students; 11% of undergraduates 25 years of age or older.

1989 FRESHMAN DATA 733 students applied for fall 1989 admission; 65% were accepted; 65% of those accepted enrolled. 2 freshmen were National Merit Scholarship Finalists. 24% of freshmen were in top 10% of secondary school class, 46% were in top 25%, 79% were in top half.

ENROLLMENT PATTERNS 80% of fall 1988 freshmen returned for fall 1989 term. 1987–89 average: 72% of entering classes graduated; 55% of students completing a degree program went on for further study.

FRESHMAN ADMISSIONS Options: early entrance, deferred entrance. Required: high school transcript, 2 recommendations, SAT or ACT, TOEFL (for foreign students). Recommended: 3 years of high school math and science, some high school foreign language. Required for some: interview. Test scores used for admission. Application deadline: rolling. College's own assessment of entrance difficulty level: moderately difficult.

TRANSFER ADMISSIONS Required: high school transcript, 2 recommendations, college transcript, minimum 2.0 grade point average. Required for some: interview. Application deadline: rolling. College's own assessment of entrance difficulty level: moderately difficult.

EXPENSES (1990–91) Comprehensive fee of $9005 includes full-time tuition ($6435), mandatory fees ($299), and college room and board ($2271). College room only: $978. Part-time tuition and fees per quarter (1 to 11 quarter hours) range from $192 to $1925.50.

FINANCIAL AID Fall 1989 full-time freshmen: 85% applied for aid, 92% of those were judged to have need, 100% of those were aided. College-administered aid for all 1989–90 undergraduates: 450 need-based scholarships (average $825); 244 non-need scholarships (average $1340); low-interest long-term loans from college funds (average $1270), from external sources (average $2910); SEOG; College Work-Study; 350 part-time jobs. Supporting data: FAF, institutional form required; IRS, state form required for some; FFS, AFSA/SAR acceptable. Priority application deadline: 5/1.

CAMPUS LIFE/STUDENT Services Dress code; mandatory chapel; drama/theater group; student-run newspaper and radio station. Institution provides health clinic, personal/psychological counseling.

ATHLETICS Member NCAA (Division III), NAIA. Intercollegiate sports: baseball/softball M, W(III); cross-country running M, W(III); soccer M; swimming and diving M, W(III); tennis M, W(III); volleyball W(III). Intramural sports: baseball/softball, basketball, football, soccer, tennis, volleyball.

MAJORS Accounting B; applied mathematics B; art education B; art/fine arts B; biblical languages B; biblical studies B; biochemistry B; biology/biological sciences B; broadcasting B; business administration/commerce/management B; chemistry B; computer science B; education B; elementary education B; English B; French B; history B; human services B; international studies B; journalism B; mathematics B; medical technology B; (pre)medicine sequence B; ministries B; music B; music education B; philosophy B; physical education B; psychology B; recreation and leisure services B; sociology B; Spanish B; speech/rhetoric/public address/debate B. Majors with highest enrollment: elementary education, business administration/commerce/management, psychology.

SPECIAL NOTE FROM THE COLLEGE As an independent nondenominational liberal arts college, Asbury strives to offer an education of academic excellence in a thoroughly Christian context by maintaining a synthesis of the liberal arts tradition and the Christian faith. In addition to offering an intellectual environment that promotes a desire for knowledge, the College seeks to stimulate individuals to understand Scripture and basic Christian doctrines, to receive Jesus Christ as Savior, to be filled with the Holy Spirit for cleansing and empowerment, and to demonstrate faith by a life of service through active membership in the church and participation in its mission to the world.

CONTACT Mr. Stan Wiggam, Dean of Admissions and Enrollment, Asbury College, Wilmore, KY 40390, 606-858-3511 Ext. 142.

AZUSA PACIFIC UNIVERSITY
Azusa, California

Total enrollment: 2,933

UG enrollment: 1,567 (56% W)

Application deadline: rolling

Tuition & fees: $8750

Room & board: $3590

Entrance: moderately difficult

SAT ≥ 500: 24% V, 38% M

ACT ≥ 21: 48%

Denominational affiliation: interdenominational

GENERAL INFORMATION Independent comprehensive coed institution. Founded 1899. Awards A (college transfer), B, M (offers associate only through external degree home-study program). Primary accreditation: regional. Small-town setting, with easy access to Los Angeles; 52-acre campus. Total enrollment: 2,933. Faculty: 180 (120 full-time, 60 part-time); 50% of full-time faculty have doctoral degrees; graduate assistants teach a few undergraduate courses. Library holdings: 95,067 bound volumes, 391,477 titles on microform, 766 periodical subscriptions, 4,678 records/tapes. Computer terminals/PCs available for student use: 82, located in computer center.

UNDERGRADUATE PROFILE Fall 1989: 1,567 undergraduates (396 freshmen) from 39 states and territories and 36 foreign countries; 8% part-time; 70% state residents; 81% financial aid recipients; 56% women; 44% men; 4% blacks; 1% Native Americans; 6% Hispanics; 13% Asian Americans; 7% international students; 7% of undergraduates 25 years of age or older.

1989 FRESHMAN DATA 957 students applied for fall 1989 admission; 68% were accepted; 61% of those accepted enrolled.

ENROLLMENT PATTERNS 84% of fall 1988 freshmen returned for fall 1989 term.

FRESHMAN ADMISSIONS Option: deferred entrance. Required: essay, high school transcript, 2 recommendations, SAT or ACT, English Composition Test (with essay), TOEFL (for foreign students). Test scores used for admission. Application deadline: rolling. Notification date: continuous. College's own assessment of entrance difficulty level: moderately difficult.

TRANSFER ADMISSIONS Required: essay, 2 recommendations, college transcript, minimum 2.0 grade point average. Required for some: standardized test scores, high school transcript. Application deadline: rolling. Notification date: continuous. College's own assessment of entrance difficulty level: moderately difficult.

EXPENSES (1990–91) Comprehensive fee of $12,340 includes full-time tuition ($8600), mandatory fees ($150), and college room and board ($3590 minimum). College room only: $1600 (minimum). Part-time tuition: $350 per unit.

FINANCIAL AID College-administered aid for all 1989–90 undergraduates: need-based scholarships; 105 non-need scholarships (average $2358); low-interest long-term loans from external sources (average $2500); SEOG; College Work-Study; part-time jobs. Supporting data: FAF, IRS, institutional form, AFSA/SAR required; state form acceptable. Priority application deadline: 3/1.

CAMPUS LIFE/STUDENT SERVICES Mandatory chapel; drama/theater group; student-run newspaper. Institution provides health clinic, personal/psychological counseling.

ATHLETICS Member NAIA. Intercollegiate sports: baseball/softball M(s), W(s); basketball M(s), W(s); cross-country running M(s), W(s); football M(s); soccer M(s), W; tennis M(s); track and field M(s), W(s); volleyball W(s). Intramural sports: badminton, baseball/softball, basketball, bowling, football, golf, racquetball, skiing (cross-country), skiing (downhill), soccer, tennis, track and field, volleyball, wrestling.

MAJORS Accounting B; applied art B; art/fine arts B; biblical languages B; biblical studies B; biology/biological sciences B; business administration/commerce/management B; chemistry B; communication B; computer information systems B; computer science B; (pre)dentistry sequence B; education B; English B; history B; international studies B; (pre)law sequence B; liberal arts/general studies A, B; marketing/retailing/merchandising B; mathematics B; (pre)medicine sequence B; ministries B; modern languages B; music B; music education B; nursing B; pastoral studies B; philosophy B; physical education B; physics B; political science/government B; psychology A, B; recreation and leisure services B; religious studies B; secondary education B; social science B; social work B; sociology B; sports medicine B; theology B; (pre)veterinary medicine sequence B; voice B. Majors with highest enrollment: business administration/commerce/management, physical education, religious studies.

SPECIAL NOTE FROM THE COLLEGE Azusa Pacific University provides an academic and personal challenge for students, inspiring in them quality of mind and character and a living faith in Jesus Christ. While education has conforming aspects, the University strives to build upon the unique strengths of each student. Azusa Pacific cares about students' development and supports them as emerging adults. The University believes that balancing academic challenge with personal support equips students with the knowledge and ethical foundation necessary to serve generously and contribute professionally in a complex, changing world.

CONTACT Mr. Guy Adams, Dean of Admissions, Azusa Pacific University, Azusa, CA 91702, 818-969-3434 Ext. 3416.

BARTLESVILLE WESLEYAN COLLEGE
Bartlesville, Oklahoma

Total enrollment: 465 (all UG)

Women: 58%

Application deadline: rolling

Tuition & fees: $5140

Room & board: $2700

Entrance: minimally difficult

SAT ≥ 500: N/R

ACT ≥ 21: 46%

Denominational affiliation: Wesleyan Church

GENERAL INFORMATION Independent 4-year coed college. Founded 1909. Awards A (college transfer), B. Primary accreditation: regional. Small-town setting, with easy access to Tulsa; 128-acre campus. Total enrollment: 465. Faculty: 64 (34 full-time, 30 part-time); 55% of full-time faculty have doctoral degrees. Library holdings: 124,722 bound volumes, 35,997 titles on microform, 300 periodical subscriptions, 1,076 records/tapes. Computer terminals/PCs available for student use: 12, located in computer center.

UNDERGRADUATE Profile Fall 1989: 465 undergraduates (131 freshmen) from 29 states and territories and 17 foreign countries; 28% part-time; 52% state residents; 16% transfers; 85% financial aid recipients; 58% women; 42% men; 2% blacks; 2% Native Americans; 1% Hispanics; 1% Asian Americans; 11% international students; 32% of undergraduates 25 years of age or older.

1989 FRESHMAN DATA 237 students applied for fall 1989 admission; 67% were accepted; 83% of those accepted enrolled. 17% of freshmen were in top 10% of secondary school class, 34% were in top 25%, 66% were in top half.

ENROLLMENT PATTERNS 73% of fall 1988 freshmen returned for fall 1989 term. 1987–89 average: 45% of entering classes graduated; 8% of students completing a bachelor's program went on for further study.

FRESHMAN ADMISSIONS Options: early entrance, deferred entrance. Required: high school transcript, 2 recommendations, SAT or ACT, TOEFL (for foreign students). Test scores used for counseling/placement. Application deadline: rolling. College's own assessment of entrance difficulty level: minimally difficult.

TRANSFER ADMISSIONS Required: high school transcript, 2 recommendations, college transcript, minimum 2.0 grade point average. Application deadline: rolling. College's own assessment of entrance difficulty level: minimally difficult.

EXPENSES (1990–91) Comprehensive fee of $7840 includes full-time tuition ($5140) and college room and board ($2700 minimum). Part-time tuition: $170 per semester hour.

FINANCIAL AID Fall 1989 full-time freshmen: 92% applied for aid, 75% of those were judged to have need, 100% of those were aided; the average aided freshman received an aid package worth $6020 (58% scholarships/grants, 42% self-help) meeting 89% of need. College-administered aid for all 1989–90 undergraduates: 128 need-based scholarships; 290 non-need scholarships (average $895); low-interest long-term loans from external sources (average $1445); SEOG; College Work-Study; 17 part-time jobs. Supporting data: FFS, IRS, state form, institutional form, AFSA/SAR required; FAF acceptable. Priority application deadline: 5/1.

CAMPUS LIFE/STUDENT SERVICES Dress code; mandatory chapel; student-run newspaper. Institution provides health clinic, personal/psychological counseling. Honor Society: Sigma Xi.

ATHLETICS Member NAIA. Intercollegiate sports: baseball/softball W; basketball M(s), W(s); golf M; soccer M(s); tennis M; volleyball W. Intramural sports: baseball/softball, basketball, football, golf, racquetball, tennis, volleyball.

MAJORS ACCOUNTING A, B; behavioral sciences A, B; biology/biological sciences A, B; business administration/commerce/management A, B; business education B; chemistry A, B; computer information systems A, B; education B; elementary education B; English B; history B; liberal arts/general studies A; mathematics B; natural sciences B; physical education B; political science/government B; science B; science education B; secondary education B; secretarial studies/office management A; theology B. Majors with highest enrollment: business administration/commerce/management, education, theology.

SPECIAL NOTE FROM THE COLLEGE Bartlesville Wesleyan College is a distinctive Christian college. The campus community strongly believes in providing a Christ-centered educational experience that will produce lifelong results. It is located in the south-central part of the United States, 45 miles north of Metropolitan Tulsa. Bartlesville is a cosmopolitan city of 40,000 and is the world headquarters of Phillips Petroleum Company. Local cultural opportunities include a choral society, a civic ballet, a theater guild, a symphony orchestra, and an annual International OK Mozart festival. The focal point of the 128-acre campus is an elegant 55-year-old, 32-room, Spanish-style mansion overlooking a beautiful lake.

CONTACT Mr. Pete Wood, Enrollment Services Administrator, Bartlesville Wesleyan College, Bartlesville, OK 74006, 918-333-6151 Ext. 236.

BELHAVEN COLLEGE
Jackson, Mississippi

Total enrollment: 721 (all UG)

Women: 59%

Application deadline: rolling

Tuition & fees: $5850

Room & board: $2100

Entrance: moderately difficult

SAT ≥ 500: 37% V, 18% M

ACT ≥ 21: 50%

Denominational affiliation: Presbyterian

GENERAL INFORMATION Independent 4-year coed college. Founded 1883. Awards B. Primary accreditation: regional. City setting; 42-acre campus. Total enrollment: 721. Faculty: 76 (34 full-time, 42 part-time); 69% of full-time faculty have doctoral degrees. Library holdings: 76,673 bound volumes, 543 titles on microform, 439 periodical subscriptions, 1,862 records/tapes. Computer terminals/PCs available for student use: 12, located in computer center.

UNDERGRADUATE Profile Fall 1989: 721 undergraduates (83 freshmen) from 20 states and territories and 16 foreign countries; 36% part-time; 84% state residents; 25% transfers; 77% financial aid recipients; 59% women; 41% men; 9% blacks; 1% Hispanics; 3% international students.

1989 FRESHMAN DATA 263 students applied for fall 1989 admission; 76% were accepted; 42% of those accepted enrolled. 21% of freshmen were in top 10% of secondary school class, 41% were in top 25%, 66% were in top half.

ENROLLMENT PATTERNS 66% of fall 1988 freshmen returned for fall 1989 term. 1987–89 average: 41% of entering classes graduated; 14% of students completing a degree program went on for further study.

FRESHMAN ADMISSIONS Options: early entrance, deferred entrance. Required: high school transcript, SAT or ACT, TOEFL (for foreign students). Test scores used for admission. Application deadline: rolling. College's own assessment of entrance difficulty level: moderately difficult.

TRANSFER ADMISSIONS REQUIRED: 2 recommendations, college transcript, minimum 2.0 grade point average. Recommended: standardized test scores, high school transcript. Application deadline: rolling. College's own assessment of entrance difficulty level: moderately difficult.

EXPENSES (1990–91) Comprehensive fee of $7950 includes full-time tuition ($5850) and college room and board ($2100).

FINANCIAL AID Fall 1989 full-time freshmen: 93% applied for aid, 55% of those were judged to have need, 100% of those were aided; the average aided freshman received an aid package worth $5520 (56% scholarships/grants, 44% self-help) meeting 92% of need. College-administered aid for all 1989–90 undergraduates: need-based scholarships; 281 non-need scholarships (average $1426); low-interest long-term loans from college funds (average $1000), from external sources (average $2760); SEOG; College Work-Study. Supporting data: FAF, IRS, institutional form required; FFS, AFSA/SAR acceptable. Priority application deadline: 5/1.

CAMPUS LIFE/STUDENT SERVICES Mandatory chapel; drama/theater group; student-run newspaper. Institution provides health clinic.

ATHLETICS Member NAIA. Intercollegiate sports: baseball/softball M(s); basketball M(s), W(s); soccer M(s); tennis M(s). Intramural sports: baseball/softball, basketball, football, soccer, swimming and diving, tennis.

MAJORS Accounting B; art/fine arts B; biblical studies B; biology/biological sciences B; business administration/commerce/management B; chemistry B; classics B; (pre)dentistry sequence B; elementary education B; English B; finance/banking B; Greek B; history B; humanities B; Latin B; liberal arts/general studies B; marketing/retailing/merchandising B; mathematics B; (pre)medicine sequence B; ministries B; music B; physical education B; piano/organ B; psychology B; Romance languages B; stringed instruments B; (pre)veterinary medicine sequence B; voice B. Majors with highest enrollment: business administration/commerce/management, elementary education, biology/biological sciences.

SPECIAL NOTE FROM THE COLLEGE Founded in 1883, Belhaven is located on approximately 42 acres in Jackson, the center of cultural, economic, educational, and political life in Mississippi. Belhaven College is a coeducational, 4-year Christian liberal arts college serving Presbyterians and other evangelical Christians throughout the Southeast and beyond. Dedicated to the promotion of academic excellence in a clearly Christian environment, Belhaven emphasizes the importance of individuals and their intellectual, spiritual, social, and physical development. Belhaven provides an atmosphere in which students are encouraged to learn to think, evaluate, make wise decisions, and judge fairly. Because academic preparation and Christian experience go hand in hand at Belhaven, students receive support from the faculty and administration in their development of a personal value system based on Christian principles. At Belhaven, the ultimate goal is to prepare students not only for their chosen vocation but also for life and service.

CONTACT Mr. Wayne Smith, Director of Admissions, Belhaven College, Jackson, MS 39202, 601-968-5940.

BETHEL COLLEGE
Mishawaka, Indiana

Total enrollment: 585

UG enrollment: 570 (60% W)

Application deadline: rolling

Tuition & fees: $6410

Room & board: $2500

Entrance: minimally difficult

SAT ≥ 500: 8% V, 28% M

ACT ≥ 21: N/R

Denominational affiliation: Missionary Church

GENERAL INFORMATION Independent comprehensive coed institution. Founded 1947. Awards A (college transfer and terminal), B, M. Primary accreditation: regional. City setting; 60-acre campus. Total enrollment: 585. Faculty: 62 (40 full-time, 22 part-time); 38% of full-time faculty have doctoral degrees; graduate assistants teach no undergraduate courses. Library holdings: 60,000 bound volumes, 3,384 titles on microform, 750 periodical subscriptions, 2,000 records/tapes. Computer terminals/PCs available for student use: 20, located in computer center.

UNDERGRADUATE PROFILE Fall 1989: 570 undergraduates (180 freshmen) from 11 states and territories and 4 foreign countries; 36% part-time; 84% state residents; 8% transfers; 60% financial aid recipients; 60% women; 40% men; 2% blacks; 1% Native Americans; 1% Hispanics.

1989 FRESHMAN DATA 277 students applied for fall 1989 admission; 72% were accepted; 90% of those accepted enrolled. 18% of freshmen were in top 10% of secondary school class, 42% were in top 25%.

ENROLLMENT PATTERNS 80% of fall 1988 freshmen returned for fall 1989 term. 1987–89 average: 49% of entering classes graduated; 15% of students completing a bachelor's program went on for further study.

FRESHMAN ADMISSIONS Options: early entrance, deferred entrance. Required: high school transcript, recommendations, SAT or ACT, TOEFL (for foreign students). Recommended: some high school foreign language, interview. Test scores used for counseling/placement. Application deadline: rolling. College's own assessment of entrance difficulty level: minimally difficult.

TRANSFER ADMISSIONS Required: standardized test scores, high school transcript, recommendations, college transcript, minimum 2.0 grade point average. Recommended: some high school foreign language, interview. Application deadline: rolling. College's own assessment of entrance difficulty level: minimally difficult.

EXPENSES (1989–90) Comprehensive fee of $8910 includes full-time tuition ($6250), mandatory fees ($160), and college room and board ($2500). Part-time fees per semester: $50.

FINANCIAL AID Fall 1989 full-time freshmen: 87% applied for aid, 90% of those were judged to have need, 100% of those were aided; the average aided freshman received an aid package worth $4002 (41% scholarships/grants, 59% self-help) meeting 90% of need. College-administered aid for all 1989–90 undergraduates: need-based scholarships (average $500); non-need scholarships (average $500); low-interest long-term loans from college funds (average $1600), from external sources (average $2000); SEOG; College Work-Study; part-time jobs. Supporting data: FAF, institutional form, AFSA/SAR required; FFS acceptable. Priority application deadline: 3/1.

CAMPUS LIFE/STUDENT SERVICES Dress code; mandatory chapel; drama/theater group; student-run newspaper and radio station. Institution provides personal/psychological counseling.

ATHLETICS Member NAIA. Intercollegiate sports: baseball/softball M(s), W(s); basketball M(s), W(s); golf M(s); soccer M(s); tennis M(s), W(s); volleyball W(s). Intramural sports: baseball/softball, basketball, cross-country running, skiing (cross-country), skiing (downhill), soccer, table tennis (ping pong), tennis, track and field, ultimate frisbee, volleyball.

MAJORS Accounting B; art/fine arts B; biblical studies A; biology/biological sciences A, B; business administration/commerce/management A, B; business education B; chemistry A, B; commercial art A, B; communication B; computer science A, B; early childhood education A; education B; elementary education B; engineering (general) B; English B; gerontology A; journalism A; liberal arts/general studies A, B; mathematics B; ministries B; music A, B; music education B; nursing B; physical education B; piano/organ A, B; psychology B; recreation and leisure services B; religious studies B; sacred music A, B; science B; science education B; secondary education B; secretarial studies/office management A; social science A, B; sociology B; voice B. Majors with highest enrollment: elementary education, business administration/commerce/management, accounting.

SPECIAL NOTE FROM THE COLLEGE Bethel College is located in northern Indiana on a beautiful 60-acre wooded campus. Bethel is a college of the Missionary Church, an evangelical denomination with roots in Methodist and Mennonite traditions. Since its founding in 1947, the hallmark of the College has been an emphasis on excellent teaching and warm student-faculty relationships. Bethel cares about its students. Bethel College has a challenging and participatory environment: students work hard in the classroom, on the athletic field, in performance, and in ministry opportunities. Bethel is a college with a deep Christian commitment. There is an open and joyful emphasis on the Christian life. Chapel meets 3 times a week and is the center of the campus culture. "With Christ at the helm" is more than a motto—it is the purpose and intent of living and studying together.

CONTACT Mr. Steve Matteson, Director of Admissions, Bethel College, Mishawaka, IN 46545, 219-259-8511 Ext. 339.

BETHEL COLLEGE
North Newton, Kansas

Total enrollment: 605 (all UG)

Women: 53%

Application deadline: 8/15

Tuition & fees: $6182

Room & board: $2800

Entrance: moderately difficult

SAT ≥ 500: N/R

ACT ≥ 21: 63%

Denominational affiliation: General Conference Mennonite Church

GENERAL INFORMATION Independent 4-year coed college Mennonite Church. Founded 1887. Awards A (terminal), B. Primary accreditation: regional. Small-town setting; 47-acre campus. Total enrollment: 605. Faculty: 59 (41 full-time, 18 part-time); 56% of full-time faculty have doctoral degrees. Library holdings: 120,500 bound volumes, 2,800 titles on microform, 750 periodical subscriptions, 300 records/tapes. Computer terminals/PCs available for student use: 20, located in computer center.

UNDERGRADUATE Profile Fall 1989: 605 undergraduates (166 freshmen) from 31 states and territories and 9 foreign countries; 15% part-time; 65% state residents; 23% transfers; 97% financial aid recipients; 53% women; 47% men; 5% blacks; 0% Native Americans; 1% Hispanics; 1% Asian Americans; 4% international students; 17% of undergraduates 25 years of age or older.

1989 FRESHMAN DATA 484 students applied for fall 1989 admission; 94% were accepted; 37% of those accepted enrolled. 25% of freshmen were in top 10% of secondary school class, 46% were in top 25%, 79% were in top half.

ENROLLMENT PATTERNS 64% of fall 1988 freshmen returned for fall 1989 term. 1987–89 average: 44% of entering classes graduated; 15% of students completing a bachelor's program went on for further study.

FRESHMAN ADMISSIONS Options: early entrance, deferred entrance. Required: high school transcript, 2 recommendations, interview, SAT or ACT, TOEFL (for foreign students). Recommended: 3 years of high school math and science, some high school foreign language. Test scores used for admission. Application deadline: 8/15. Notification date: continuous. College's own assessment of entrance difficulty level: moderately difficult.

TRANSFER Admissions Required: standardized test scores, high school transcript, interview, college transcript, minimum 2.0 grade point average. Recommended: 3 years of high school math and science, some high school foreign language. Application deadline: 8/15. Notification date: continuous. College's own assessment of entrance difficulty level: moderately difficult.

EXPENSES (1989–90) Comprehensive fee of $8982 includes full-time tuition ($5990), mandatory fees ($192), and college room and board ($2800). College room only: $1300. Part-time tuition per credit hour: $107 for the first 5 credit hours, $214 for the next 6 credit hours.

FINANCIAL AID Fall 1989 full-time freshmen: 96% applied for aid, 70% of those were judged to have need, 100% of those were aided; the average aided freshman received an aid package worth $6000 meeting 80% of need. College-administered aid for all 1989–90 undergraduates: 369 need-based scholarships (average $715); 400 non-need scholarships (average $1753); low-interest long-term loans from external sources (average $2600); SEOG; College Work-Study; 130 part-time jobs. Supporting data: FFS, FAF, IRS, institutional form, AFSA/SAR acceptable. Priority application deadline: 3/1.

CAMPUS LIFE/STUDENT SERVICES Drama/theater group; student-run newspaper and radio station. Institution provides health clinic, personal/psychological counseling.

ATHLETICS Member NAIA. Intercollegiate sports: basketball M(s), W(s); football M(s); soccer M(s); tennis M(s), W(s); track and field M(s), W(s); volleyball W(s). Intramural sports: badminton, baseball/softball, basketball, bowling, football, tennis, track and field, volleyball, weight lifting.

MAJORS Accounting B; agricultural business A; agricultural sciences A; art education B; art/fine arts B; biblical studies B; biology/biological sciences B; business administration/commerce/management B; business education B; ceramic art and design B; chemistry B; communication B; computer science B; (pre)dentistry sequence B; early childhood education B; economics B; education B; elementary education B; (pre)engineering sequence A; English B; environmental sciences B; fashion merchandising B; German B; health education B; history B; home economics B; home economics education B; industrial arts A, B; interdisciplinary studies B; interior design B; international studies B; (pre)law sequence B; liberal arts/general studies A, B; mathematics B; medical technology B; (pre)medicine sequence B; music B; music education B; natural sciences B; nursing B; painting/drawing B; peace studies B; philosophy B; physical education B; physics B; political science/government B; psychology B; public relations B; publishing B; religious studies B; science B; science education B; secondary education B; social work B; special education B; speech/rhetoric/public address/debate B; theater arts/drama B; theology B. Majors with highest enrollment: nursing, elementary education, history.

SPECIAL NOTE FROM THE COLLEGE At Bethel College in Kansas, both scholarship and service are important. Bethel graduates are in exciting and challenging careers as a result of their strong, problem-solving, liberal arts background. Professors are readily available for Bethel students. Bethel's emphasis on service is also renowned. Bethel College students are set to travel to disaster sites and to serve community needs in the witness of the College's heritage. Students are invited to Bethel to discover if its story might become theirs. The mission of Bethel College is to graduate educated, caring Christians.

CONTACT Mr. James N. Huxman, Director of Admissions, Bethel College, North Newton, KS 67117, 316-283-2500 Ext. 230.

BETHEL COLLEGE
St. Paul, Minnesota

Total enrollment: 1,832 (all UG)

Women: 68%

Application deadline: 8/15

Tuition & fees: $9250

Room & board: $3380

Entrance: moderately difficult

SAT ≥ 500: 30% V, 57% M

ACT ≥ 21: 62%

Denominational affiliation: Baptist General Conference

GENERAL INFORMATION Independent 4-year coed college. Founded 1871. Awards A (college transfer), B. Primary accreditation: regional. Metropolitan setting; 231-acre campus. Total enrollment: 1,832. Faculty: 151 (107 full-time, 44 part-time); 60% of full-time faculty have doctoral degrees. Library holdings: 129,000 bound volumes, 640 periodical subscriptions, 3,700 records/tapes. Computer terminals/PCs available for student use: 74, located in computer center, dormitories.

UNDERGRADUATE Profile·Fall 1989: 1,832 undergraduates (419 freshmen); 6% part-time; 65% state residents; 7% transfers; 82% financial aid recipients; 68% women; 32% men; 1% blacks; 1% Hispanics; 1% Asian Americans; 1% international students; 1% of undergraduates 25 years of age or older.

1989 FRESHMAN DATA 831 students applied for fall 1989 admission; 86% were accepted; 59% of those accepted enrolled. 24% of freshmen were in top 10% of secondary school class, 54% were in top 25%, 84% were in top half.

FRESHMAN ADMISSIONS Options: early entrance, deferred entrance. Required: essay, high school transcript, 3 recommendations, SAT or ACT, TOEFL (for foreign students), PSAT. Recommended: 3 years of high school math and science, interview. Test scores used for admission. Application deadline: 8/15. College's own assessment of entrance difficulty level: moderately difficult.

TRANSFER ADMISSIONS Required: essay, standardized test scores, 3 recommendations, college transcript, minimum 2.0 grade point average. Required for some: high school transcript. Application deadline: 8/15. College's own assessment of entrance difficulty level: moderately difficult.

EXPENSES (1990–91) Comprehensive fee of $12,630 includes full-time tuition ($9250) and college room and board ($3380). College room only: $1860. Part-time tuition: $350 per credit hour.

FINANCIAL AID Fall 1989 full-time freshmen: 88% applied for aid, 76% of those were judged to have need, 100% of those were aided; the average aided freshman received an aid package worth $8320 (60% scholarships/grants, 40% self-help) meeting 98% of need. College-administered aid for all 1989–90 undergraduates: 1,170 need-based scholarships (average $1674); non-need scholarships (average $800); short-term loans (average $300); low-interest long-term loans from external sources (average $2400); SEOG; College Work-Study; 430 part-time jobs. Supporting data: IRS, institutional form required; FFS, state form required for some; FAF acceptable. Priority application deadline: 4/15.

CAMPUS LIFE/STUDENT SERVICES Drama/theater group; student-run newspaper and radio station. Institution provides health clinic, personal/psychological counseling.

ATHLETICS Member NCAA (Division III). Intercollegiate sports: baseball/softball M(III); basketball M(III), W(III); cross-country running M(III), W(III); football M(III); golf M(III); ice hockey M(III); soccer M(III); tennis M(III), W(III); track and field M(III), W(III); volleyball W(III). Intramural sports: baseball/softball, basketball, football, golf, racquetball, table tennis (ping pong), tennis, track and field, volleyball, weight lifting.

MAJORS Accounting B; adult and continuing education B; anthropology B; art education B; art/fine arts B; art history B; biblical studies B; biology/biological sciences B; business administration/commerce/management B; chemistry B; child care/child and family studies B; child psychology/child development B; communication B; computer science B; creative writing B; (pre)dentistry sequence B; early childhood education B; economics B; education B; elementary education B; (pre)engineering sequence A; English B; finance/banking B; health education B; history B; international studies B; (pre)law sequence B; liberal arts/general studies A; literature B; management information systems B; mathematics B; (pre)medicine sequence B; music B; music education B; natural sciences B; nursing B; philosophy B; physical education B; physics B; political science/government B; psychology B; sacred music B; science education B; secondary education B; social science B; social work B; sociology B; Spanish B; speech/rhetoric/public address/debate B; studio art B; theater arts/drama B; theology B; (pre)veterinary medicine sequence B. Majors with highest enrollment: business administration/commerce/management, psychology, education.

SPECIAL NOTE FROM THE COLLEGE From the first day of classes at Bethel, students find an atmosphere of active questioning, both intellectual and spiritual. Bethel believes that this questioning results in clearer understanding and a deepening faith. Students at Bethel find not only an educational experience but also spiritual maturity. Life and learning are celebrated at Bethel.

CONTACT Mr. Douglas Briggs, Director of Admissions, Bethel College, St. Paul, MN 55112, 612-638-6242 or toll-free 800-255-8706.

BIOLA UNIVERSITY
La Mirada, California

Total enrollment: 2,566

UG enrollment: 1,827 (59% W)

Application deadline: 6/1

Tuition & fees: $9172

Room & board: $3820

Entrance: moderately difficult

Denominational affiliation: nondenominational

GENERAL INFORMATION Independent coed university. Founded 1908. Awards B, M, D. Primary accreditation: regional. Small-town setting, with easy access to Los Angeles; 100-acre campus. Total enrollment: 2,566. Faculty: 222 (140 full-time, 82 part-time); 65% of full-time faculty have doctoral degrees; graduate assistants teach a few undergraduate courses. Library holdings: 200,000 bound volumes, 4,550 titles on microform, 1,146 periodical subscriptions, 4,200 records/tapes. Computer terminals/PCs available for student use: 60, located in computer center, dormitories, computer labs.

UNDERGRADUATE Profile Fall 1989: 1,827 undergraduates (631 freshmen); 6% part-time; 70% state residents; 23% transfers; 85% financial aid recipients; 59% women; 41% men; 2% blacks; 0% Native Americans; 4% Hispanics; 10% Asian Americans; 7% international students.

1989 FRESHMAN DATA 1,363 students applied for fall 1989 admission; 71% were accepted; 65% of those accepted enrolled.

ENROLLMENT PATTERNS 75% of fall 1988 freshmen returned for fall 1989 term. 1987–89 average: 65% of entering classes graduated.

FRESHMAN ADMISSIONS Options: early entrance, deferred entrance. Required: high school transcript, 2 recommendations, interview, SAT or ACT, TOEFL (for foreign students). Recommended: 3 years of high school math and science, some high school foreign language. Test scores used for admission. Application deadline: 6/1. College's own assessment of entrance difficulty level: moderately difficult.

TRANSFER ADMISSIONS Required: high school transcript, 2 recommendations, interview, college transcript, minimum 2.0 grade point average. Recommended: 3 years of high school math and science, some high school foreign language, minimum 3.0 grade point average. Required for some: standardized test scores. Application deadline: 6/1. College's own assessment of entrance difficulty level: moderately difficult.

EXPENSES (1990–91) Comprehensive fee of $12,992 includes full-time tuition ($9172) and college room and board ($3820). Part-time tuition: $382 per unit.

FINANCIAL AID College-administered aid for all 1989–90 undergraduates: 1,300 need-based scholarships (average $4674); 628 non-need scholarships (average $4000); low-interest long-term loans from external sources (average $3100); SEOG; College Work-Study; 350 part-time jobs. Supporting data: FAF, state form required for some. Priority application deadline: 3/2.

CAMPUS LIFE Dress code; mandatory chapel; drama/theater group; student-run newspaper and radio station.

ATHLETICS Member NAIA. Intercollegiate sports: baseball/softball M(s); basketball M(s), W(s); cross-country running M(s), W(s); soccer M(s); tennis W(s); track and field M(s), W(s); volleyball W(s). Intramural sports: badminton, baseball/softball, basketball, cross-country running, football, racquetball, skiing (cross-country), skiing (downhill), soccer, table tennis (ping pong), tennis, track and field, volleyball, water polo.

MAJORS Accounting B; anthropology B; art education B; art/fine arts B; art therapy B; biblical studies B; biochemistry B; biology/biological sciences B; broadcasting B; business administration/commerce/management B; business economics B; business education B; business machine technologies B; chemistry B; communication B; computer information systems B; computer programming B; computer science B; economics B; education B; elementary education B; English B; European studies B; film studies B; Greek B; history B; humanities B; international studies B; journalism B; liberal arts/general studies B; literature B; marketing/retailing/merchandising B; mathematics B; (pre)medicine sequence B; ministries B; modern languages B; music B; music education B; nursing B; painting/drawing B; pastoral studies B; philosophy B; physical education B; physical sciences B; physics B; piano/organ B; psychology B; public relations B; radio and television studies B; religious education B; religious studies B; social science B; sociology B; Spanish B; speech pathology and audiology B; speech therapy B; theater arts/drama B; theology B. Majors with highest enrollment: business administration/commerce/management, communication, nursing.

SPECIAL NOTE FROM THE COLLEGE The administration and faculty at Biola University believe relationships to Jesus Christ touch every aspect of life. Biola's commitment to students starts with a solid biblical foundation—almost a second major. Its university setting provides the academic environment essential for true Christian scholarship. Students can choose from 1 of 123 programs and enjoy close contact with a highly qualified, caring faculty. Biola is ranked by the Carnegie Commission as a doctoral level II degree-granting institution: 1 of 2 such within the Christian College Coalition. A commitment to spiritual development and openness to academic risk are the twin hallmarks of Biola University.

CONTACT Mr. Greg Vaughan, Director of Admissions, Biola University, La Mirada, CA 90639, 213-903-4752.

CALIFORNIA BAPTIST COLLEGE
Riverside, California

Total enrollment: 673

UG enrollment: 630 (52% W)

Application deadline: rolling

Tuition & fees: $5346

Room & board: $2990

Entrance: minimally difficult

Denominational affiliation: Southern Baptist

GENERAL INFORMATION Independent comprehensive coed institution. Founded 1950. Awards B, M. Primary accreditation: regional. City setting, with easy access to Los Angeles; 75-acre campus. Total enrollment: 673. Faculty: 82 (44 full-time, 38 part-time); 64% of full-time faculty have doctoral degrees; graduate assistants teach no undergraduate courses. Library holdings: 70,000 bound volumes, 8,200 titles on microform, 400 periodical subscriptions, 2,500 records/tapes. Computer terminals/PCs available for student use: 43, located in computer center, business administration department.

UNDERGRADUATE PROFILE Fall 1989: 630 undergraduates (157 freshmen) from 30 states and territories and 21 foreign countries; 16% part-time; 69% state residents; 38% transfers; 88% financial aid recipients; 52% women; 48% men; 7% blacks; 1% Native Americans; 5% Hispanics; 2% Asian Americans; 7% international students.

1989 FRESHMAN DATA 308 students applied for fall 1989 admission; 85% were accepted; 60% of those accepted enrolled. 37% of freshmen were in top 25% of secondary school class, 72% were in top half.

FRESHMAN ADMISSIONS Required: high school transcript, 2 recommendations, SAT or ACT, TOEFL (for foreign students). Recommended: 3 years of high school math and science, some high school foreign language, Achievement Tests, English Composition Test. Test scores used for admission and counseling/placement. Application deadline: rolling. College's own assessment of entrance difficulty level: minimally difficult.

TRANSFER ADMISSIONS Required: 2 recommendations, college transcript, minimum 2.0 grade point average. Required for some: standardized test scores, high school transcript. Application deadline: rolling.

EXPENSES (1990–91) Comprehensive fee of $8336 includes full-time tuition ($5070), mandatory fees ($276), and college room and board ($2990 minimum). College room only: $1480 (minimum). Part-time tuition: $195 per unit.

FINANCIAL AID College-administered aid for all 1989–90 undergraduates: 540 need-based scholarships; 300 non-need scholarships (average $2405); low-interest long-term loans from external sources (average $2625); SEOG; College Work-Study; 76 part-time jobs. Supporting data: FAF, IRS, institutional form, AFSA/SAR required; state form required for some. Priority application deadline: 4/15.

CAMPUS LIFE/STUDENT SERVICES Dress code; mandatory chapel; drama/theater group; student-run newspaper. Institution provides health clinic, personal/psychological counseling. <EP>

ATHLETICS Member NAIA. Intercollegiate sports: baseball/softball M(s), W(s); basketball M(s), W(s); soccer M(s); tennis M(s); volleyball W(s). Intramural sports: baseball/softball, basketball, football, golf, volleyball.

MAJORS Art/fine arts B; behavioral sciences B; biology/biological sciences B; business administration/commerce/management B; communication B; education B; elementary education B; English B; history B; liberal arts/general studies B; music B; physical education B; physical sciences B; political science/government B; psychology B; public administration B; recreation and leisure services B; religious studies B; secondary education B; social science B; sociology B; Spanish B; theater arts/drama B. Majors with highest enrollment: business administration/commerce/management, religious studies, liberal arts/general studies.

SPECIAL NOTE FROM THE COLLEGE California Baptist College is located in southern California's Inland Empire, which is one of the most rapidly growing areas in the nation. Cal Baptist, with 17 undergraduate majors and a master's degree in marriage, family, and child counseling, offers a diverse and challenging academic program and the opportunity for active participation in experiential learning and development. Opportunities include, but are not limited to, studies abroad in China and the USSR; summer missions; and internships in juvenile hall ministries, political science, religion and counseling, and social science. At California Baptist College, knowledge is tested through personal experience.

CONTACT Mr. John E. Potter, Associate Vice President for Student Life, California Baptist College, Riverside, CA 92504, 714-689-5771 Ext. 212.

CALVIN COLLEGE
Grand Rapids, Michigan

Total enrollment: 4,325

UG enrollment: 4,179 (54% W)

Application deadline: rolling

Tuition & fees: $7350

Room & board: $3100

Entrance: moderately difficult

SAT ≥ 500: 44% V, 67% M

ACT ≥ 21: 71%

Denominational affiliation: Christian Reformed Church

GENERAL INFORMATION Independent comprehensive coed institution. Founded 1876. Awards B, M. Primary accreditation: regional. Metropolitan setting; 370-acre campus. Total enrollment: 4,325. Faculty: 308 (253 full-time, 55 part-time); 75% of full-time faculty have doctoral degrees; graduate assistants teach no undergraduate courses. Library holdings: 500,000 bound volumes, 390,000 titles on microform, 2,700 periodical subscriptions, 16,500 records/tapes. Computer terminals/PCs available for student use: 200, located in computer center, student center, library, dormitories.

UNDERGRADUATE PROFILE Fall 1989: 4,179 undergraduates (992 freshmen) from 48 states and territories and 32 foreign countries; 5% part-time; 54% state residents; 4% transfers; 90% financial aid recipients; 54% women; 46% men; 1% blacks; 1% Hispanics; 1% Asian Americans; 1% international students; 6% of undergraduates 25 years of age or older.

1989 FRESHMAN DATA 1,698 students applied for fall 1989 admission; 96% were accepted; 61% of those accepted enrolled. 20 freshmen were National Merit Scholarship Finalists; 17 received a National Merit Scholarship. 24% of freshmen were in top 10% of secondary school class, 54% were in top 25%, 75% were in top half.

ENROLLMENT PATTERNS 92% of fall 1988 freshmen returned for fall 1989 term. 1987–89 average: 52% of entering classes graduated; 21% of students completing a degree program went on for further study.

FRESHMAN ADMISSIONS Options: early entrance, deferred entrance. Required: high school transcript, 1 recommendation, SAT or ACT, TOEFL (for foreign students). Recommended: 3 years of high school math and science, 2 years of high school foreign language. Test scores used for admission and counseling/placement. Application deadline: rolling. College's own assessment of entrance difficulty level: moderately difficult.

TRANSFER ADMISSIONS Required: standardized test scores, high school transcript, 1 recommendation, college transcript, minimum 2.0 grade point average. Recommended: 3 years of high school math and science. Application deadline: rolling. College's own assessment of entrance difficulty level: moderately difficult.

EXPENSES (1990–91) Comprehensive fee of $10,450 includes full-time tuition ($7350) and college room and board ($3100). Part-time tuition: $930 per course. Tuition prepayment plan available.

FINANCIAL AID Fall 1989 full-time freshmen: 72% applied for aid, 80% of those were judged to have need, 100% of those were aided; the average aided freshman received an aid package worth $5843 (65% scholarships/grants, 35% self-help) meeting 91% of need. College-administered aid for all 1989–90 undergraduates: 1,625 need-based scholarships (average $1525); 4,320 non-need scholarships (average $630); short-term loans (average $70); low-interest long-term loans from college funds (average $2150), from external sources (average $2450); SEOG; College Work-Study; 600 part-time jobs. Supporting data: FAF required; IRS required for some; FFS acceptable. Priority application deadline: 2/15.

CAMPUS LIFE/STUDENT SERVICES Drama/theater group; student-run newspaper and radio station. Institution provides health clinic, personal/psychological counseling.

ATHLETICS Member NCAA (Division III). Intercollegiate sports: baseball/softball M(III), W(III); basketball M(III), W(III); cross-country running M(III), W(III); field hockey W(III); golf M(III); ice hockey M(III); soccer M(III), W(III); swimming and diving M(III), W(III); tennis M(III), W(III); track and field M(III), W(III); volleyball W(III). Intramural sports: baseball/softball, basketball, football, golf, ice hockey, racquetball, soccer, ultimate frisbee, volleyball, weight lifting.

MAJORS Accounting B; art education B; art/fine arts B; art history B; biology/biological sciences B; business administration/commerce/management B; business economics B; chemistry B; civil engineering B; classics B; communication B; computer science B; criminal justice B; (pre)dentistry sequence B; ecology/environmental studies B; economics B; education B; electrical engineering B; elementary education B; engineering (general) B; English B; environmental sciences B; European studies B; French B; geology B; German B; Germanic languages and literature B; Greek B; history B; humanities B; Latin B; (pre)law sequence B; liberal arts/general studies B; literature B; mathematics B; mechanical engineering B; medical technology B; (pre)medicine sequence B; music B; music education B; nursing B; philosophy B; physical education B; physical sciences B; physics B; political science/government B; psychology B; recreation and leisure services B; religious education B; religious studies B; sacred music B; science B; science education B; secondary education B; social science B; social work B; sociology B; Spanish B; special education B; speech/rhetoric/public address/debate B; telecommunications B; theology B; (pre)veterinary medicine sequence B; voice B. Majors with highest enrollment: education, business administration/commerce/management, engineering (general).

SPECIAL NOTE FROM THE COLLEGE Calvin College is one of the largest, oldest, and most respected of the Coalition schools. Calvin's modern 370-acre campus provides the setting for over 4,000 students and 250 faculty members to explore a broad range of majors and programs. While awarding over half of its degrees in accredited professional programs such as education, engineering, nursing, and business, Calvin remains committed to a liberal arts approach to learning. Eager to become a partner with students in their Christian maturation, the College encourages students to make faithful and responsible decisions about how they will use their time and talents—without imposing an excessive list of rules and regulations.

CONTACT Mr. Donald Lautenbach, Director of Admissions, Calvin College, Grand Rapids, MI 49546, 616-957-6106.

CAMPBELLSVILLE COLLEGE
Campbellsville, Kentucky

Total enrollment: 642 (all UG)

Women: 59%

Application deadline: rolling

Tuition & fees: $4500

Room & board: $2760

Entrance: moderately difficult

SAT ≥ 500: N/R

ACT ≥ 21: 30%

Denominational affiliation: Baptist

GENERAL INFORMATION Independent 4-year coed college. Founded 1906. Awards A (college transfer and terminal), B. Primary accreditation: regional. Small-town setting; 35-acre campus. Total enrollment: 642. Faculty: 56 (43 full-time, 13 part-time); 42% of full-time faculty have doctoral degrees. Library holdings: 108,000 bound volumes, 160 titles on microform, 500 periodical subscriptions, 1,816 records/tapes. Computer terminals/PCs available for student use: 30, located in computer center, library, classrooms.

UNDERGRADUATE PROFILE Fall 1989: 642 undergraduates (203 freshmen) from 15 states and territories and 6 foreign countries; 18% part-time; 90% state residents; 8% transfers; 85% financial aid recipients; 59% women; 41% men; 4% blacks; 1% Asian Americans; 1% international students; 27% of undergraduates 25 years of age or older.

1989 FRESHMAN DATA 575 students applied for fall 1989 admission; 67% were accepted; 53% of those accepted enrolled. 11% of freshmen were in top 10% of secondary school class, 25% were in top 25%, 73% were in top half.

ENROLLMENT PATTERNS 60% of fall 1988 freshmen returned for fall 1989 term. 1987–89 average: 33% of entering classes graduated; 43% of students completing a bachelor's program went on for further study.

FRESHMAN ADMISSIONS Options: early entrance, deferred entrance. Required: high school transcript, SAT or ACT, TOEFL (for foreign students). Test scores used for admission. Application deadline: rolling. Notification date: continuous. College's own assessment of entrance difficulty level: moderately difficult.

TRANSFER ADMISSIONS Required: college transcript, minimum 2.0 grade point average. Required for some: standardized test scores, high school transcript. Application deadline: rolling. Notification date: continuous. College's own assessment of entrance difficulty level: moderately difficult.

EXPENSES (1990–91) Comprehensive fee of $7260 includes full-time tuition ($4500) and college room and board ($2760). College room only: $980. Part-time tuition: $190 per credit.

FINANCIAL AID College-administered aid for all 1989–90 undergraduates: 40 need-based scholarships; 222 non-need scholarships (average $700); short-term loans (average $800); low-interest long-term loans from college funds (average $1000), from external sources (average $2500); SEOG; College Work-Study; 10 part-time jobs. Supporting data: FAF, institutional form required; IRS required for some; AFSA/SAR acceptable. Priority application deadline: 5/15.

CAMPUS LIFE/STUDENT SERVICES Dress code; mandatory chapel; drama/theater group; student-run newspaper. Institution provides health clinic, personal/psychological counseling.

ATHLETICS Member NAIA. Intercollegiate sports: baseball/softball M(s), W; basketball M(s), W(s); football M; golf M(s); swimming and diving M(s), W(s); tennis M(s), W(s). Intramural sports: basketball, football, soccer, table tennis (ping pong), tennis, volleyball.

MAJORS Accounting B; art education B; art/fine arts B; biblical studies B; biology/biological sciences B; business administration/commerce/management A, B; business economics B; business education B; chemistry B; communication B; computer information systems A, B; criminal justice A; data processing A; (pre)dentistry sequence B; economics B; elementary education B; (pre)engineering sequence A; English B; health education B; history B; (pre)law sequence B; mathematics B; medical technology B; (pre)medicine sequence B; ministries B; music B; music education B; natural sciences B; pastoral studies B; physical education B; piano/organ B; political science/government B; psychology B; recreation and leisure services B; religious education B; religious studies B; sacred music B; science education B; secondary education B; secretarial studies/office management A, B; social science B; sociology B; (pre)veterinary medicine sequence B; voice B. Majors with highest enrollment: elementary education, business administration/commerce/management, psychology.

SPECIAL NOTE FROM THE COLLEGE Campbellsville College is a 4-year liberal arts and sciences institution of the Kentucky Baptist Convention. Campbellsville is situated in central Kentucky, minutes from the beautiful Green River Reservoir and Lake. Approximately 600 students benefit from individual attention from the 118 full-time, caring, dedicated faculty and staff members. Academic work at Campbellsville is not confined only to the classroom. This past year, study groups traveled to Europe, Israel, New York, and the western states. Students are active in many phases of mission work. As Dr. W. R. Davenport, president of Campbellsville College, has said, "Campbellsville College is a place where significant areas of life are being explored. In a Christian college of the liberal arts, beautiful things happen in the lives of many people as they follow God's leadership in higher education."

CONTACT Mr. Philip L. Hanna, Director of Admissions, Campbellsville College, Campbellsville, KY 42718, 502-465-8158 Ext. 6220.

CAMPBELL UNIVERSITY
Buies Creek, North Carolina

Total enrollment: 4,820

UG enrollment: 3,773 (49% W)

Application deadline: 8/1

Tuition & fees: $6386

Room & board: $2515

Entrance: moderately difficult

SAT ≥ 500: 38% V, 33% M

ACT ≥ 21: 25%

Denominational affiliation: Baptist

GENERAL INFORMATION Independent coed university. Founded 1887. Awards A (college transfer), B, M, D. Primary accreditation: regional. Rural setting; 1,200-acre campus. Total enrollment: 4,820. Faculty: 243 (165 full-time, 78 part-time); 85% of full-time faculty have doctoral degrees; graduate assistants teach no undergraduate courses. Library holdings: 245,000 bound volumes, 291,000 titles on microform, 826 periodical subscriptions, 4,100 records/tapes. Computer terminals/PCs available for student use: 35, located in computer center.

UNDERGRADUATE PROFILE Fall 1989: 3,773 undergraduates (1,498 freshmen) from 41 states and territories and 38 foreign countries; 11% part-time; 68% state residents; 14% transfers; 84% financial aid recipients; 49% women; 51% men; 8% blacks; 1% Native Americans; 1% Hispanics; 8% Asian Americans; 7% international students; 14% of undergraduates 25 years of age or older.

1989 FRESHMAN DATA 2,612 students applied for fall 1989 admission; 75% were accepted; 77% of those accepted enrolled. 16% of freshmen were in top 10% of secondary school class, 25% were in top 25%, 65% were in top half.

ENROLLMENT PATTERNS 91% of fall 1988 freshmen returned for fall 1989 term. 1987–89 average: 53% of entering classes graduated; 27% of students completing a bachelor's program went on for further study.

FRESHMAN ADMISSIONS Options: early entrance, deferred entrance. Required: high school transcript, SAT or ACT, TOEFL (for foreign students). Recommended: 3 years of high school math and science, some high school foreign language, interview. Required for some: recommendations. Test scores used for admission and counseling/placement. Application deadline: 8/1. Notification date: continuous. College's own assessment of entrance difficulty level: moderately difficult.

TRANSFER ADMISSIONS Required: high school transcript, college transcript, minimum 2.0 grade point average, good standing at previous institution. Recommended: standardized test scores, interview. Required for some: recommendations, minimum 3.0 grade point average. Application deadline: 8/1. Notification date: continuous.

EXPENSES (1989–90) Comprehensive fee of $8901 includes full-time tuition ($6386) and college room and board ($2515). College room only: $920. Part-time tuition: $95 per semester hour.

FINANCIAL AID Fall 1989 full-time freshmen: 82% applied for aid, 54% of those were judged to have need, 100% of those were aided; the average aided freshman received an aid package worth $4980 meeting 84% of need. College-administered aid for all 1989–90 undergraduates: 2,100 need-based scholarships (average $4712); 649 non-need scholarships (average $1800); low-interest long-term loans from external sources (average $3000); SEOG; College Work-Study; 300 part-time jobs. Supporting data: FFS, institutional form, AFSA/SAR required; IRS, state form required for some; FAF acceptable. Priority application deadline: 3/15.

CAMPUS LIFE/STUDENT SERVICES Dress code; mandatory chapel; drama/theater group; student-run newspaper and radio station. Institution provides health clinic, personal/psychological counseling.

ATHLETICS Member NCAA (Division I). Intercollegiate sports: baseball/softball M(I,s), W(s); basketball M(I,s), W(s); cross-country running M(I,s), W(s); golf M(I,s), W(s); soccer M(I,s); tennis M(I,s), W(s); track and field M(I,s), W(s); volleyball W(s); wrestling M(I,s). Intramural sports: baseball/softball, basketball, golf, soccer, swimming and diving, tennis, track and field, volleyball, wrestling.

MAJORS Accounting B; applied mathematics B; art/fine arts B; biblical studies B; biology/biological sciences B; biomedical technologies B; broadcasting B; business administration/commerce/management B; business economics B; chemistry B; child care/child and family studies B; communication B; computer information systems B; data processing B; (pre)dentistry sequence B; early childhood education B; earth science B; economics B; education B; educational administration B; elementary education B; English B; fashion merchandising B; finance/banking B; food services management B; French B; health education B; health science B; history B; home economics B; home economics education B; interior design B; journalism B; (pre)law sequence B; liberal arts/general studies A; mathematics B; medical technology B; (pre)medicine sequence B; military science B; music B; music education B; natural sciences B; pastoral studies B; physical education B; piano/organ B; political science/government B; psychology B; public relations B; radio and television studies B; religious education B; sacred music B; science education B; secondary education B; social science B; social work B; Spanish B; sports administration B; studio art B; theater arts/drama B; theology B; (pre)veterinary medicine sequence B; voice B. Majors with highest enrollment: business administration/commerce/management, (pre)law sequence, communication.

SPECIAL NOTE FROM THE COLLEGE Campbell University is a private liberal arts institution in southeastern North Carolina, born of a vision 100 years ago—a vision that lives on today. Campbell's curriculum meets individual needs and interests and offers the range of majors that today's students expect from a high-quality institution, including preprofessional and professional studies. A comprehensive financial aid program helps families meet educational costs. The University has adapted to changing times and needs without losing sight of its heritage and mission to provide educational opportunities in a Christian environment.

CONTACT Mr. Herbert V. Kerner Jr., Dean of Admissions, Financial Aid, and Veterans' Affairs, Campbell University, Buies Creek, NC 27506, 919-893-4111 Ext. 2275 or toll-free 800-334-4111 (out-of-state).

CENTRAL WESLEYAN COLLEGE
Central, South Carolina

Total enrollment: 439 (all UG)

Women: 56%

Application deadline: 8/20

Tuition & fees: $6500

Room & board: $2820

Entrance: minimally difficult

SAT ≥ 500: 17% V, 20% M

ACT ≥ 21: 17%

Denominational affiliation: Wesleyan Church

GENERAL INFORMATION Independent 4-year coed college. Founded 1906. Awards B. Primary accreditation: regional. Small-town setting; 140-acre campus. Total enrollment: 439. Faculty: 50 (36 full-time, 14 part-time); 49% of full-time faculty have doctoral degrees. Library holdings: 71,090 bound volumes, 345 titles on microform, 427 periodical subscriptions, 2,537 records/tapes. Computer terminals/PCs available for student use: 42, located in computer center.

UNDERGRADUATE PROFILE Fall 1989: 439 undergraduates (76 freshmen) from 21 states and territories and 5 foreign countries; 6% part-time; 81% state residents; 14% transfers; 95% financial aid recipients; 56% women; 44% men; 7% blacks; 1% Native Americans; 1% Hispanics; 1% Asian Americans; 1% international students.

1989 FRESHMAN DATA 157 students applied for fall 1989 admission; 83% were accepted; 58% of those accepted enrolled. 10% of freshmen were in top 10% of secondary school class, 56% were in top 25%, 66% were in top half.

ENROLLMENT PATTERNS 68% of fall 1988 freshmen returned for fall 1989 term. 1987–89 average: 35% of entering classes graduated.

FRESHMAN ADMISSIONS Options: early entrance, deferred entrance. Required: high school transcript, SAT or ACT, TOEFL (for foreign students). Required for some: recommendations, interview. Test scores used for admission. Application deadline:

8/20. Notification date: continuous. College's own assessment of entrance difficulty level: minimally difficult.

TRANSFER ADMISSIONS Required: college transcript. Recommended: minimum 2.0 grade point average. Required for some: standardized test scores, high school transcript, recommendations, interview. College's own assessment of entrance difficulty level: minimally difficult.

EXPENSES (1990–91) Comprehensive fee of $9320 includes full-time tuition ($6380), mandatory fees ($120), and college room and board ($2820). College room only: $950. Part-time tuition: $220 per hour. Tuition prepayment plan available.

FINANCIAL AID Fall 1989 full-time freshmen: 100% applied for aid, 95% of those were judged to have need, 100% of those were aided; the average aided freshman received an aid package worth $6624 (72% scholarships/grants, 28% self-help) meeting 93% of need. College-administered aid for all 1989–90 undergraduates: need-based scholarships; 345 non-need scholarships (average $1931); low-interest long-term loans from external sources (average $2482); SEOG; College Work-Study; 25 part-time jobs. Supporting data: FAF, institutional form required; IRS, state form, AFSA/SAR required for some; FFS acceptable. Priority application deadline: 4/15.

CAMPUS LIFE/STUDENT SERVICES Dress code; mandatory chapel; student-run newspaper. Institution provides health clinic, personal/psychological counseling.

ATHLETICS Member NAIA. Intercollegiate sports: baseball/softball M(s), W(s); basketball M(s), W(s); golf M(s); soccer M(s); volleyball W(s). Intramural sports: baseball/softball, basketball, soccer, table tennis (ping pong), tennis, volleyball.

MAJORS Accounting B; biblical studies B; biology/biological sciences B; business administration/commerce/management B; chemistry B; early childhood education B; education B; elementary education B; English B; Greek B; history B; mathematics B; medical technology B; ministries B; music B; music education B; nursing B; pastoral studies B; physical education B; psychology B; religious studies B; sacred music B; social science B; special education B; theology B. Majors with highest enrollment: business administration/commerce/management, elementary education, religious studies.

SPECIAL NOTE FROM THE COLLEGE Central Wesleyan College is committed to providing a high-quality education from a very Christian perspective. The issues of faith are explored in each course of study and practiced in daily life. The faculty's personal dedication and skills enable it to serve students from a wide variety of backgrounds—ranging from those who might be underprepared to National Merit Finalists—by providing the right amount of support and the right amount of challenge. A cooperative program with nearby Clemson University allows Central Wesleyan's students to experience the atmosphere and fellowship of a Christian campus and the academic diversity of a large university. Graduates have distinguished themselves in their careers while maintaining active involvement in service to their communities and churches. An education at Central Wesleyan provides what's needed for a career and for a satisfying and balanced life.

CONTACT Mr. Tim Wilkerson, Dean of Enrollment Management, Central Wesleyan College, Central, SC 29630, 803-639-2453 Ext. 326.

COLORADO CHRISTIAN UNIVERSITY
Lakewood, Colorado

Total enrollment: 781

UG enrollment: 729 (48% W)

Application deadline: rolling

Tuition & fees: $4380

Room & board: $1980

Entrance: moderately difficult

SAT ≥ 500: 21% V, 26% M

ACT ≥ 21: 50%

Denominational affiliation: interdenominational

GENERAL INFORMATION Independent comprehensive coed institution. Founded 1914. Awards A (college transfer), B, M. Primary accreditation: regional and AABC. City setting, with easy access to Denver; 25-acre campus. Total enrollment: 781. Faculty: 57 (24 full-time, 33 part-time); graduate assistants teach no undergraduate courses. Library holdings: 50,000 bound volumes, 25 titles on microform, 280 periodical subscriptions, 1,530 records/tapes. Computer terminals/PCs available for student use: 32, located in computer center.

UNDERGRADUATE PROFILE Fall 1989: 729 undergraduates (265 freshmen) from 38 states and territories and 4 foreign countries; 10% part-time; 68% state residents; 42% transfers; 80% financial aid recipients; 48% women; 52% men; 2% blacks; 1% Native Americans; 3% Hispanics; 1% Asian Americans; 1% international students; 35% of undergraduates 25 years of age or older.

1989 FRESHMAN DATA 491 students applied for fall 1989 admission; 69% were accepted; 78% of those accepted enrolled. 19% of freshmen were in top 10% of secondary school class, 50% were in top 25%, 67% were in top half.

FRESHMAN ADMISSIONS Options: early entrance, deferred entrance. Required: essay, high school transcript, SAT or ACT, TOEFL (for foreign students). Recommended: 3 years of high school math and science, some high school foreign language,

English Composition Test (with essay). Required for some: 3 recommendations, interview. Test scores used for admission. Application deadline: rolling. College's own assessment of entrance difficulty level: moderately difficult.

TRANSFER ADMISSIONS Required: essay, college transcript, minimum 2.0 grade point average. Required for some: high school transcript, 3 recommendations, interview. Application deadline: rolling. College's own assessment of entrance difficulty level: moderately difficult.

EXPENSES (1990–91) Comprehensive fee of $6360 includes full-time tuition ($4080), mandatory fees ($300), and college room and board ($1980). College room only: $1350. Part-time tuition: $170 per semester hour.

FINANCIAL AID Fall 1989 full-time freshmen: 96% applied for aid, 64% of those were judged to have need, 100% of those were aided; the average aided freshman received an aid package worth $5222 (65% scholarships/grants, 35% self-help) meeting 93% of need. College-administered aid for all 1989–90 undergraduates: need-based scholarships; non-need scholarships; short-term loans; low-interest long-term loans from external sources (average $2000); SEOG; College Work-Study. Supporting data: FFS, IRS, institutional form, AFSA/SAR required; state form required for some; FAF acceptable. Priority application deadline: 4/1.

CAMPUS LIFE/STUDENT SERVICES Mandatory chapel; drama/theater group; student-run newspaper. Institution provides personal/psychological counseling.

ATHLETICS Member NCAA (Division II). Intercollegiate sports: basketball M(II,s), W(II,s); football M; golf M(II); soccer M(II,s), W(II,s); tennis M(II,s), W(II,s); volleyball W(II,s).

MAJORS Accounting B; biblical studies A, B; biology/biological sciences B; business administration/commerce/management B; communication B; computer information systems A, B; elementary education B; English B; history B; humanities B; human services B; liberal arts/general studies A, B; ministries B; music B; music education B; pastoral studies B; psychology B; sacred music B; theater arts/drama B. Majors with highest enrollment: ministries, psychology, business administration/commerce/management.

SPECIAL NOTE FROM THE COLLEGE Colorado Christian University emphasizes the integration of biblical principles into every aspect of the student's life. Educating the whole person is the focus; preparing each student for a successful life of leadership and service is the goal. In an ideal setting of dynamic urban Denver, the Colorado Christian student benefits from various internship opportunities as well as cultural stimulation to help prepare for the realities of the everyday world. The campus offers natural open space and a caring community to encourage creative educational growth. The University's location in Colorado allows every student a wealth of recreational opportunities, including skiing, hiking, camping, and biking. Students are invited to come and experience an education at Colorado Christian University—an education designed for life.

CONTACT Mr. Mark Middlebrooks, Admissions Office Manager, Colorado Christian University, 180 South Garrison Street, Lakewood, CO 80226, 303-238-5386 Ext. 125.

COVENANT COLLEGE
Lookout Mountain, Georgia

Total enrollment: 580 (all UG)

Women: 51%

Application deadline: rolling

Tuition & fees: $7550

Room & board: $3250

Entrance: moderately difficult

SAT ≥ 500: 49% V, 54% M

ACT ≥ 21: 54%

Denominational affiliation: Presbyterian Church in America

GENERAL INFORMATION Independent 4-year coed college. Founded 1955. Awards A (college transfer and terminal), B. Primary accreditation: regional. Small-town setting; 70-acre campus. Total enrollment: 580. Faculty: 64 (37 full-time, 27 part-time); 68% of full-time faculty have doctoral degrees. Library holdings: 65,061 bound volumes, 26,776 titles on microform, 504 periodical subscriptions, 6,327 records/tapes. Computer terminals/PCs available for student use: 26, located in computer center, library.

UNDERGRADUATE PROFILE Fall 1989: 580 undergraduates (174 freshmen) from 39 states and territories and 19 foreign countries; 5% part-time; 18% state residents; 5% transfers; 86% financial aid recipients; 51% women; 49% men; 2% blacks; 1% Native Americans; 1% Hispanics; 2% Asian Americans; 5% international students; 10% of undergraduates 25 years of age or older.

1989 FRESHMAN DATA 359 students applied for fall 1989 admission; 67% were accepted; 73% of those accepted enrolled. 20% of freshmen were in top 10% of secondary school class, 44% were in top 25%, 74% were in top half.

ENROLLMENT PATTERNS 69% of fall 1988 freshmen returned for fall 1989 term. 1987–89 average: 35% of entering classes graduated.

FRESHMAN ADMISSIONS Options: early entrance, deferred entrance. Required: essay, high school transcript, 3 years of high school math and science, interview, SAT or ACT, TOEFL (for foreign students). Recommended: 2 years of high school foreign language, 1 recommendation, English Composition Test. Test scores used for admission. Application deadline: rolling. College's own assessment of entrance difficulty level: moderately difficult.

TRANSFER ADMISSIONS Required: essay, high school transcript, 3 years of high school math and science, interview, college transcript, minimum 2.0 grade point average. Recommended: standardized test scores, 2 years of high school foreign language, 1 recommendation. Application deadline: rolling. College's own assessment of entrance difficulty level: moderately difficult.

EXPENSES (1990–91) Comprehensive fee of $10,800 includes full-time tuition ($7400), mandatory fees ($150), and college room and board ($3250). College room only: $1650.

FINANCIAL AID Fall 1989 full-time freshmen: 97% applied for aid, 68% of those were judged to have need, 99% of those were aided; the average aided freshman received an aid package worth $5115 (59% scholarships/grants, 41% self-help) meeting 92% of need. College-administered aid for all 1989–90 undergraduates: 179 need-based scholarships (average $1412); 259 non-need scholarships (average $1383); low-interest long-term loans from external sources (average $2074); SEOG; College Work-Study; 52 part-time jobs. Supporting data: FAF, IRS required; AFSA/SAR required for some; FFS acceptable. Priority application deadline: 3/31.

CAMPUS LIFE/STUDENT SERVICES Mandatory chapel; drama/theater group; student-run newspaper. Institution provides health clinic, personal/psychological counseling.

ATHLETICS Member NAIA. Intercollegiate sports: basketball M(s), W(s); cross-country running M, W; soccer M(s); volleyball W. Intramural sports: baseball/softball, basketball, football, soccer, tennis, volleyball.

MAJORS Biblical studies A, B; biology/biological sciences B; business administration/commerce/management A, B; chemistry B; computer science B; elementary education B; English B; health science A; history B; interdisciplinary studies B; (pre)law sequence B; (pre)medicine sequence B; music B; music education B; natural sciences B; piano/organ B; psychology B; sociology B; stringed instruments B; voice B; wind and percussion instruments B. Majors with highest enrollment: business administration/commerce/management, elementary education, psychology.

SPECIAL NOTE FROM THE COLLEGE "In all things . . . Christ preeminent" is more than a motto at Covenant College. It is a way of teaching, a way of learning, and a way of living. Covenant College provides a broad liberal arts education emphasizing a personal commitment to Christ. The College offers both associate and baccalaureate degrees in liberal arts disciplines and selected preprofessional programs. The primary goal is to provide an environment of academic excellence that encourages students to develop an active Christian mind. More than two thirds of the faculty members have earned doctorates. More than 500 students come to Covenant from 39 states and 19 foreign countries. Christian commitment and academic excellence are knit together in a warm spirit of friendship that makes Covenant unique.

CONTACT Mr. Nick Arnett, Director of Admissions Counseling, Covenant College, Lookout Mountain, GA 30750, 404-820-1560 Ext. 147.

DALLAS BAPTIST UNIVERSITY
Dallas, Texas

Total enrollment: 2,269

UG enrollment: 1,759 (51% W)

Application deadline: rolling

Tuition & fees: $4620

Room & board: $2928

Entrance: moderately difficult

SAT ≥ 500: N/R

ACT ≥ 21: 40%

Denominational affiliation: Southern Baptist

GENERAL INFORMATION Independent comprehensive coed institution. Founded 1898. Awards B, M. Primary accreditation: regional. Metropolitan setting; 200-acre campus. Total enrollment: 2,269. Faculty: 115 (54 full-time, 61 part-time); 59% of full-time faculty have doctoral degrees; graduate assistants teach no undergraduate courses. Library holdings: 123,508 bound volumes, 265,931 titles on microform, 820 periodical subscriptions, 2,164 records/tapes. Computer terminals/PCs available for student use: 30, located in computer center, library.

UNDERGRADUATE PROFILE Fall 1989: 1,759 undergraduates (110 freshmen) from 33 states and territories and 35 foreign countries; 60% part-time; 94% state residents; 41% transfers; 67% financial aid recipients; 51% women; 49% men; 20% blacks; 1% Native Americans; 4% Hispanics; 3% Asian Americans; 5% international students; 70% of undergraduates 25 years of age or older.

1989 FRESHMAN DATA 310 students applied for fall 1989 admission; 98% were accepted; 36% of those accepted enrolled. 21% of freshmen were in top 10% of secondary school class, 46% were in top 25%, 72% were in top half.

ENROLLMENT PATTERNS 59% of fall 1988 freshmen returned for fall 1989 term.

FRESHMAN ADMISSIONS Options: early entrance, deferred entrance. Required: high school transcript, SAT or ACT, TOEFL (for foreign students). Recommended: 3 years of high school math and science, some high school foreign language. Required for some: recommendations, interview. Test scores used for admission. Application deadline: rolling. Notification date: continuous. College's own assessment of entrance difficulty level: moderately difficult.

TRANSFER ADMISSIONS Required: college transcript, minimum 2.0 grade point average. Required for some: standardized test scores, high school transcript, recommendations, interview. Application deadline: rolling. Notification date: continuous. College's own assessment of entrance difficulty level: minimally difficult.

EXPENSES (1990–91) Comprehensive fee of $7548 includes full-time tuition ($4620) and college room and board ($2928). College room only: $1060. Part-time tuition: $154 per credit hour.

FINANCIAL AID College-administered aid for all 1989–90 undergraduates: 103 need-based scholarships (average $1100); 788 non-need scholarships (average $1776); low-interest long-term loans from college funds (average $2500), from external sources (average $3426); SEOG; College Work-Study. Supporting data: FAF, IRS, institutional form, AFSA/SAR required. Priority application deadline: 6/1.

CAMPUS LIFE/STUDENT SERVICES Dress code; mandatory chapel; drama/theater group; student-run newspaper. Institution provides legal services, health clinic, personal/psychological counseling. Social organizations: local fraternities, local sororities, social clubs.

ATHLETICS Member NAIA. Intercollegiate sports: baseball/ softball M(s); basketball M(s); volleyball W(s). Intramural sports: badminton, baseball/softball, basketball, bowling, football, golf, soccer, table tennis (ping pong), tennis, track and field, ultimate frisbee, volleyball, weight lifting.

MAJORS Accounting B; art/fine arts B; biblical studies B; biology/biological sciences B; business administration/ commerce/management B; business economics B; business education B; communication B; computer science B; criminal justice B; deaf interpreter training B; (pre)dentistry sequence B; early childhood education B; economics B; education B; elementary education B; engineering and applied sciences B; English B; finance/banking B; history B; interdisciplinary studies B; (pre)law sequence B; liberal arts/general studies B; marketing/ retailing/merchandising B; mathematics B; (pre)medicine sequence B; ministries B; music B; music education B; nursing B; paralegal studies B; physical education B; piano/organ B; political science/government B; psychology B; religious education B; religious studies B; sacred music B; science education B; secondary education B; sociology B; (pre)veterinary medicine sequence B; voice B. Majors with highest enrollment: business administration/ commerce/management, accounting, religious studies.

SPECIAL NOTE FROM THE COLLEGE Dallas Baptist University is located in the "hill country" of Dallas. It is 20 minutes from downtown Dallas and 30 minutes from downtown Fort Worth, between one of the most exciting cosmopolitan centers in the United States and "where the West really begins." In 1983, as part of its computer literacy program, DBU became the first private college or university in the nation to require every entering freshman to lease or purchase a microcomputer. Freshmen are also required to write a paper integrating biblical principles with their intended majors. DBU provides a high-quality education in a Christian context.

CONTACT Mrs. Jill Lewis, Admissions Office Manager, Dallas Baptist University, 7777 West Kiest Boulevard, Dallas, TX 75211, 214-333-5360.

DORDT COLLEGE
Sioux Center, Iowa

Total enrollment: 1,038 (all UG)

Women: 50%

Application deadline: 9/1

Tuition & fees: $6400

Room & board: $2240

Entrance: moderately difficult

Denominational affiliation: Christian Reformed

GENERAL INFORMATION Independent 4-year coed college. Founded 1955. Awards A (terminal), B. Primary accreditation: regional. Rural setting; 45-acre campus. Total enrollment: 1,038. Faculty: 82 (70 full-time, 12 part-time); 56% of full-time faculty have doctoral degrees. Library holdings: 120,000 bound volumes, 14,500 titles on microform, 698 periodical subscriptions, 850 records/tapes. Computer terminals/PCs available for student use: 100, located in computer center, student center, library.

UNDERGRADUATE PROFILE Fall 1989: 1,038 undergraduates (313 freshmen) from 28 states and territories; 4% part-time; 45% state residents; 5% transfers; 95% financial aid recipients; 50% women; 50% men; 0% blacks; 0% Native Americans; 0% Hispanics; 2% Asian Americans; 0% international students; 8% of undergraduates 25 years of age or older.

1989 FRESHMAN DATA 468 students applied for fall 1989 admission; 83% were accepted; 80% of those accepted enrolled. 18% of freshmen were in top 10% of secondary school class, 38% were in top 25%, 70% were in top half.

ENROLLMENT PATTERNS 85% of fall 1988 freshmen returned for fall 1989 term. 1987–89 average: 60% of entering classes graduated; 18% of students completing a bachelor's program went on for further study.

FRESHMAN ADMISSIONS Options: early entrance, deferred entrance. Required: high school transcript, SAT or ACT. Recommended: some high school foreign language. Required for some: interview. Test scores used for counseling/placement. Application deadline: 9/1. Notification date: continuous until 9/1. College's own assessment of entrance difficulty level: moderately difficult.

TRANSFER ADMISSIONS Required: high school transcript, college transcript, minimum 2.0 grade point average. Required

for some: interview. Application deadline: 9/1. Notification date: continuous until 9/1.

EXPENSES (1989–90) Comprehensive fee of $8640 includes full-time tuition ($6400) and college room and board ($2240). College room only: $1100. Part-time tuition: $265 per semester hour. Part-time mandatory fees per semester: $10.

FINANCIAL AID Fall 1989 full-time freshmen: 87% applied for aid, 99% of those were judged to have need, 100% of those were aided; the average aided freshman received an aid package worth $6067 (57% scholarships/grants, 43% self-help) meeting 100% of need. College-administered aid for all 1989–90 undergraduates: need-based scholarships; non-need scholarships (average $1000); low-interest long-term loans from college funds (average $700), from external sources (average $3200); SEOG; College Work-Study; 710 part-time jobs. Supporting data: institutional form required; IRS required for some; FFS, FAF, AFSA/SAR acceptable. Priority application deadline: 4/15.

CAMPUS LIFE/STUDENT SERVICES Mandatory chapel; drama/theater group; student-run newspaper. Institution provides health clinic, personal/psychological counseling.

ATHLETICS Member NAIA. Intercollegiate sports: baseball/softball M, W; basketball M, W; golf M, W; ice hockey M; soccer M; swimming and diving M, W; tennis M, W; track and field M, W; volleyball W. Intramural sports: baseball/softball, basketball, bowling, field hockey, gymnastics, ice hockey, soccer, swimming and diving, table tennis (ping pong), tennis, track and field, volleyball.

MAJORS Accounting B; agricultural business A, B; agricultural sciences B; art/fine arts B; biology/biological sciences B; business administration/commerce/management B; business education B; chemistry B; communication B; computer science B; (pre)dentistry sequence B; education B; electrical engineering B; elementary education B; engineering (general) B; engineering mechanics B; English B; environmental sciences B; German B; history B; journalism B; management information systems B; mathematics B; medical technology B; (pre)medicine sequence B; music B; music education B; natural sciences B; philosophy B; physical education B; physics B; political science/government B; psychology B; religious studies B; secondary education B; secretarial studies/office management A; social science B; social work B; sociology B; Spanish B; theater arts/drama B; theology B; (pre)veterinary medicine sequence B. Majors with highest enrollment: business administration/commerce/management, elementary education, agricultural sciences.

SPECIAL NOTE FROM THE COLLEGE Dordt College seeks to provide an education that is thoroughly and vitally Christian. It is committed to making a Dordt education both academically excellent and broadly useful. There are more than 40 programs of study to choose from. Faculty members and students work together to develop knowledge and insight and strive to find ways to use that knowledge and insight in a life of service. Because of Dordt's size—just over 1,000 students—and the fact that students and faculty share a common goal—to glorify God in all they do—the Dordt community is close-knit. This provides an environment in which students are encouraged and supported in reaching their full potential academically, spiritually, and socially.

CONTACT Mr. Howard J. Hall, Director of Admissions and Financial Aid, Dordt College, Sioux Center, IA 51250, 712-722-6080 or toll-free 800-343-6738.

EASTERN COLLEGE
Saint Davids, Pennsylvania

Total enrollment: 1,282

UG enrollment: 1,037 (60% W)

Application deadline: 8/15

Tuition & fees: $8720

Room & board: $3470

Entrance: moderately difficult

SAT ≥ 500: 28% V, 42% M

ACT ≥ 21: 72%

Denominational affiliation: American Baptist

GENERAL INFORMATION Independent comprehensive coed institution. Founded 1932. Awards B, M. Primary accreditation: regional. Small-town setting, with easy access to Philadelphia; 100-acre campus. Total enrollment: 1,282. Faculty: 108 (40 full-time, 68 part-time); 63% of full-time faculty have doctoral degrees; graduate assistants teach a few undergraduate courses. Library holdings: 137,000 bound volumes, 56,828 titles on microform, 763 periodical subscriptions, 2,154 records/tapes. Computer terminals/PCs available for student use: 50, located in computer center, classroom building.

UNDERGRADUATE PROFILE Fall 1989: 1,037 undergraduates (225 freshmen) from 31 states and territories and 10 foreign countries; 39% part-time; 75% state residents; 30% transfers; 66% financial aid recipients; 60% women; 40% men; 6% blacks; 0% Native Americans; 1% Hispanics; 1% Asian Americans; 1% international students; 37% of undergraduates 25 years of age or older.

1989 FRESHMAN DATA 539 students applied for fall 1989 admission; 76% were accepted; 55% of those accepted enrolled. 5 freshmen were National Merit Scholarship Finalists; 1 received a National Merit Scholarship. 11% of freshmen were in top 10% of secondary school class, 23% were in top 25%, 47% were in top half.

ENROLLMENT PATTERNS 74% of fall 1988 freshmen returned for fall 1989 term. 1987–89 average: 50% of entering classes graduated; 29% of students completing a degree program went on for further study.

FRESHMAN ADMISSIONS Options: early entrance, deferred entrance. Required: essay, high school transcript, 1 recommendation, SAT or ACT, TOEFL (for foreign students). Recommended: 3 years of high school math and science, some high school foreign language, interview, English Composition Test. Test scores used for admission. Application deadline: 8/15. Notification date: continuous. College's own assessment of entrance difficulty level: moderately difficult.

TRANSFER ADMISSIONS Required: essay, standardized test scores, high school transcript, 1 recommendation, college transcript, minimum 2.0 grade point average. Recommended: 3 years of high school math and science, some high school foreign language, interview. Application deadline: 8/15. Notification date: continuous. College's own assessment of entrance difficulty level: moderately difficult.

EXPENSES (1990–91 estimated) Comprehensive fee of $12,190 includes full-time tuition ($8720) and college room and board ($3470). Part-time tuition: $225 per credit.

FINANCIAL AID Fall 1989 full-time freshmen: 79% applied for aid, 90% of those were judged to have need, 83% of those were aided; the average aided freshman received an aid package worth $10,829 (55% scholarships/grants, 45% self-help) meeting 85% of need. College-administered aid for all 1989–90 undergraduates: 436 need-based scholarships (average $1576); non-need scholarships; low-interest long-term loans from external sources (average $598); SEOG; College Work-Study; 47 part-time jobs. Supporting data: IRS, state form, institutional form required; FFS, FAF, AFSA/SAR acceptable. Priority application deadline: 6/1.

CAMPUS LIFE/STUDENT SERVICES Drama/theater group; student-run newspaper and radio station. Institution provides health clinic, personal/psychological counseling.

ATHLETICS Member NAIA. Intercollegiate sports: baseball/softball M(s), W(s); basketball M(s), W(s); cross-country running M(s), W(s); field hockey W(s); lacrosse W(s); soccer M(s); tennis M, W; volleyball W(s). Intramural sports: baseball/softball, basketball, bowling, football, soccer, table tennis (ping pong), tennis, volleyball.

MAJORS Accounting B; American studies B; art history B; biblical studies B; biology/biological sciences B; business administration/commerce/management B; chemistry B; communication B; creative writing B; (pre)dentistry sequence B; economics B; elementary education B; French B; health services administration B; history B; literature B; mathematics B; medical technology B; (pre)medicine sequence B; ministries B; nursing B; philosophy B; physical education B; physical sciences B; political science/government B; psychology B; religious studies B; secondary education B; social work B; sociology B; Spanish B; studio art B. Majors with highest enrollment: nursing, elementary education, business administration/commerce/management.

SPECIAL NOTE FROM THE COLLEGE Eastern College is set on a 100-acre, wooded campus in suburban Philadelphia, thereby offering students easy access to the Northeast metropolitan corridor's abundant resources. The many creative academic programs at Eastern not only help students explore a diverse world but also change it. Dedicated faculty members sharpen critical thinking and encourage seekers; yet each student is challenged to seek first the Kingdom. The resulting Christian commitment reaches out beyond the campus to all humanity. Eastern's unique MBA program in economic development, for example, is truly international, enrolling students from around the world. At Eastern, the success of the College is gauged by students' thoughtful, involved lives of service.

CONTACT Dr. Ronald L. Keller, Vice President for Enrollment Management, Eastern College, Saint Davids, PA 19087, 215-341-5967.

EASTERN MENNONITE COLLEGE
Harrisonburg, Virginia

Total enrollment: 969 (all UG)

Women: 60%

Application deadline: 8/1

Tuition & fees: $6895

Room & board: $3080

Entrance: moderately difficult

SAT ≥ 500: 39% V, 55% M

ACT ≥ 21: 69%

Denominational affiliation: Mennonite

GENERAL INFORMATION Independent 4-year coed college. Administratively affiliated with Eastern Mennonite Seminary. Founded 1917. Awards A (college transfer and terminal), B. Primary accreditation: regional. Small-town setting; 88-acre campus. Total enrollment: 969. Faculty: 85 (53 full-time, 32 part-time); 50% of full-time faculty have doctoral degrees. Library holdings: 119,000 bound volumes, 30,000 titles on microform, 857 periodical subscriptions, 4,900 records/tapes. Computer terminals/PCs available for student use: 40, located in computer center, library, dormitories, science center.

UNDERGRADUATE PROFILE Fall 1989: 969 undergraduates (195 freshmen) from 33 states and territories and 12 foreign countries; 5% part-time; 38% state residents; 12% transfers; 88% financial aid recipients; 60% women; 40% men; 2% blacks; 0% Native Americans; 2% Hispanics; 0% Asian Americans; 2% international students; 3% of undergraduates 25 years of age or older.

1989 FRESHMAN DATA 441 students applied for fall 1989 admission; 79% were accepted; 56% of those accepted enrolled. 4 freshmen were National Merit Scholarship Finalists. 22% of freshmen were in top 10% of secondary school class, 45% were in top 25%, 71% were in top half.

ENROLLMENT PATTERNS 76% of fall 1988 freshmen returned for fall 1989 term. 1987–89 average: 63% of entering classes graduated; 12% of students completing a bachelor's program went on for further study.

FRESHMAN ADMISSIONS Options: early entrance, deferred entrance. Required: essay, high school transcript, 2 recommendations, statement of commitment, SAT or ACT, TOEFL (for foreign students). Recommended: 3 years of high school math and science, 2 years of high school foreign language, interview. Test scores used for admission. Application deadline: 8/1. Notification date: continuous until 8/1. College's own assessment of entrance difficulty level: moderately difficult.

TRANSFER ADMISSIONS Required: essay, high school transcript, 2 recommendations, college transcript, minimum 2.0 grade point average, statement of commitment. Recommended: standardized test scores, 3 years of high school math and science, 2 years of high school foreign language, interview. Application deadline: 8/1. Notification date: continuous until 8/1. College's own assessment of entrance difficulty level: moderately difficult.

EXPENSES (1990–91) Comprehensive fee of $9975 includes full-time tuition ($6895) and college room and board ($3080). Part-time tuition: $285 per semester hour.

FINANCIAL AID Fall 1989 full-time freshmen: 86% applied for aid, 86% of those were judged to have need, 100% of those were aided; the average aided freshman received an aid package worth $6591 (54% scholarships/grants, 46% self-help) meeting 92% of need. College-administered aid for all 1989–90 undergraduates: 430 need-based scholarships (average $1050); 652 non-need scholarships (average $825); low-interest long-term loans from college funds (average $1712), from external sources (average $1700); SEOG; College Work-Study; 149 part-time jobs. Supporting data: FAF, IRS, institutional form, AFSA/SAR required; state form required for some; FFS acceptable. Priority application deadline: 4/15. k-Study; 149 part-time jobs. Supporting data: FAF, IRS, institter group; student-run newspaper and radio station. Institution provides health clinic, personal/psychological counseling.

CAMPUS LIFE/STUDENT SERVICES Mandatory chapel; drama/theater group; student-run newspaper and radio station. Institution provides health clinic, personal/psychological counseling.

ATHLETICS Member NCAA (Division III). Intercollegiate sports: baseball/softball M(III), W(III); basketball M(III), W(III); cross-country running M(III), W(III); field hockey W(III); soccer M(III); tennis M(III), W(III); track and field M(III), W(III); volleyball W(III). Intramural sports: baseball/softball, basketball, football, soccer, table tennis (ping pong), tennis, volleyball, weight lifting.

MAJORS Accounting B; agricultural sciences B; art/fine arts B; biblical studies A, B; biology/biological sciences B; business administration/commerce/management B; chemistry B; community services B; computer information systems B; computer programming A; computer science B; data processing A; (pre)dentistry sequence B; dietetics B; early childhood education B; education A, B; elementary education B; (pre)engineering sequence A; English B; food services management B; French B; German B; history B; (pre)law sequence B; liberal arts/general studies A, B; mathematics B; medical technology B; (pre)medicine sequence B; ministries B; modern languages B; music B; music education B; nursing B; nutrition B; paralegal studies A; pastoral studies B; peace studies B; philosophy B; physical education B; psychology B; recreation and leisure services B; religious studies B; science education B; secondary education B; social work B; sociology B; Spanish B; special education B; teacher aide studies A; teaching English as a second language B; theology B; (pre)veterinary medicine sequence B. Majors with highest enrollment: business administration/commerce/management, biology/biological sciences, nursing.

SPECIAL NOTE FROM THE COLLEGE EMC students discover what it means to be a Christian and a world citizen. EMC's Global Village curriculum integrates the liberal arts and sciences with Christian values and personal contact with people of other cultures. Students spend a semester in the Middle East, Latin America, or Europe; a summer in China, Ireland, New Zealand, Appalachia, Mexico, South Africa, or Southeast Asia; or a year in Washington, DC, in a study-service program. Graduates are equipped with a distinctive intellectual framework and extraordinary, often life-transforming, experience in human relations. EMC alumni find that they are well prepared for advanced study and report that their careers and professional practice are profoundly enriched by a global perspective. Students come to see life as an opportunity for faithful Christian service and peacemaking in a needy world. All of this begins in a friendly campus community in the heart of the scenic and historic Shenandoah Valley of Virginia.

CONTACT Mr. Jerry A. Miller, Director of Admissions, Eastern Mennonite College, Harrisonburg, VA 22801, 703-433-2771 Ext. 118 or toll-free 800-368-2665 (out-of-state).

EASTERN NAZARENE COLLEGE
Quincy, Massachusetts

Total enrollment: 912

UG enrollment: 750 (57% W)

Application deadline: rolling

Tuition & fees: $7020

Room & board: $3100

Entrance: moderately difficult

SAT ≥ 500: 26% V, 42% M

ACT ≥ 21: N/R

Denominational affiliation: Church of the Nazarene

GENERAL INFORMATION Independent comprehensive coed institution. Founded 1918. Awards A (college transfer and terminal), B, M. Primary accreditation: regional. City setting, with easy access to Boston; 15-acre campus. Total enrollment: 912. Faculty: 62 (48 full-time, 14 part-time); 55% of full-time faculty have doctoral degrees; graduate assistants teach no undergraduate courses. Library holdings: 112,750 bound volumes, 240 titles on microform, 550 periodical subscriptions, 530 records/tapes. Computer terminals/PCs available for student use: 70, located in computer center, library.

UNDERGRADUATE PROFILE Fall 1989: 750 undergraduates (214 freshmen) from 31 states and territories and 26 foreign countries; 7% part-time; 38% state residents; 18% transfers; 89% financial aid recipients; 57% women; 43% men; 3% blacks; 0% Native Americans; 2% Hispanics; 1% Asian Americans; 4% international students; 10% of undergraduates 25 years of age or older.

1989 FRESHMAN DATA 552 students applied for fall 1989 admission; 75% were accepted; 51% of those accepted enrolled. 21% of freshmen were in top 10% of secondary school class, 37% were in top 25%, 75% were in top half.

ENROLLMENT PATTERNS 72% of fall 1988 freshmen returned for fall 1989 term.

FRESHMAN ADMISSIONS Options: early entrance, deferred entrance. Required: high school transcript, 1 recommendation, SAT or ACT, TOEFL (for foreign students). Recommended: essay, 3 years of high school math and science, some high school foreign language, interview. Test scores used for counseling/placement. Application deadline: rolling. Notification date: continuous.

College's own assessment of entrance difficulty level: moderately difficult.

TRANSFER ADMISSIONS Required: standardized test scores, high school transcript, 1 recommendation, college transcript, minimum 2.0 grade point average. Recommended: interview. Application deadline: rolling. Notification date: continuous.

EXPENSES (1990–91) Comprehensive fee of $10,120 includes full-time tuition ($6650), mandatory fees ($370), and college room and board ($3100). Part-time tuition: $295 per hour.

FINANCIAL AID Fall 1989 full-time freshmen: 85% applied for aid, 80% of those were judged to have need, 100% of those were aided; the average aided freshman received an aid package worth $6150 meeting 90% of need. College-administered aid for all 1989–90 undergraduates: 300 need-based scholarships (average $1500); 500 non-need scholarships (average $1000); short-term loans (average $400); low-interest long-term loans from external sources (average $3800); SEOG; College Work-Study; 175 part-time jobs. Supporting data: FAF, IRS, state form, institutional form, AFSA/SAR required. Priority application deadline: 3/1.

CAMPUS LIFE/STUDENT SERVICES Mandatory chapel; drama/theater group; student-run newspaper and radio station. Institution provides health clinic, personal/psychological counseling.

ATHLETICS Member NCAA (Division III). Intercollegiate sports: baseball/softball M(III), W(III); basketball M(III), W(III); cross-country running M(III), W(III); soccer M(III); tennis M(III), W(III); volleyball W(III). Intramural sports: basketball, soccer, volleyball.

MAJORS Aerospace engineering B; biology/biological sciences B; biomedical engineering B; business administration/commerce/management B; chemistry B; communication B; computer engineering B; computer information systems B; computer science B; (pre)dentistry sequence B; early childhood education A, B; education B; electrical engineering B; elementary education B; engineering physics B; English B; French B; history B; (pre)law sequence B; liberal arts/general studies A; manufacturing engineering B; mathematics B; mechanical engineering B; (pre)medicine sequence B; music B; music education B; pastoral studies B; physical education B; physics B; psychology B; religious education A, B; religious studies B; science B; social science B; social work B; sociology B; Spanish B; systems engineering B; (pre)veterinary medicine sequence B. Majors with highest enrollment: business administration/commerce/management, psychology, education.

SPECIAL NOTE FROM THE COLLEGE Eastern Nazarene College offers a strong commitment to a liberal arts education in a small-school, Christian-oriented setting. ENC has been producing graduates in Quincy, Massachusetts, for over 70 years and has maintained a reputation for being a caring, yet academically demanding, school. Boston's libraries, universities, conservatories, museums, historic sights, and churches offer unsurpassed educational opportunities and abundant possibilities for employment and entertainment. ENC believes that the solid academic programs, supportive faculty, Christian values, and Boston area location provide students with unparalleled opportunities for personal growth. Moreover, Eastern Nazarene seeks to develop in each person a Christian world view and to encourage each person to become God's creative and redemptive agent in today's world.

CONTACT Mr. William Nichols, Director of Admissions, Eastern Nazarene College, Quincy, MA 02170, 617-773-2373.

EVANGEL COLLEGE
Springfield, Missouri

Total enrollment: 1,525 (all UG)

Women: 55%

Application deadline: 8/15

Tuition & fees: $5278

Room & board: $2730

Entrance: moderately difficult

SAT ≥ 500: N/R

ACT ≥ 21: 39%

Denominational affiliation: Assemblies of God

GENERAL INFORMATION Independent 4-year coed college. Founded 1955. Awards A (terminal), B. Primary accreditation: regional. City setting; 80-acre campus. Total enrollment: 1,525. Faculty: 122 (86 full-time, 36 part-time); 50% of full-time faculty have doctoral degrees. Library holdings: 105,000 bound volumes, 23,000 titles on microform, 610 periodical subscriptions, 3,000 records/tapes. Computer terminals/PCs available for student use: 58, located in computer center, labs.

UNDERGRADUATE PROFILE Fall 1989: 1,525 undergraduates (411 freshmen) from 47 states and territories and 11 foreign countries; 7% part-time; 29% state residents; 8% transfers; 84% financial aid recipients; 55% women; 45% men; 3% blacks; 1% Hispanics; 2% international students; 1% of undergraduates 25 years of age or older.

1989 FRESHMAN DATA 661 students applied for fall 1989 admission; 67% were accepted; 93% of those accepted enrolled. 19% of freshmen were in top 10% of secondary school class, 45% were in top 25%, 77% were in top half.

ENROLLMENT PATTERNS 55% of fall 1988 freshmen returned for fall 1989 term. 1987–89 average: 44% of entering classes graduated; 29% of students completing a bachelor's program went on for further study.

FRESHMAN ADMISSIONS Option: deferred entrance. Required: high school transcript, SAT or ACT, TOEFL (for foreign students). Recommended: 3 years of high school math and science, some high school foreign language. Test scores used for admission. Application deadline: 8/15. Notification date: continuous. College's own assessment of entrance difficulty level: moderately difficult.

TRANSFER ADMISSIONS Required: college transcript, minimum 2.0 grade point average. Required for some: high school transcript. Application deadline: 8/15. Notification date: continuous. College's own assessment of entrance difficulty level: moderately difficult.

EXPENSES (1990–91) Comprehensive fee of $8008 includes full-time tuition ($5190), mandatory fees ($88), and college room and board ($2730). College room only: $1280. Part-time tuition: $216 per credit hour. Part-time mandatory fees per semester: $47.

FINANCIAL AID College-administered aid for all 1989–90 undergraduates: need-based scholarships; 866 non-need scholarships (average $751); low-interest long-term loans from college funds (average $973), from external sources (average $2410); SEOG; College Work-Study; 104 part-time jobs. Supporting data: FAF, institutional form required; IRS required for some; AFSA/SAR acceptable. Priority application deadline: 4/1.

CAMPUS LIFE/STUDENT SERVICES Dress code; mandatory chapel; drama/theater group; student-run newspaper and radio station. Institution provides health clinic, personal/psychological counseling.

ATHLETICS Member NAIA. Intercollegiate sports: baseball/softball M(s), W(s); basketball M(s), W(s); cross-country running M(s), W(s); football M(s); track and field M(s), W(s); volleyball W(s). Intramural sports: baseball/softball, basketball, football, soccer, volleyball.

MAJORS Accounting A, B; art education B; art/fine arts B; behavioral sciences B; biblical studies B; biology/biological sciences B; broadcasting A, B; business administration/commerce/management B; business education B; chemistry B; child care/child and family studies A; communication A, B; computer science B; (pre)dentistry sequence B; early childhood education B; education A, B; elementary education B; English B; history B; journalism A, B; laboratory technologies A; (pre)law sequence B; mathematics B; medical technology B; (pre)medicine sequence B; mental health/rehabilitation counseling A, B; music B; music education B; physical education B; political science/government B; psychology B; public administration B; radio and television studies B; recreation and leisure services B; science education B; secondary education B; secretarial studies/office management A, B; social science A, B; social work B; sociology B; Spanish B; special education B; speech/rhetoric/public address/debate B; (pre)veterinary medicine sequence B. Majors with highest enrollment: business administration/commerce/management, education, music education.

SPECIAL NOTE FROM THE COLLEGE Evangel, the national Assemblies of God college of arts and sciences, is located near the international headquarters of the Assemblies of God, six other colleges, and a seminary. It is a residential college, with 80% of the students living on campus in modern residence halls. As a national college, Evangel draws these students from an average of 48 states and 10 foreign countries. Evangel offers over 30 academic majors, from premedicine to journalism to engineering, operating with the theme, "An education you can work with." The Student Development Department, headed by the dean of students, provides planned programs that contribute to the student's intellectual, social, vocational, physical, emotional, and spiritual development. Finally, Springfield is the gateway to the Ozark Mountain recreational haven and is close to numerous lakes, parks, historic sites, and the Silver Dollar City theme park. After all, recreation is a vital part of the total education process.

CONTACT Mr. David Schoolfield, Executive Director of Enrollment, Evangel College, Springfield, MO 65802, 417-865-2811 Ext. 202 or toll-free 800-EVANGEL (out-of-state).

FRESNO PACIFIC COLLEGE
Fresno, California

Total enrollment: 1,364

UG enrollment: 698 (66% W)

Application deadline: rolling

Tuition & fees: $7650

Room & board: $3310

Entrance: moderately difficult

SAT ≥ 500: 27% V, 40% M

ACT ≥ 21: N/R

Denominational affiliation: Mennonite Brethren Church

GENERAL INFORMATION Independent comprehensive coed institution. Founded 1944. Awards A (college transfer), B, M. Primary accreditation: regional. City setting; 40-acre campus. Total enrollment: 1,364. Faculty: 43 (35 full-time, 8 part-time); 50% of full-time faculty have doctoral degrees; graduate assistants teach a few undergraduate courses. Library holdings: 125,000 bound volumes, 150,000 titles on microform, 900 periodical subscriptions, 4,000 records/tapes. Computer terminals/PCs available for student use: 45, located in computer center, student center, library.

UNDERGRADUATE PROFILE Fall 1989: 698 undergraduates (97 freshmen) from 14 states and territories; 29% part-time; 85% state residents; 20% transfers; 82% financial aid recipients; 66% women; 34% men; 2% blacks; 1% Native Americans; 8% Hispanics; 1% Asian Americans; 3% international students; 21% of undergraduates 25 years of age or older.

1989 FRESHMAN DATA 196 students applied for fall 1989 admission; 82% were accepted; 61% of those accepted enrolled.

ENROLLMENT PATTERNS 74% of fall 1988 freshmen returned for fall 1989 term. 1987–89 average: 45% of entering classes graduated.

FRESHMAN ADMISSIONS Options: early entrance, deferred entrance. Required: essay, high school transcript, 1 recommendation, SAT or ACT. Recommended: some high school foreign language, TOEFL (for foreign students). Required for some: interview. Test scores used for admission. Application deadline: rolling. Notification date: continuous until 7/31. College's own assessment of entrance difficulty level: moderately difficult.

TRANSFER ADMISSIONS Required: essay, high school transcript, 1 recommendation, college transcript, minimum 2.0 grade point average. Recommended: minimum 3.0 grade point average. Required for some: standardized test scores, interview. Application deadline: rolling. Notification date: continuous until 7/31. College's own assessment of entrance difficulty level: moderately difficult.

EXPENSES (1990–91) Comprehensive fee of $10,960 includes full-time tuition ($7500), mandatory fees ($150), and college room and board ($3310). College room only: $1380. Part-time tuition: $270 per unit.

FINANCIAL AID Fall 1989 full-time freshmen: 98% applied for aid, 64% of those were judged to have need, 100% of those were aided; the average aided freshman received an aid package worth $7276 (80% scholarships/grants, 20% self-help) meeting 75% of need. College-administered aid for all 1989–90 undergraduates: 250 need-based scholarships; non-need scholarships; short-term loans (average $300); low-interest long-term loans from external sources (average $1219); SEOG; College Work-Study; 250 part-time jobs. Supporting data: FAF, institutional form, AFSA/SAR required; IRS required for some. Priority application deadline: 3/2.

CAMPUS LIFE/STUDENT SERVICES Mandatory chapel; drama/theater group; student-run newspaper. Institution provides health clinic, personal/psychological counseling.

ATHLETICS Member NAIA. Intercollegiate sports: basketball M(s), W(s); cross-country running M(s), W(s); soccer M(s); track and field M(s), W(s); volleyball W. Intramural sports: baseball/softball, basketball, bowling, cross-country running, football, racquetball, skiing (cross-country), skiing (downhill), soccer, tennis, track and field, ultimate frisbee, volleyball.

MAJORS Accounting B; biblical studies A, B; biology/biological sciences A, B; business administration/commerce/management A, B; business education B; child psychology/child development A, B; communication A, B; education B; elementary education B; English A, B; history A, B; humanities B; (pre)law sequence B; liberal arts/general studies A, B; literature B; management information systems B; mathematics A, B; (pre)medicine sequence B; ministries B; music A, B; natural sciences A, B; physical education A, B; political science/government A, B; psychology A, B; religious studies B; secondary education B; social science B; sociology A, B; Spanish B. Majors with highest enrollment: education, ministries, business administration/commerce/management.

SPECIAL NOTE FROM THE COLLEGE Fresno Pacific offers an academically and spiritually rigorous experience in an unusual setting. The tree-covered main campus lies in the vast agricultural valley of central California, an hour's drive from the College's 5-acre retreat center in the High Sierras and 2½ hours from Pacific Ocean beaches. The curriculum prepares each student for leadership in a profession by creatively integrating Christian truth and values in a liberal arts paradigm of stories, systems, skills development, and problem solving. The program includes a unique core course sequence, practical Christian service, extensive cocurricular activities, and professional internships. At Fresno Pacific, special emphasis is placed on developing responsible personal freedom and strong Christian community.

CONTACT Mr. Cary W. Templeton, Director of Admissions, Fresno Pacific College, Fresno, CA 93702, 209-453-2039.

GENEVA COLLEGE
Beaver Falls, Pennsylvania

Total enrollment: 1,308

UG enrollment: 1,264 (46% W)

Application deadline: rolling

Tuition & fees: $7184

Room & board: $3480

Entrance: moderately difficult

Denominational affiliation: Reformed Presbyterian Church

GENERAL INFORMATION Independent comprehensive coed institution. Founded 1848. Awards A (college transfer and terminal), B, M. Primary accreditation: regional. Small-town setting, with easy access to Pittsburgh; 55-acre campus. Total enrollment: 1,308. Faculty: 79 (49 full-time, 30 part-time); 67% of full-time faculty have doctoral degrees; graduate assistants teach no undergraduate courses. Library holdings: 141,084 bound volumes, 67,582 titles on microform, 714 periodical subscriptions, 9,411 records/tapes. Computer terminals/PCs available for student use: 70, located in computer center, library, education department.

UNDERGRADUATE PROFILE Fall 1989: 1,264 undergraduates (205 freshmen) from 33 states and territories and 12 foreign countries; 16% part-time; 78% state residents; 31% transfers; 90% financial aid recipients; 46% women; 54% men; 3% blacks; 0% Native Americans; 0% Hispanics; 1% Asian Americans; 1% international students.

1989 FRESHMAN DATA 519 students applied for fall 1989 admission; 88% were accepted; 45% of those accepted enrolled. 13% of freshmen were in top 10% of secondary school class, 67% were in top half.

ENROLLMENT PATTERNS 77% of fall 1988 freshmen returned for fall 1989 term. 1987–89 average: 55% of entering classes graduated; 14% of students completing a bachelor's program went on for further study.

FRESHMAN ADMISSIONS Options: early entrance, deferred entrance. Required: essay, high school transcript, 2 years of high school foreign language, SAT or ACT, TOEFL (for foreign students). Required for some: recommendations, interview. Test scores used for admission. Application deadline: rolling. Notification date: continuous. College's own assessment of entrance difficulty level: moderately difficult.

TRANSFER ADMISSIONS Required: essay, standardized test scores, high school transcript, 2 years of high school foreign language, college transcript, minimum 2.0 grade point average.

Required for some: recommendations, interview. Application deadline: rolling. Notification date: continuous. College's own assessment of entrance difficulty level: moderately difficult.

EXPENSES (1990–91) Comprehensive fee of $10,664 includes full-time tuition ($7140), mandatory fees ($44), and college room and board ($3480). Part-time tuition: $210 per credit.

FINANCIAL AID Fall 1989 full-time freshmen: 87% applied for aid, 84% of those were judged to have need, 99% of those were aided; the average aided freshman received an aid package worth $7382 (60% scholarships/grants, 40% self-help) meeting 97% of need. College-administered aid for all 1989–90 undergraduates: 1,233 need-based scholarships (average $1037); 421 non-need scholarships (average $576); short-term loans (average $50); low-interest long-term loans from external sources (average $2092); SEOG; College Work-Study; 366 part-time jobs. Supporting data: institutional form required; FAF, IRS, state form required for some; FFS, AFSA/SAR acceptable. Priority application deadline: 4/15.

CAMPUS LIFE/STUDENT SERVICES Mandatory chapel; drama/theater group; student-run newspaper and radio station. Institution provides health clinic, personal/psychological counseling.

ATHLETICS Member NAIA. Intercollegiate sports: baseball/softball M(s), W(s); basketball M(s), W(s); cross-country running M(s), W; football M(s); soccer M(s), W(s); tennis M(s), W(s); track and field M(s), W; volleyball M(c), W(s). Intramural sports: baseball/softball, basketball, bowling, football, ice hockey, racquetball, skiing (downhill), soccer, volleyball.

MAJORS Accounting B; applied mathematics B; aviation administration B; biblical studies B; biology/biological sciences B; broadcasting B; business administration/commerce/management A, B; business education B; chemical engineering B; chemistry B; civil engineering B; communication B; computer science B; economics B; education B; electrical engineering B; elementary education B; engineering (general) A, B; English B; guidance and counseling B; history B; industrial engineering B; journalism B; Latin American studies B; (pre)law sequence B; management information systems B; mathematics B; mechanical engineering B; medical secretarial studies A, B; medical technology B; (pre)medicine sequence B; ministries B; music B; music business B; music education B; pastoral studies B; philosophy B; physics B; political science/government B; psychology B; radio and television studies B; science B; secondary education B; secretarial studies/office management A, B; sociology B; Spanish B; speech pathology and audiology B; speech/rhetoric/public address/debate B. Majors with highest enrollment: engineering (general), business administration/commerce/management, accounting.

SPECIAL NOTE FROM THE COLLEGE Founded in 1848, Geneva is one of the oldest evangelical Christian colleges in the nation, the second oldest in the Christian College Coalition. It offers an education that articulates the implications of Christ's sovereignty over all his creation. Majors include engineering, speech pathology, and cardiovascular technology. Through a cooperative program, students can combine degrees in aviation, air traffic control, or aerospace management with a business degree. All students complete a core program, which integrates courses in history, music, art, literature, and culture from a Christian perspective. Cocurricular activities include intercollegiate programs in all major sports, theater, choir, an FM radio station, and marching and concert bands. Although Geneva seeks students with a biblical world/life view, all students are welcome.

CONTACT Ms. Robin Ware, Director of Admissions, Geneva College, Beaver Falls, PA 15010, 412-847-6500 or toll-free 800-847-2428 (in-state), 800-847-8255 (out-of-state).

GEORGE FOX COLLEGE
Newberg, Oregon

Total enrollment: 944 (all UG)

Women: 54%

Application deadline: 8/1

Tuition & fees: $8135

Room & board: $3400

Entrance: moderately difficult

SAT ≥ 500: 34% V, 41% M

ACT ≥ 21: N/R

Denominational affiliation: Friends

GENERAL INFORMATION Independent 4-year coed college. Founded 1891. Awards B. Primary accreditation: regional. Small-town setting, with easy access to Portland; 60-acre campus. Total enrollment: 944. Faculty: 74 (51 full-time, 23 part-time); 71% of full-time faculty have doctoral degrees. Library holdings: 98,000 bound volumes, 1,300 titles on microform, 541 periodical subscriptions, 980 records/tapes. Computer terminals/PCs available for student use: 78, located in computer center, library.

UNDERGRADUATE PROFILE Fall 1989: 944 undergraduates (236 freshmen) from 24 states and territories and 12 foreign countries; 5% part-time; 54% state residents; 22% transfers; 84% financial aid recipients; 54% women; 46% men; 2% blacks; 1% Native Americans; 2% Hispanics; 2% Asian Americans; 4% international students; 22% of undergraduates 25 years of age or older.

1989 FRESHMAN DATA 641 students applied for fall 1989 admission; 88% were accepted; 42% of those accepted enrolled. 3 freshmen were National Merit Scholarship Finalists; all received a National Merit Scholarship. 18% of freshmen were in top 10% of secondary school class, 43% were in top 25%, 76% were in top half.

ENROLLMENT PATTERNS 71% of fall 1988 freshmen returned for fall 1989 term. 1987–89 average: 39% of entering classes graduated; 16% of students completing a degree program went on for further study.

FRESHMAN ADMISSIONS Options: early entrance, deferred entrance. Required: essay, high school transcript, 1 recommendation, SAT or ACT, TOEFL (for foreign students), WPCT. Recommended: 3 years of high school math and science, some high school foreign language. Required for some: interview. Test scores used for admission and counseling/placement.

Application deadline: 8/1. College's own assessment of entrance difficulty level: moderately difficult.

TRANSFER ADMISSIONS Required: 1 recommendation, college transcript, minimum 2.0 grade point average. Recommended: interview. Application deadline: 8/1. College's own assessment of entrance difficulty level: minimally difficult.

EXPENSES (1990–91 estimated) Comprehensive fee of $11,535 includes full-time tuition ($8000), mandatory fees ($135 minimum), and college room and board ($3400). College room only: $1700. Part-time tuition: $250 per semester hour.

FINANCIAL AID Fall 1989 full-time freshmen: 82% applied for aid, 90% of those were judged to have need, 100% of those were aided; the average aided freshman received an aid package worth $7916 (52% scholarships/grants, 48% self-help) meeting 91% of need. College-administered aid for all 1989–90 undergraduates: need-based scholarships (average $1200); non-need scholarships (average $950); low-interest long-term loans from external sources (average $2400); SEOG; College Work-Study; part-time jobs. Supporting data: FAF, AFSA/SAR required; IRS required for some. Priority application deadline: 8/1.

CAMPUS LIFE/STUDENT SERVICES Mandatory chapel; drama/theater group; student-run newspaper and radio station. Institution provides health clinic, personal/psychological counseling.

ATHLETICS Member NAIA. Intercollegiate sports: baseball/softball M(s), W(s); basketball M(s), W(s); cross-country running M(s), W(s); soccer M(s); track and field M(s), W(s); volleyball W(s). Intramural sports: badminton, baseball/softball, basketball, football, racquetball, soccer, table tennis (ping pong), tennis, volleyball, weight lifting.

MAJORS Biblical studies B; biology/biological sciences B; broadcasting B; business administration/commerce/management B; business economics B; chemistry B; civil engineering B; communication B; computer engineering B; computer information systems B; computer science B; (pre)dentistry sequence B; economics B; education B; electrical engineering B; elementary education B; engineering (general) B; engineering sciences B; English B; history B; home economics B; home economics education B; human resources B; interdisciplinary studies B; international studies B; (pre)law sequence B; liberal arts/general studies B; literature B; mathematics B; (pre)medicine sequence B; ministries B; music B; music education B; physical education B; psychology B; religious studies B; science B; science education B; secondary education B; social work B; sociology B; sports medicine B; telecommunications B; (pre)veterinary medicine sequence B. Majors with highest enrollment: business economics, secondary education, elementary education.

SPECIAL NOTE FROM THE COLLEGE Freedom or faith. A college decision may seem like a choice between the two: sacrifice your faith or put your mind on the shelf. At George Fox College, academic freedom and Christian faith go hand in hand. Students find faculty members who encourage questions, who value their uniqueness, and who challenge them to explore truth from a foundation of faith. Students find a community of friends who accept them as they are, not as they are "supposed to be." Graduates of George Fox leave with more than a competitive degree from a well-respected school. They leave with the ability to think critically, to express themselves, and to take their faith into today's world. At George Fox College, students have the freedom to think and the freedom to believe.

CONTACT Mr. Jeff Rickey, Director of Admissions, George Fox College, Newberg, OR 97132, 503-538-8383 Ext. 235.

GORDON COLLEGE
Wenham, Massachusetts

Total enrollment: 1,216 (all UG)

Women: 59%

Application deadline: rolling

Tuition & fees: $10,700

Room & board: $3406

Entrance: moderately difficult

SAT ≥ 500: 46% V, 56% M

ACT ≥ 21: N/R

Denominational affiliation: interdenominational

GENERAL INFORMATION Independent 4-year coed college. Founded 1889. Awards B. Primary accreditation: regional. Small-town setting, with easy access to Boston; 800-acre campus. Total enrollment: 1,216. Faculty: 94 (64 full-time, 30 part-time); 77% of full-time faculty have doctoral degrees. Library holdings: 220,000 bound volumes, 22,500 titles on microform, 8,000 records/tapes. Computer terminals/PCs available for student use: 78, located in computer center, library.

UNDERGRADUATE PROFILE Fall 1989: 1,216 undergraduates (275 freshmen) from 38 states and territories and 10 foreign countries; 4% part-time; 35% state residents; 21% transfers; 80% financial aid recipients; 59% women; 41% men; 3% blacks; 0% Native Americans; 2% Hispanics; 2% Asian Americans; 1% international students; 1% of undergraduates 25 years of age or older.

1989 FRESHMAN DATA 579 students applied for fall 1989 admission; 88% were accepted; 54% of those accepted enrolled. 24% of freshmen were in top 10% of secondary school class, 63% were in top 25%, 86% were in top half.

ENROLLMENT PATTERNS 86% of fall 1988 freshmen returned for fall 1989 term. 1987–89 average: 56% of entering classes graduated.

FRESHMAN ADMISSIONS Options: early entrance, early decision, deferred entrance. Required: essay, high school transcript, 1 recommendation, interview, SAT or ACT, TOEFL (for foreign students). Recommended: 3 years of high school math and science, 3 years of high school foreign language, Achievement Tests. Test scores used for admission. Application

deadlines: rolling, 12/15 for early decision. College's own assessment of entrance difficulty level: moderately difficult.

TRANSFER ADMISSIONS Required: essay, standardized test scores, 1 recommendation, interview, college transcript. Recommended: high school transcript, 3 years of high school math and science, 3 years of high school foreign language, minimum 2.0 grade point average. Application deadline: rolling. College's own assessment of entrance difficulty level: moderately difficult.

EXPENSES (1990–91) Comprehensive fee of $14,106 includes full-time tuition ($10,269), mandatory fees ($431), and college room and board ($3406). College room only: $2125 (minimum). Tuition prepayment plan available.

FINANCIAL AID College-administered aid for all 1989–90 undergraduates: 701 need-based scholarships (average $3721); non-need scholarships (average $1000); short-term loans (average $50); low-interest long-term loans from external sources (average $2464); SEOG; College Work-Study; 150 part-time jobs. Supporting data: FAF, state form, institutional form, AFSA/SAR required; IRS required for some; FFS acceptable. Priority application deadline: 3/15.

CAMPUS LIFE/STUDENT SERVICES Mandatory chapel; drama/theater group; student-run newspaper. Institution provides health clinic, personal/psychological counseling.

ATHLETICS Member NCAA (Division III). Intercollegiate sports: baseball/softball M(III), W(III); basketball M(III), W(III); cross-country running M(III), W(III); field hockey W(III); ice hockey M(c); lacrosse M(c); soccer M(III), W(c); tennis M(III), W(III); volleyball W(III). Intramural sports: baseball/softball, basketball, football, ice hockey, skiing (cross-country), skiing (downhill), soccer, volleyball.

MAJORS Accounting B; biblical languages B; biblical studies B; biology/biological sciences B; business administration/commerce/management B; business economics B; chemistry B; computer science B; early childhood education B; economics B; education B; elementary education B; English B; French B; German B; history B; (pre)law sequence B; linguistics B; literature B; mathematics B; (pre)medicine sequence B; ministries B; music B; music education B; philosophy B; physical fitness/human movement B; physics B; political science/government B; psychology B; recreation and leisure services B; religious studies B; secondary education B; social science B; social work B; sociology B; Spanish B; special education B; theology B; (pre)veterinary medicine sequence B. Majors with highest enrollment: business economics, psychology, biblical studies.

SPECIAL NOTE FROM THE COLLEGE Gordon College, located on a wooded 800-acre campus 25 miles north of Boston, is New England's leading Christian liberal arts college. Described by *New York Times* education editor Edward B. Fiske as a "major intellectual bastion of Protestant evangelicalism," Gordon has won widespread recognition for quality. For example, Gordon's cooperative education program, through which students may alternate 6 months of study with 6 months of paid employment, has been ranked 2nd out of 381 such programs by the US Department of Education. The Academy for Educational Development has ranked Gordon's faculty development programs among the top 10 in the nation for attracting and retaining young, highly competent faculty members. Also, along with only 2 other Massachusetts schools, Gordon is profiled in Times Books' The Best Buys in College Education, a consumer's guide to 221 colleges that offer high-quality education at a reasonable cost.

CONTACT Mr. Mark Sylvester, Dean of Admissions and Financial Aid, Gordon College, Wenham, MA 01984, 508-927-2300 Ext. 4217 or toll-free 800-322-0463 (in-state), 800-343-1379 (out-of-state).

GOSHEN COLLEGE
Goshen, Indiana

Total enrollment: 1,152 (all UG)

Women: 55%

Application deadline: rolling

Tuition & fees: $7205

Room & board: $3105

Entrance: moderately difficult

SAT ≥ 500: 41% V, 58% M

ACT ≥ 21: N/R

Denominational affiliation: Mennonite

GENERAL INFORMATION Independent 4-year coed college. Founded 1894. Awards B. Primary accreditation: regional. Small-town setting; 135-acre campus. Total enrollment: 1,152. Faculty: 112 (79 full-time, 33 part-time); 62% of full-time faculty have doctoral degrees. Library holdings: 120,000 bound volumes, 100 titles on microform, 800 periodical subscriptions, 1,500 records/tapes. Computer terminals/PCs available for student use: 75, located in computer center, dormitories.

UNDERGRADUATE PROFILE Fall 1989: 1,152 undergraduates (224 freshmen) from 34 states and territories and 26 foreign countries; 10% part-time; 41% state residents; 9% transfers; 86% financial aid recipients; 55% women; 45% men; 2% blacks; 0% Native Americans; 3% Hispanics; 1% Asian Americans; 8% international students; 14% of undergraduates 25 years of age or older.

1989 FRESHMAN DATA 457 students applied for fall 1989 admission; 90% were accepted; 54% of those accepted enrolled. 9 freshmen were National Merit Scholarship Finalists; all received a National Merit Scholarship. 24% of freshmen were in top 10% of secondary school class, 51% were in top 25%, 71% were in top half.

ENROLLMENT PATTERNS 81% of fall 1988 freshmen returned for fall 1989 term. 1987–89 average: 62% of entering classes graduated; 18% of students completing a degree program went on for further study.

FRESHMAN ADMISSIONS Options: early entrance, deferred entrance. Required: high school transcript, 1 recommendation, SAT or ACT, TOEFL (for foreign students). Recommended: 3 years of high school math and science, some high school foreign language, interview. Test scores used for admission. Application deadline: rolling. Notification date: continuous. College's own assessment of entrance difficulty level: moderately difficult.

TRANSFER ADMISSIONS Required: high school transcript, 2 recommendations, college transcript, minimum 2.0 grade point average. Recommended: 3 years of high school math and science, some high school foreign language, interview. Application deadline: rolling. Notification date: continuous. College's own assessment of entrance difficulty level: moderately difficult.

EXPENSES (1990–91) Comprehensive fee of $10,310 includes full-time tuition ($7205) and college room and board ($3105). College room only: $1504. Part-time tuition: $285 per credit hour. Discounted part-time tuition for students enrolled in 1 to 5 credit hours ranges from $100 to $150 per credit hour according to program.

FINANCIAL AID Fall 1989 full-time freshmen: 79% applied for aid, 78% of those were judged to have need, 100% of those were aided; the average aided freshman received an aid package worth $6866 (64% scholarships/grants, 36% self-help) meeting 100% of need. College-administered aid for all 1989–90 undergraduates: 774 need-based scholarships (average $826); 1,177 non-need scholarships (average $940); low-interest long-term loans from college funds (average $1545), from external sources (average $2109); SEOG; College Work-Study; 60 part-time jobs. Supporting data: FAF, IRS, institutional form required; AFSA/SAR required for some; FFS acceptable. Priority application deadline: 3/1.

CAMPUS LIFE/STUDENT SERVICES Mandatory chapel; drama/theater group; student-run newspaper and radio station. Institution provides health clinic, personal/psychological counseling, women's center.

ATHLETICS Member NAIA. Intercollegiate sports: baseball/softball M; basketball M, W; cross-country running M, W; field hockey W; golf M; soccer M; tennis M, W; track and field M, W; volleyball W. Intramural sports: badminton, baseball/softball, basketball, cross-country running, skiing (cross-country), soccer, table tennis (ping pong), tennis, volleyball.

MAJORS Accounting B; art education B; art/fine arts B; art therapy B; biblical studies B; bilingual/bicultural education B; biology/biological sciences B; broadcasting B; business administration/commerce/management B; business education B; chemistry B; child care/child and family studies B; communication B; computer information systems B; computer science B; (pre)dentistry sequence B; dietetics B; early childhood education B; economics B; education B; elementary education B; English B; family services B; German B; Hispanic studies B; history B; journalism B; (pre)law sequence B; liberal arts/general studies B; mathematics B; (pre)medicine sequence B; music B; music education B; natural sciences B; nursing B; nutrition B; physical education B; physical sciences B; physics B; political science/government B; psychology B; religious studies B; science education B; secondary education B; social work B; sociology B; Spanish B; teaching English as a second language B; theater arts/drama B; (pre)veterinary medicine sequence B. Majors with highest enrollment: business administration/commerce/management, elementary education, nursing.

SPECIAL NOTE FROM THE COLLEGE Goshen College is an institution at which theory is translated into action. GC was 1 of 3 institutions of higher learning named by *U.S. News & World Report* as a place where values are lived as well as taught. GC's Study-Service Term program (SST) has been nationally recognized for its innovative approach. SST students stay in a "significantly different" country for 13 weeks, studying language, history, and culture for 7 weeks and giving service to the people for 6 weeks. The environmental studies minor, starting in fall 1990, will prepare students to be managers and decision makers in environmental areas. The peace studies minor enables students to examine familiar issues from a fresh perspective.

CONTACT Mr. Stan Miller, Interim Director of Admissions, Goshen College, Goshen, IN 46526, 219-535-7535 Ext. 526 or toll-free 800-348-7422 (out-of-state).

GRACE COLLEGE
Winona Lake, Indiana

Total enrollment: 738 (all UG)

Women: 57%

Application deadline: 8/1

Tuition & fees: $6550

Room & board: $3200

Entrance: moderately difficult

SAT ≥ 500: N/App

ACT ≥ 21: 41%

Denominational affiliation: Fellowship of Grace Brethren Churches

GENERAL INFORMATION Independent 4-year coed college. Administratively affiliated with Grace Theological Seminary. Founded 1948. Awards A (terminal), B. Primary accreditation: regional. Small-town setting; 150-acre campus. Total enrollment: 738. Faculty: 61 (31 full-time, 30 part-time); 45% of full-time faculty have doctoral degrees; graduate assistants teach a few undergraduate courses. Library holdings: 136,700 bound volumes, 590 periodical subscriptions, 6,500 records/tapes. Computer terminals/PCs available for student use: 38, located in computer center, library.

UNDERGRADUATE PROFILE Fall 1989: 738 undergraduates (158 freshmen) from 36 states and territories and 8 foreign countries; 15% part-time; 44% state residents; 6% transfers; 82% financial aid recipients; 57% women; 43% men; 1% blacks; 1% Native Americans; 0% Hispanics; 0% Asian Americans; 2% international students; 6% of undergraduates 25 years of age or older.

1989 FRESHMAN DATA 292 students applied for fall 1989 admission; 91% were accepted; 60% of those accepted enrolled. 23% of freshmen were in top 10% of secondary school class, 51% were in top 25%, 80% were in top half.

ENROLLMENT PATTERNS 77% of fall 1988 freshmen returned for fall 1989 term. 1987–89 average: 48% of entering classes graduated; 23% of students completing a bachelor's program went on for further study.

FRESHMAN ADMISSIONS Options: early entrance, deferred entrance. Required: high school transcript, 3 recommendations, ACT. Recommended: some high school foreign language. Required for some: 3 years of high school math and science,

interview. Test scores used for admission. Application deadline: 8/1. Notification date: continuous until 8/15. College's own assessment of entrance difficulty level: moderately difficult.

TRANSFER ADMISSIONS Required: high school transcript, 3 recommendations, college transcript, minimum 2.0 grade point average. Recommended: some high school foreign language. Required for some: 3 years of high school math and science, interview. Application deadline: 8/1. Notification date: continuous until 8/15. College's own assessment of entrance difficulty level: moderately difficult.

EXPENSES (1990–91 estimated) Comprehensive fee of $9750 includes full-time tuition ($6200), mandatory fees ($350), and college room and board ($3200). Part-time tuition: $200 per semester hour.

FINANCIAL AID Fall 1989 full-time freshmen: 90% applied for aid, 80% of those were judged to have need, 100% of those were aided; the average aided freshman received an aid package worth $4500 (58% scholarships/grants, 42% self-help) meeting 100% of need. College-administered aid for all 1989–90 undergraduates: need-based scholarships (average $1100); non-need scholarships (average $500); low-interest long-term loans from college funds, from external sources (average $1800); SEOG; College Work-Study; 200 part-time jobs. Supporting data: FAF, institutional form, AFSA/SAR required; FFS, IRS acceptable. Priority application deadline: 4/1.

CAMPUS LIFE/STUDENT SERVICES Dress code; mandatory chapel; drama/theater group; student-run newspaper. Institution provides health clinic, personal/psychological counseling.

ATHLETICS Member NAIA. Intercollegiate sports: baseball/ softball M(s), W(s); basketball M(s), W(s); golf M(s); soccer M(s); tennis M(s); volleyball W(s). Intramural sports: baseball/softball, basketball, football, volleyball.

MAJORS Accounting B; art education B; art/fine arts B; behavioral sciences B; biblical languages B; biblical studies B; biology/biological sciences B; business administration/ commerce/management B; commercial art B; communication B; computer science B; criminal justice B; elementary education B; English B; French B; German B; Greek B; history B; (pre)law sequence B; mathematics B; (pre)medicine sequence B; music B; music education B; nursing A; physical education B; piano/ organ B; psychology B; sacred music B; science education B; secretarial studies/office management A; sociology B; Spanish B; speech/rhetoric/public address/debate B. Majors with highest enrollment: elementary education, business administration/ commerce/management, psychology.

SPECIAL NOTE FROM THE COLLEGE Grace College offers an opportunity for students to discover and develop personal interests and crucial, life-guiding values. Highly qualified professors, aggressive learning, and fully integrated biblical presuppositions are the foundation of Grace and lead to meaningful career/ministry action. The combination of a strong academic program and a host of creative on-campus activities aimed at cultivating proper interpersonal relationships serve to prepare students for life after college. Throughout each student's college experience, from personal assistance in receiving financial aid to careful help in career/ministry placement upon graduation, Grace College is dedicated to providing high-quality, personalized service.

CONTACT Mr. Ron Henry, Director of Enrollment, Grace College, Winona Lake, IN 46590, 219-372-5128 or toll-free 800-845-2930 (in-state), 800-54 GRACE (out-of-state).

GRAND CANYON UNIVERSITY
Phoenix, Arizona

Total enrollment: 1,842

UG enrollment: 1,730 (60% W)

Application deadline: 8/1

Tuition & fees: $4928

Room & board: $2280

Entrance: moderately difficult

SAT ≥ 500: N/R

ACT ≥ 21: 38%

Denominational affiliation: Southern Baptist

GENERAL INFORMATION Independent comprehensive coed institution. Founded 1949. Awards B, M. Primary accreditation: regional. Metropolitan setting; 70-acre campus. Total enrollment: 1,842. Faculty: 161 (70 full-time, 91 part-time); 52% of full-time faculty have doctoral degrees; graduate assistants teach no undergraduate courses. Library holdings: 102,500 bound volumes, 528 periodical subscriptions, 3,300 records/tapes. Computer terminals/PCs available for student use: 60, located in computer center, library, audio-visual lab.

UNDERGRADUATE PROFILE Fall 1989: 1,730 undergraduates (348 freshmen) from 38 states and territories and 21 foreign countries; 22% part-time; 82% state residents; 57% transfers; 80% financial aid recipients; 60% women; 40% men; 4% blacks; 3% Native Americans; 6% Hispanics; 1% Asian Americans; 2% international students; 17% of undergraduates 25 years of age or older.

1989 FRESHMAN DATA 519 students applied for fall 1989 admission; 80% were accepted; 84% of those accepted enrolled. 1 freshman received a National Merit Scholarship. 20% of freshmen were in top 10% of secondary school class, 40% were in top 25%, 85% were in top half.

ENROLLMENT PATTERNS 70% of fall 1988 freshmen returned for fall 1989 term. 1987–89 average: 65% of entering classes graduated; 10% of students completing a degree program went on for further study.

FRESHMAN ADMISSIONS Option: early entrance. Required: essay, high school transcript, SAT or ACT, TOEFL (for foreign students). Recommended: 3 years of high school math and science, some high school foreign language. Required for some: 3 recommendations, campus interview. Test scores used for admission and counseling/placement. Application deadline: 8/1. Notification date: continuous until 8/15. College's own assessment of entrance difficulty level: moderately difficult.

TRANSFER ADMISSIONS Required: essay, college transcript, minimum 2.0 grade point average. Recommended: standardized test scores, high school transcript, 3 years of high school math and science, some high school foreign language. Required for some: 3 recommendations, campus interview. Application deadline: 8/1. Notification date: continuous until 8/15. College's own assessment of entrance difficulty level: moderately difficult.

EXPENSES (1990–91 estimated) Comprehensive fee of $7208 includes full-time tuition ($4608), mandatory fees ($320), and college room and board ($2280). Part-time tuition: $144 per semester hour.

FINANCIAL AID Fall 1989 full-time freshmen: 81% applied for aid, 70% of those were judged to have need, 92% of those were aided; the average aided freshman received an aid package worth $4298 (51% scholarships/grants, 49% self-help) meeting 72% of need. College-administered aid for all 1989–90 undergraduates: 30 need-based scholarships (average $300); 911 non-need scholarships (average $1238); short-term loans (average $300); low-interest long-term loans from external sources (average $3000); SEOG; College Work-Study; 12 part-time jobs. Supporting data: FFS, institutional form required; IRS required for some; FAF, state form, AFSA/SAR acceptable. Priority application deadline: 4/15.

CAMPUS LIFE/STUDENT SERVICES Dress code; mandatory chapel; drama/theater group; student-run newspaper. Institution provides health clinic, personal/psychological counseling.

ATHLETICS Member NAIA. Intercollegiate sports: baseball/softball M(s); basketball M(s), W(s); cross-country running M(s), W(s); golf M(s); soccer M(s); tennis W(s); volleyball W(s). Intramural sports: baseball/softball, basketball, football, volleyball.

MAJORS Accounting B; art education B; art/fine arts B; biblical studies B; biology/biological sciences B; business administration/commerce/management B; business economics B; business education B; chemistry B; communication B; computer science B; criminal justice B; (pre)dentistry sequence B; economics B; elementary education B; English B; environmental biology B; finance/banking B; history B; human resources B; international business B; (pre)law sequence B; liberal arts/general studies B; literature B; marketing/retailing/merchandising B; mathematics B; (pre)medicine sequence B; ministries B; music B; music business B; music education B; nursing B; physical education B; piano/organ B; psychology B; religious studies B; sacred music B; science education B; secondary education B; social science B; sociology B; special education B; speech/rhetoric/public address/debate B; studio art B; theater arts/drama B; theology B; (pre)veterinary medicine sequence B; voice B; wind and percussion instruments B. Majors with highest enrollment: elementary education, business administration/commerce/management, nursing.

SPECIAL NOTE FROM THE COLLEGE It is a small world, and it grows more crowded and divisive every day. Grand Canyon University is keenly aware that changing that world means infusing it with a different kind of person—a Christian. The University believes that the people who will spread the gospel most effectively will be those who live it out in a vital profession, whether that is nursing, teaching, engineering, or law. Grand Canyon tries to bring an international perspective to every aspect of the institution by giving students ample opportunities to visit and minister in foreign countries, as well as in the mission fields at home.

CONTACT Mr. Don Browning, Director of Admissions, Grand Canyon University, Phoenix, AZ 85061, 602-589-2850.

GREENVILLE COLLEGE
Greenville, Illinois

Total enrollment: 743 (all UG)

Women: 53%

Application deadline: rolling

Tuition & fees: $7761

Room & board: $3300

Entrance: moderately difficult

SAT ≥ 500: N/R

ACT ≥ 21: 44%

Denominational affiliation: Free Methodist

GENERAL INFORMATION Independent 4-year coed college. Founded 1892. Awards B. Primary accreditation: regional. Small-town setting, with easy access to St. Louis; 12-acre campus. Total enrollment: 743. Faculty: 64 (53 full-time, 11 part-time); 51% of full-time faculty have doctoral degrees. Library holdings: 109,465 bound volumes, 2,961 titles on microform, 508 periodical subscriptions, 1,699 records/tapes. Computer terminals/PCs available for student use: 14, located in computer center.

UNDERGRADUATE PROFILE Fall 1989: 743 undergraduates (230 freshmen) from 34 states and territories and 11 foreign countries; 10% part-time; 68% state residents; 9% transfers; 85% financial aid recipients; 53% women; 47% men; 5% blacks; 0% Native Americans; 5% Hispanics; 1% Asian Americans; 1% international students; 11% of undergraduates 25 years of age or older.

1989 FRESHMAN DATA 746 students applied for fall 1989 admission; 73% were accepted; 42% of those accepted enrolled. 21% of freshmen were in top 10% of secondary school class, 49% were in top 25%, 74% were in top half.

ENROLLMENT PATTERNS 83% of fall 1988 freshmen returned for fall 1989 term. 1987–89 average: 55% of entering classes graduated; 25% of students completing a degree program went on for further study.

FRESHMAN ADMISSIONS Options: early entrance, deferred entrance. Required: high school transcript, 2 recommendations, agreement to code of conduct, SAT or ACT, TOEFL (for foreign students). Recommended: 3 years of high school foreign language. Required for some: interview. Test scores used for counseling/placement. Application deadline: rolling. College's own assessment of entrance difficulty level: moderately difficult.

TRANSFER ADMISSIONS Required: standardized test scores, 2 recommendations, college transcript, minimum 2.0 grade point average, agreement to code of conduct. Recommended: high school transcript, 3 years of high school foreign language. Required for some: interview. Application deadline: rolling. College's own assessment of entrance difficulty level: moderately difficult.

EXPENSES (1990–91 estimated) Comprehensive fee of $11,061 includes full-time tuition ($7500), mandatory fees ($261), and college room and board ($3300). Part-time tuition: $255 per credit hour.

FINANCIAL AID Fall 1989 full-time freshmen: 92% applied for aid, 96% of those were judged to have need, 100% of those were aided; the average aided freshman received an aid package worth $6000 meeting 100% of need. College-administered aid for all 1989–90 undergraduates: 525 need-based scholarships; 75 non-need scholarships (average $950); low-interest long-term loans from college funds (average $1000), from external sources (average $2500); SEOG; College Work-Study; 230 part-time jobs. Supporting data: FAF, AFSA/SAR required; IRS required for some. Priority application deadline: 6/1.

CAMPUS LIFE/STUDENT SERVICES Mandatory chapel; drama/theater group; student-run newspaper and radio station. Institution provides personal/psychological counseling.

ATHLETICS Member NAIA. Intercollegiate sports: baseball/softball M, W; basketball M, W; cross-country running M, W; football M; golf M; soccer M; tennis M, W; track and field M, W; volleyball W. Intramural sports: badminton, baseball/softball, basketball, football, table tennis (ping pong), volleyball.

MAJORS Accounting B; art education B; art/fine arts B; biblical studies B; biology/biological sciences B; business administration/commerce/management B; business education B; chemistry B; communication B; computer science B; (pre)dentistry sequence B; early childhood education B; economics B; education B; elementary education B; English B; French B; gerontology B; history B; (pre)law sequence B; liberal arts/general studies B; marketing/retailing/merchandising B; mathematics B; medical technology B; (pre)medicine sequence B; ministries B; modern languages B; music B; music education B; pastoral studies B; philosophy B; physical education B; physics B; political science/government B; psychology B; recreation and leisure services B; religious studies B; sacred music B; secondary education B; social work B; sociology B; Spanish B; special education B; speech/rhetoric/public address/debate B; theater arts/drama B; theology B; (pre)veterinary medicine sequence B. Majors with highest enrollment: education, business administration/commerce/management, biology/biological sciences.

SPECIAL NOTE FROM THE COLLEGE Greenville College is located just 50 minutes east of downtown St. Louis, in beautiful central Illinois. Established in 1892, Greenville is fully accredited. Greenville has structured a thoroughly evangelical environment that supports and encourages growth of the whole person—spiritually, academically, and socially. Greenville graduates excel. For example, alumnus James Buick is president of Zondervan Corporation; Bob Briner is president of ProServ Television; Chaz Corzine is vice president of Blanton/Herrell, Inc. (the talent management firm of Amy Grant and Michael W. Smith); Dr. Ernest Boyer, former US Commissioner of Education, is currently president of the Carnegie Foundation for the Advancement of Teaching; and hundreds of other graduates are teachers, doctors, businesspeople, missionaries, and laypeople in churches all over the world. Greenville College graduates are making a difference.

CONTACT Dr. H. Kent Krober, Director of Admissions, Greenville College, Greenville, IL 62246, 618-664-1840 Ext. 218 or toll-free 800-248-2288 (in-state), 800-345-4440 (out-of-state).

HOUGHTON COLLEGE
Houghton, New York

Total enrollment: 1,164 (all UG)

Women: 61%

Application deadline: 8/1

Tuition & fees: $8123

Room & board: $3044

Entrance: moderately difficult

SAT ≥ 500: 59% V, 72% M

ACT ≥ 21: 67%

Denominational affiliation: Wesleyan

GENERAL INFORMATION Independent 4-year coed college. Founded 1883. Awards A (college transfer), B. Primary accreditation: regional. Rural setting, with easy access to Buffalo and Rochester; 1,300-acre campus. Total enrollment: 1,164. Faculty: 104 (75 full-time, 29 part-time); 63% of full-time faculty have doctoral degrees. Library holdings: 171,094 bound volumes, 269 titles on microform, 627 periodical subscriptions, 5,612 records/tapes. Computer terminals/PCs available for student use: 110, located in computer center, library, dormitories, computer lab, divisional offices.

UNDERGRADUATE PROFILE Fall 1989: 1,164 undergraduates (320 freshmen) from 25 states and territories and over 30 foreign countries; 5% part-time; 65% state residents; 14% transfers; 87% financial aid recipients; 61% women; 39% men; 2% blacks; 1% Native Americans; 1% Hispanics; 1% Asian Americans; 5% international students; 8% of undergraduates 25 years of age or older.

1989 FRESHMAN DATA 667 students applied for fall 1989 admission; 95% were accepted; 51% of those accepted enrolled. 1 freshman was a National Merit Scholarship Finalist and received a National Merit Scholarship. 31% of freshmen were in top 10% of secondary school class, 63% were in top 25%, 92% were in top half.

ENROLLMENT PATTERNS 81% of fall 1988 freshmen returned for fall 1989 term. 1987–89 average: 61% of entering classes graduated; 32% of students completing a bachelor's program went on for further study.

FRESHMAN ADMISSIONS Preference given to evangelical Christians. Options: early entrance, deferred entrance. Required: essay, high school transcript, 1 recommendation, SAT or ACT, TOEFL (for foreign students). Recommended: 3 years of high school math, some high school foreign language, interview. Test scores used for admission. Application deadline: 8/1. Notification date: continuous. College's own assessment of entrance difficulty level: moderately difficult.

TRANSFER ADMISSIONS Required: essay, high school transcript, 1 recommendation, college transcript, minimum 2.0 grade point average. Recommended: 3 years of high school math, some high school foreign language, interview. Required for some: standardized test scores. Application deadline: 8/1. Notification date: continuous. College's own assessment of entrance difficulty level: moderately difficult.

EXPENSES (1990–91) Comprehensive fee of $11,167 includes full-time tuition ($7800 minimum), mandatory fees ($323), and college room and board ($3044). College room only: $1428.

FINANCIAL AID Fall 1989 full-time freshmen: 94% applied for aid, 98% of those were judged to have need, 100% of those were aided; the average aided freshman received an aid package worth $7279 (62% scholarships/grants, 38% self-help) meeting 94% of need. College-administered aid for all 1989–90 undergraduates: 780 need-based scholarships (average $1263); 482 non-need scholarships (average $1158); short-term loans (average $950); low-interest long-term loans from external sources (average $2600); SEOG; College Work-Study; 210 part-time jobs. Supporting data: FAF, institutional form required; state form required for some; FFS acceptable. Priority application deadline: 3/15.

CAMPUS LIFE/STUDENT SERVICES Mandatory chapel; drama/theater group; student-run newspaper and radio station. Institution provides health clinic, personal/psychological counseling.

ATHLETICS Member NAIA. Intercollegiate sports: basketball M(s), W(s); cross-country running M, W; field hockey W(s); soccer M(s), W(s); track and field M(s), W(s); volleyball W(s). Intramural sports: baseball/softball, basketball, equestrian sports, football, racquetball, skiing (cross-country), skiing (downhill), soccer, swimming and diving, table tennis (ping pong), tennis, volleyball, water polo, weight lifting.

MAJORS Accounting B; art education B; art/fine arts B; biblical studies A, B; biology/biological sciences B; business administration/commerce/management B; chemistry B; communication B; computer science B; creative writing B; (pre)dentistry sequence B; early childhood education B; education B; elementary education B; (pre)engineering sequence A; English B; French B; history B; humanities B; (pre)law sequence B; literature B; mathematics B; medical technology B; (pre)medicine sequence B; ministries B; music B; music education B; natural sciences B; pastoral studies B; philosophy B; physical education B; physical sciences B; physics B; piano/organ B; psychology B; recreation and leisure services B; religious education A, B; religious studies B; sacred music B; science B; science education B; secondary education B; social science B; sociology B; Spanish B; sports administration B; stringed instruments B; (pre)veterinary medicine sequence B; voice B; wind and percussion instruments B. Majors with highest enrollment: biology/biological sciences, business administration/commerce/management, elementary education.

SPECIAL NOTE FROM THE COLLEGE For over 100 years Houghton College has provided an educational experience that integrates high academic quality with the Christian faith. The College is fully accredited and rated highly by national college publications. Physical facilities at Houghton include an equestrian farm, comprehensive art studios, downhill and cross-country ski trails, an initiatives ropes course, and 4 major residence halls. Houghton offers 45 majors and programs on 2 campuses. The 1,300-acre Houghton campus in the beautiful countryside of western New York has 1,150 students. Students in programs calling for an urban focus may spend time on the 50-acre suburban campus near Buffalo. Programs in the sciences, education, music, and art are highly respected, and the religion department is rated among the best in the country. Over 100 international students and MKs (missionary's kids) come from over 30 countries to attend Houghton. Internships and study-abroad options are available.

CONTACT Mr. Timothy R. Fuller, Director of Admissions/Retention, Houghton College, Houghton, NY 14744, 716-567-9353 or toll-free 800-777-2556.

HUNTINGTON COLLEGE
Huntington, Indiana

Total enrollment: 611

UG enrollment: 549 (51% W)

Application deadline: 8/15

Tuition & fees: $7370

Room & board: $3010

Entrance: moderately difficult

SAT ≥ 500: 9% V, 29% M

ACT ≥ 21: 38%

Denominational affiliation: Church of the United Brethren in Christ

GENERAL INFORMATION Independent comprehensive coed institution. Founded 1897. Awards A (college transfer and terminal), B, M. Primary accreditation: regional. Small-town setting; 100-acre campus. Total enrollment: 611. Faculty: 44 (37 full-time, 7 part-time); 60% of full-time faculty have doctoral degrees; graduate assistants teach no undergraduate courses. Library holdings: 98,807 bound volumes, 20,992 titles on microform, 542 periodical subscriptions, 1,313 records/tapes. Computer terminals/PCs available for student use: 52, located in computer center, library.

UNDERGRADUATE PROFILE Fall 1989: 549 undergraduates (163 freshmen) from 15 states and territories and 19 foreign countries; 12% part-time; 60% state residents; 6% transfers; 90% financial aid recipients; 51% women; 49% men; 1% blacks; 0% Native Americans; 0% Hispanics; 1% Asian Americans; 4% international students; 20% of undergraduates 25 years of age or older.

1989 FRESHMAN DATA 498 students applied for fall 1989 admission; 79% were accepted; 42% of those accepted enrolled. 4 freshmen were National Merit Scholarship Finalists. 15% of freshmen were in top 10% of secondary school class, 40% were in top 25%, 75% were in top half.

ENROLLMENT PATTERNS 70% of fall 1988 freshmen returned for fall 1989 term. 1987–89 average: 61% of entering classes graduated; 20% of students completing a college-transfer associate program went on to 4-year colleges; 24% of students completing a bachelor's program went on for further study.

FRESHMAN ADMISSIONS Options: early entrance, deferred entrance. Required: high school transcript, SAT or ACT, TOEFL (for foreign students). Recommended: 3 years of high school math and science, 1 year of high school foreign language. Required for some: interview. Test scores used for counseling/

placement. Application deadline: 8/15. College's own assessment of entrance difficulty level: moderately difficult.

TRANSFER ADMISSIONS Required: standardized test scores, high school transcript, college transcript. Recommended: 3 years of high school math and science, 1 year of high school foreign language, interview, minimum 2.0 grade point average. Application deadline: 8/15. College's own assessment of entrance difficulty level: moderately difficult.

EXPENSES (1990–91) Comprehensive fee of $10,380 includes full-time tuition ($7250), mandatory fees ($120), and college room and board ($3010). College room only: $1250. Part-time tuition: $200 per semester hour.

FINANCIAL AID Fall 1989 full-time freshmen: 93% applied for aid, 72% of those were judged to have need, 100% of those were aided; the average aided freshman received an aid package worth $6682 (64% scholarships/grants, 36% self-help) meeting 99% of need. College-administered aid for all 1989–90 undergraduates: need-based scholarships; non-need scholarships; low-interest long-term loans from external sources (average $1500); SEOG; College Work-Study; part-time jobs. Supporting data: FAF, IRS, state form, AFSA/SAR required; FFS acceptable. Priority application deadline: 3/1.

CAMPUS LIFE/STUDENT SERVICES Mandatory chapel; drama/theater group; student-run newspaper. Institution provides health clinic, personal/psychological counseling. Social organizations: 1 national fraternity, 1 national sorority; 7% of eligible undergraduate men and 10% of eligible undergraduate women are members.

ATHLETICS Member NAIA. Intercollegiate sports: baseball/softball M(s), W(s); basketball M(s), W(s); cross-country running M(s), W(s); golf M(s), W(s); soccer M(s); tennis M(s), W(s); track and field M(s), W(s); volleyball W(s). Intramural sports: baseball/softball, basketball, football, soccer, tennis, volleyball.

MAJORS Accounting A, B; biblical studies B; biology/biological sciences B; business administration/commerce/management A, B; business economics B; business education B; chemistry B; communication B; computer science A, B; (pre)dentistry sequence B; economics B; education B; elementary education B; (pre)engineering sequence A; English B; history B; (pre)law sequence B; mathematics B; medical technology B; (pre)medicine sequence B; ministries B; music B; music education B; natural resource management B; philosophy B; physical education B; piano/organ B; psychology B; recreation and leisure services B; religious studies B; science B; science education B; secondary education B; secretarial studies/office management A; sociology B; special education B; theology B; (pre)veterinary medicine sequence B; voice B. Majors with highest enrollment: business administration/commerce/management, elementary education, recreation and leisure services.

SPECIAL NOTE FROM THE COLLEGE Huntington College provides the opportunity for its students to learn in the best of both worlds. Students receive the individual attention of a small college and are challenged academically in state-of-the-art library, fine arts center, physical education center, and classrooms. Huntington College professors are dedicated to teaching academic and spiritual truth. Students live in an environment that provides campus dramatics, orchestras, and choral groups. They have the opportunity to write for the college newspaper or yearbook; compete on athletic teams recognized yearly for excellence; and serve on community, national, and international missions. There are air-conditioned residence halls and married student apartments. Huntington College has been recognized for excellence in education by the Templeton Foundation and Dr. James L. Fisher, president emeritus of the Council for Advancement and Support of Education.

CONTACT Mr. Chantler Thompson, Dean of Admissions and Financial Aid, Huntington College, Huntington, IN 46750, 219-356-6000 Ext. 1016.

INDIANA WESLEYAN UNIVERSITY
Marion, Indiana

Total enrollment: 1,068

UG enrollment: 1,022 (62% W)

Application deadline: rolling

Tuition & fees: $6420

Room & board: $2930

Entrance: moderately difficult

SAT ≥ 500: 12% V, 27% M

ACT ≥ 21: 59%

Denominational affiliation: Wesleyan

GENERAL INFORMATION Independent comprehensive coed institution. Founded 1920. Awards A (college transfer and terminal), B, M. Primary accreditation: regional. Small-town setting, with easy access to Indianapolis; 75-acre campus. Total enrollment: 1,068. Faculty: 100 (65 full-time, 35 part-time); 80% of full-time faculty have doctoral degrees; graduate assistants teach no undergraduate courses. Library holdings: 103,572 bound volumes, 7,382 titles on microform, 382 periodical subscriptions, 18,604 records/tapes. Computer terminals/PCs available for student use: 50, located in computer center, writing center, learning center.

UNDERGRADUATE PROFILE Fall 1989: 1,022 undergraduates (220 freshmen) from 30 states and territories and 6 foreign countries; 28% part-time; 83% state residents; 5% transfers; 79% financial aid recipients; 62% women; 38% men; 4% blacks; 0% Native Americans; 1% Hispanics; 1% Asian Americans; 3% international students.

1989 FRESHMAN DATA 595 students applied for fall 1989 admission; 57% were accepted; 65% of those accepted enrolled. 20% of freshmen were in top 10% of secondary school class, 28% were in top 25%, 75% were in top half.

ENROLLMENT PATTERNS 80% of fall 1988 freshmen returned for fall 1989 term. 1987–89 average: 46% of entering classes graduated; 41% of students completing a bachelor's program went on for further study.

FRESHMAN ADMISSIONS Options: early entrance, deferred entrance. Required: essay, high school transcript, 1 recommendation, SAT or ACT, TOEFL (for foreign students). Recommended: interview. Required for some: interview. Test scores used for counseling/placement. Application deadline: rolling. Notification date: continuous. College's own assessment of entrance difficulty level: moderately difficult.

TRANSFER ADMISSIONS Required: essay, high school transcript, 1 recommendation, college transcript, minimum 2.0 grade point average. Recommended: standardized test scores, interview. Required for some: interview. Application deadline: rolling. Notification date: continuous. College's own assessment of entrance difficulty level: moderately difficult.

EXPENSES (1989–90) Comprehensive fee of $9350 includes full-time tuition ($6420) and college room and board ($2930). College room only: $1120. Part-time tuition and fees per semester (1 to 11 semester hours) range from $125 to $2475.

FINANCIAL AID College-administered aid for all 1989–90 undergraduates: 870 need-based scholarships (average $2000); 499 non-need scholarships (average $700); low-interest long-term loans from external sources (average $2000); SEOG; College Work-Study; 100 part-time jobs. Supporting data: FAF, institutional form, AFSA/SAR required; IRS required for some; FFS acceptable. Priority application deadline: 4/15.

CAMPUS LIFE/STUDENT SERVICES Dress code; mandatory chapel; student-run newspaper and radio station. Institution provides health clinic, personal/psychological counseling.

ATHLETICS Member NAIA. Intercollegiate sports: baseball/softball M(s), W(s); basketball M(s), W(s); cross-country running M(s); field hockey W(s); golf M(s); soccer M(s); tennis M(s); track and field M(s), W(s); volleyball W(s). Intramural sports: badminton, baseball/softball, basketball, bowling, football, golf, racquetball, soccer, tennis, volleyball.

MAJORS Accounting A, B; art education B; art/fine arts A, B; biblical studies A, B; biology/biological sciences B; business administration/commerce/management A, B; chemistry B; computer information systems A, B; creative writing B; criminal justice A, B; (pre)dentistry sequence B; economics B; education B; elementary education B; (pre)engineering sequence A; English A, B; history B; law enforcement/police sciences A; (pre)law sequence B; liberal arts/general studies A, B; mathematics B; medical laboratory technology A; medical technology B; (pre)medicine sequence B; mental health/rehabilitation counseling A; ministries A, B; music A, B; music business B; music education B; nursing B; pastoral studies A, B; philosophy B; physical education B; physical sciences B; piano/organ B; political science/government B; psychology B; recreational facilities management B; recreation and leisure services A; religious education A, B; religious studies B; sacred music B; science A, B; science education B; secondary education B; secretarial studies/office management A; social science A, B; social work B; sociology B; Spanish B; studio art B; theology B; (pre)veterinary medicine sequence B; voice B; wind and percussion instruments B. Majors with highest enrollment: nursing, business administration/commerce/management, education.

SPECIAL NOTE FROM THE COLLEGE Indiana Wesleyan University is located between Indianapolis and Fort Wayne, Indiana. IWU has provided a high-quality Christian liberal arts education for over 70 years. The University offers more than 35 majors, such as art, business, education, nursing, and psychology and several associate degrees in special areas, such as addictions counseling, criminal justice, and medical laboratory technology. Professors have been educated in America's finest graduate schools and demonstrate a genuine caring attitude toward each student and concern for the student's development as an individual.

CONTACT Mr. J. Charles Mealy, Director of Admissions, Indiana Wesleyan University, Marion, IN 46953, 317-674-6901 Ext. 138.

JOHN BROWN UNIVERSITY
Siloam Springs, Arkansas

Total enrollment: 930 (all UG)

Women: 51%

Application deadline: rolling

Tuition & fees: $4980

Room & board: $2860

Entrance: moderately difficult

SAT ≥ 500: 31% V, 44% M

ACT ≥ 21: 51%

Denominational affiliation: nondenominational

GENERAL INFORMATION Independent 4-year coed college. Founded 1919. Awards A (college transfer and terminal), B. Primary accreditation: regional. Rural setting; 200-acre campus. Total enrollment: 930. Faculty: 80 (60 full-time, 20 part-time); 64% of full-time faculty have doctoral degrees. Library holdings: 95,000 bound volumes, 29,000 titles on microform, 430 periodical subscriptions, 2,550 records/tapes. Computer terminals/PCs available for student use: 70, located in computer center, classrooms.

UNDERGRADUATE PROFILE Fall 1989: 930 undergraduates (245 freshmen) from 38 states and territories and 21 foreign countries; 11% part-time; 35% state residents; 12% transfers; 70% financial aid recipients; 51% women; 49% men; 1% blacks; 1% Native Americans; 2% Hispanics; 1% Asian Americans; 9% international students; 16% of undergraduates 25 years of age or older.

1989 FRESHMAN DATA 407 students applied for fall 1989 admission; 77% were accepted; 78% of those accepted enrolled. 2 freshmen were National Merit Scholarship Finalists; all received a National Merit Scholarship. 14% of freshmen were in top 10% of secondary school class, 47% were in top 25%, 78% were in top half.

ENROLLMENT PATTERNS 75% of fall 1988 freshmen returned for fall 1989 term. 1987–89 average: 42% of entering classes graduated; 15% of students completing a bachelor's program went on for further study.

FRESHMAN ADMISSIONS Options: early entrance, deferred entrance. Required: high school transcript, 3 years of high school math, 2 recommendations, SAT or ACT, TOEFL (for foreign students). Recommended: 3 years of high school science, some high school foreign language. Required for some: essay, interview. Test scores used for admission. Application deadline: rolling.

College's own assessment of entrance difficulty level: moderately difficult.

TRANSFER ADMISSIONS Required: 2 recommendations, college transcript, minimum 2.0 grade point average. Required for some: essay, standardized test scores, high school transcript, 3 years of high school math and science, interview. College's own assessment of entrance difficulty level: moderately difficult.

EXPENSES (1990–91) Comprehensive fee of $7840 includes full-time tuition ($4900), mandatory fees ($80), and college room and board ($2860). College room only: $1080. Part-time tuition: $210 per semester hour. Tuition prepayment plan available.

FINANCIAL AID Fall 1989 full-time freshmen: 65% applied for aid, 75% of those were judged to have need, 99% of those were aided; the average aided freshman received an aid package worth $5125 (52% scholarships/grants, 48% self-help) meeting 80% of need. College-administered aid for all 1989–90 undergraduates: 621 need-based scholarships (average $515); 519 non-need scholarships (average $1350); low-interest long-term loans from college funds (average $2000), from external sources (average $2575); SEOG; College Work-Study; 241 part-time jobs. Supporting data: IRS required; FFS, state form required for some; FAF, AFSA/SAR acceptable. Priority application deadline: 4/1.

CAMPUS LIFE/STUDENT SERVICES Mandatory chapel; drama/theater group; student-run newspaper and radio station. Institution provides health clinic, personal/psychological counseling.

ATHLETICS Member NAIA. Intercollegiate sports: basketball M(s), W(s); cross-country running M(s), W(s); soccer M(s); swimming and diving M(s), W(s); tennis M(s), W(s); track and field M(s), W(s); volleyball W(s). Intramural sports: baseball/softball, basketball, cross-country running, football, racquetball, rugby, soccer, tennis, volleyball.

MAJORS Accounting B; art/fine arts A; biblical studies A, B; biology/biological sciences B; broadcasting A, B; business administration/commerce/management B; business education B; chemistry B; construction engineering B; construction management A, B; early childhood education B; education B; electrical engineering B; elementary education B; engineering (general) B; engineering technology A; English B; health education B; history B; interdisciplinary studies B; journalism A, B; liberal arts/general studies A; mathematics B; mechanical engineering B; medical technology B; music A, B; music education B; physical education B; physical fitness/human movement B; piano/organ A; psychology B; public relations A, B; radio and television studies B; religious studies B; secondary education B; secretarial studies/office management A, B; social science B; special education B; voice B. Majors with highest enrollment: business administration/commerce/management, broadcasting, elementary education.

SPECIAL NOTE FROM THE COLLEGE The most distinctive feature of John Brown University is its career orientation. This orientation is reflected in some of JBU's programs: engineering, broadcasting, building construction, and office administration. It is also the cornerstone of traditional programs: business, teacher education, and science. At JBU, career orientation is found in more than its programs—it is an attitude. JBU wants it graduates to be successful in their careers—no matter what career—no matter how they define success. JBU's second most distinctive feature is its intercultural perspective. With 100 international students and over 70 Third World culture missionary's kids, JBU offers a global approach to Christian higher education right in northwest Arkansas.

CONTACT Mr. Don Crandall, Director of Enrollment Management, John Brown University, Siloam Springs, AR 72761, 501-524-3131 Ext. 150 or toll-free 800-634-6969.

JUDSON COLLEGE
Elgin, Illinois

Total enrollment: 522 (all UG)

Women: 56%

Application deadline: 8/15

Tuition & fees: $7040

Room & board: $3590

Entrance: moderately difficult

SAT ≥ 500: N/R

ACT ≥ 21: 38%

Denominational affiliation: Baptist

GENERAL INFORMATION Independent 4-year coed college. Founded 1963. Awards B. Primary accreditation: regional. City setting, with easy access to Chicago; 80-acre campus. Total enrollment: 522. Faculty: 70 (29 full-time, 41 part-time); 40% of full-time faculty have doctoral degrees. Library holdings: 75,000 bound volumes, 28,000 titles on microform, 425 periodical subscriptions, 6,200 records/tapes. Computer terminals/PCs available for student use: 50, located in computer center, library.

UNDERGRADUATE PROFILE Fall 1989: 522 undergraduates (118 freshmen) from 21 states and territories and 7 foreign countries; 10% part-time; 69% state residents; 11% transfers; 97% financial aid recipients; 56% women; 44% men; 7% blacks; 1% Hispanics; 1% Asian Americans; 2% international students; 15% of undergraduates 25 years of age or older.

1989 FRESHMAN DATA 331 students applied for fall 1989 admission; 76% were accepted; 47% of those accepted enrolled. 13% of freshmen were in top 10% of secondary school class, 29% were in top 25%, 60% were in top half.

ENROLLMENT PATTERNS 70% of fall 1988 freshmen returned for fall 1989 term. 1987–89 average: 34% of entering classes graduated; 51% of students completing a degree program went on for further study.

FRESHMAN ADMISSIONS Option: deferred entrance. Required: essay, high school transcript, SAT or ACT, TOEFL (for foreign students). Required for some: 1 recommendation, campus interview. Test scores used for admission. Application deadline: 8/15. Notification date: continuous. College's own assessment of entrance difficulty level: moderately difficult.

TRANSFER ADMISSIONS Required: essay, college transcript, minimum 2.0 grade point average. Required for some: standardized test scores, high school transcript, 1 recommendation, campus interview. Application deadline: 8/15. Notification date: continuous. College's own assessment of entrance difficulty level: moderately difficult.

EXPENSES (1989–90) Comprehensive fee of $10,630 includes full-time tuition ($6690), mandatory fees ($350), and college room and board ($3590). Part-time tuition: $220 per semester hour.

FINANCIAL AID Fall 1989 full-time freshmen: 83% applied for aid, 94% of those were judged to have need, 100% of those were aided; the average aided freshman received an aid package worth $6852 (65% scholarships/grants, 35% self-help) meeting 91% of need. College-administered aid for all 1989–90 undergraduates: 345 need-based scholarships (average $1112); 604 non-need scholarships (average $1086); low-interest long-term loans from external sources (average $2610); SEOG; College Work-Study; 70 part-time jobs. Supporting data: FAF required; FFS, IRS, AFSA/SAR acceptable. Priority application deadline: 5/1.

CAMPUS LIFE/STUDENT SERVICES Mandatory chapel; drama/theater group; student-run radio station. Institution provides health clinic, personal/psychological counseling.

ATHLETICS Member NAIA. Intercollegiate sports: baseball/softball M(s), W(s); basketball M(s), W(s); soccer M(s); tennis M(s), W; volleyball M, W(s). Intramural sports: badminton, baseball/softball, basketball, football, soccer, tennis, volleyball.

MAJORS Accounting B; anthropology B; art/fine arts B; biblical studies B; biology/biological sciences B; business administration/commerce/management B; chemistry B; communication B; computer information systems B; computer science B; education B; elementary education B; English B; history B; (pre)law sequence B; linguistics B; literature B; mathematics B; (pre)medicine sequence B; music B; nursing B; painting/drawing B; philosophy B; physical education B; physical sciences B; psychology B; religious studies B; science B; social science B; sociology B; speech/rhetoric/public address/debate B; theater arts/drama B; voice B. Majors with highest enrollment: social science, elementary education, business administration/commerce/management.

SPECIAL NOTE FROM THE COLLEGE The Judson community experience is designed to equip graduates to be decisive leaders and active participants in church and society, articulate proponents of biblical Christianity, honest advocates for the sovereignty of God over all life, and ambassadors for Christ to a troubled world. Judson is committed to a broad-based liberal arts education based on a Christian world view—educating the spirit, mind, and body. Courses are taught by a highly qualified and competent Christian faculty that encourages students to claim ideas and concepts that can sharpen their insights and establish the pattern for a lifelong quest for learning. The curriculum is designed to prepare graduates for a vocation and/or graduate study. The College is close to Chicago, which provides exciting cultural opportunities for ministry, education, and recreation.

CONTACT Mr. Jack P. Powell, Director of Enrollment Services, Judson College, Elgin, IL 60123, 708-695-2500 Ext. 160.

KING COLLEGE
Bristol, Tennessee

Total enrollment: 588 (all UG)

Women: 50%

Application deadline: 8/1

Tuition & fees: $5900

Room & board: $3050

Entrance: moderately difficult

SAT ≥ 500: 35% V, 54% M

ACT ≥ 21: 52%

Denominational affiliation: Presbyterian Church (U.S.A.)

GENERAL INFORMATION Independent 4-year coed college (U.S.A.). Founded 1867. Awards B. Primary accreditation: regional. City setting; 135-acre campus. Total enrollment: 588. Faculty: 63 (33 full-time, 30 part-time); 70% of full-time faculty have doctoral degrees.

UNDERGRADUATE PROFILE Fall 1989: 588 undergraduates (238 freshmen) from 22 states and territories and 17 foreign countries; 13% part-time; 34% state residents; 12% transfers; 80% financial aid recipients; 50% women; 50% men; 6% blacks; 0% Native Americans; 2% Hispanics; 1% Asian Americans; 16% international students; 5% of undergraduates 25 years of age or older.

1989 FRESHMAN DATA 592 students applied for fall 1989 admission; 72% were accepted; 55% of those accepted enrolled. 1 freshman was a National Merit Scholarship Finalist. 28% of freshmen were in top 10% of secondary school class, 65% were in top 25%, 81% were in top half.

ENROLLMENT PATTERNS 75% of fall 1988 freshmen returned for fall 1989 term. 1987–89 average: 85% of entering classes graduated; 40% of students completing a degree program went on for further study.

FRESHMAN ADMISSIONS Option: early entrance. Required: essay, high school transcript, SAT or ACT. Recommended: 3 years of high school math and science, some high school foreign language, interview, TOEFL (for foreign students). Required for some: recommendations, interview. Test scores used for admission. Application deadline: 8/1. College's own assessment of entrance difficulty level: moderately difficult.

TRANSFER ADMISSIONS Required: essay, college transcript, minimum 2.0 grade point average, dean's evaluation form. Recommended: standardized test scores, high school transcript, 3 years of high school math and science, some high school foreign language, interview. Required for some: interview. Application deadline: 8/1. College's own assessment of entrance difficulty level: moderately difficult.

EXPENSES (1990–91 estimated) Comprehensive fee of $8950 includes full-time tuition ($5500), mandatory fees ($400), and college room and board ($3050). College room only: $1500. Part-time tuition: $200 per semester hour.

FINANCIAL AID Fall 1989 full-time freshmen: 97% applied for aid, 78% of those were judged to have need, 100% of those were aided; the average aided freshman received an aid package worth $6693 (70% scholarships/grants, 30% self-help) meeting 85% of need. College-administered aid for all 1989–90 undergraduates: 252 need-based scholarships (average $3931); non-need scholarships (average $931); low-interest long-term loans from college funds (average $800), from external sources (average $2375); SEOG; College Work-Study; 173 part-time jobs. Supporting data: FAF, IRS, institutional form, AFSA/SAR required; Financial Aid Transcript required for some. Priority application deadline: 3/15.

CAMPUS LIFE/STUDENT SERVICES Mandatory chapel; drama/theater group; student-run newspaper. Institution provides health clinic, personal/psychological counseling.

ATHLETICS Member NAIA. Intercollegiate sports: baseball/softball M(s); basketball M(s), W(s); soccer M(s); tennis M; volleyball W(s). Intramural sports: baseball/softball, basketball, football, golf, skiing (downhill), soccer, swimming and diving, table tennis (ping pong), tennis, ultimate frisbee, volleyball, weight lifting.

MAJORS Accounting B; art/fine arts B; biblical studies B; biology/biological sciences B; business administration/commerce/management B; business economics B; chemistry B; (pre)dentistry sequence B; economics B; education B; elementary education B; English B; history B; international business B; (pre)law sequence B; mathematics B; medical technology B; (pre)medicine sequence B; music B; physics B; political science/government B; psychology B; religious studies B; science B; theater arts/drama B; (pre)veterinary medicine sequence B. Majors with highest enrollment: economics, English, political science/government.

SPECIAL NOTE FROM THE COLLEGE King College is a Presbyterian liberal arts college that is evangelical and reformed. As such, it is a community of scholars that takes seriously both academic excellence and Christian faith and regards the two as integral parts of its primary educational purpose—to glorify God. Its academic program is rigorous, preparing gifted and capable students to enter the finest graduate and professional schools in the nation or make an immediate contribution in the marketplace upon graduation.

CONTACT Mr. Edwin Seaver, Dean of Admissions, King College, Bristol, TN 37620, 615-968-1787.

KING'S COLLEGE
Briarcliff Manor, New York

Total enrollment: 513 (all UG)

Women: 61%

Application deadline: rolling

Tuition & fees: $7515

Room & board: $3520

Entrance: moderately difficult

SAT ≥ 500: 22% V, 36% M

ACT ≥ 21: N/R

Denominational affiliation: nondenominational

GENERAL INFORMATION Independent 4-year coed college. Founded 1938. Awards A (college transfer), B. Primary accreditation: regional. Small-town setting, with easy access to New York City; 80-acre campus. Total enrollment: 513. Faculty: 68 (50 full-time, 18 part-time); 54% of full-time faculty have doctoral degrees. Library holdings: 89,000 bound volumes, 12,000 titles on microform, 560 periodical subscriptions, 1,400 records/ tapes. Computer terminals/PCs available for student use: 50, located in computer center, library, dormitories.

UNDERGRADUATE PROFILE Fall 1989: 513 undergraduates (145 freshmen) from 25 states and territories and 10 foreign countries; 4% part-time; 45% state residents; 5% transfers; 80% financial aid recipients; 61% women; 39% men; 6% blacks; 0% Native Americans; 5% Hispanics; 5% Asian Americans; 3% international students; 5% of undergraduates 25 years of age or older.

1989 FRESHMAN DATA 374 students applied for fall 1989 admission; 93% were accepted; 42% of those accepted enrolled. 14% of freshmen were in top 10% of secondary school class, 38% were in top 25%, 79% were in top half.

ENROLLMENT PATTERNS 76% of fall 1988 freshmen returned for fall 1989 term. 1987–89 average: 45% of entering classes graduated.

FRESHMAN ADMISSIONS Options: early entrance, deferred entrance. Required: essay, high school transcript, 2 recommendations, SAT or ACT, TOEFL (for foreign students). Recommended: 3 years of high school math and science, some high school foreign language. Required for some: campus interview. Test scores used for admission. Application deadline: rolling. College's own assessment of entrance difficulty level: moderately difficult.

TRANSFER ADMISSIONS Required: essay, 2 recommendations, college transcript, minimum 2.0 grade point average. Recommended: standardized test scores, 3 years of high school math and science, some high school foreign language. Required for some: standardized test scores, high school transcript, campus interview. Application deadline: rolling. College's own assessment of entrance difficulty level: moderately difficult.

EXPENSES (1989–90) Comprehensive fee of $11,035 includes full-time tuition ($7440), mandatory fees ($75), and college room and board ($3520). College room only: $1792. Part-time tuition: $245 per semester hour.

FINANCIAL AID Fall 1989 full-time freshmen: 97% of those who applied for aid were judged to have need, 100% of those were aided; the average aided freshman received an aid package worth $7432 (61% scholarships/grants, 39% self-help) meeting 90% of need. College-administered aid for all 1989–90 undergraduates: 220 need-based scholarships (average $1285); 423 non-need scholarships (average $860); low-interest long-term loans from external sources (average $2610); SEOG; College Work-Study; 234 part-time jobs. Supporting data: FAF, IRS, institutional form required; state form required for some; FFS, AFSA/SAR acceptable. Priority application deadline: 4/1.

CAMPUS LIFE/STUDENT SERVICES Mandatory chapel; drama/theater group; student-run newspaper. Institution provides health clinic, personal/psychological counseling.

ATHLETICS Member NAIA. Intercollegiate sports: baseball/ softball M(s), W(s); basketball M(s), W(s); cross-country running M(s), W(s); soccer M(s), W(s); track and field M(s), W(s); volleyball W(s). Intramural sports: baseball/softball, basketball, football, golf, volleyball, weight lifting.

MAJORS Accounting B; biblical studies B; biology/biological sciences B; business administration/commerce/management B; chemistry B; computer science B; elementary education B; English B; history B; liberal arts/general studies A; mathematics B; medical technology B; modern languages B; music B; music education B; nursing B; physical education B; psychology B; religious education B; religious studies B; secondary education B; sociology B. Majors with highest enrollment: business administration/commerce/ management, elementary education, accounting.

SPECIAL NOTE FROM THE COLLEGE The King's College is uniquely situated between Manhattan and the mountains of New York State. TKC has the best of both worlds when it comes to location—a quiet, safe, wooded suburban campus with access to the excitement of unparalleled cultural opportunities in New York City, just a 45-minute train ride away. King's is a conservative, evangelical college with a dedicated Christian faculty and staff assembled to serve students. This cosmopolitan college offers a comprehensive liberal arts education. King's College has the warmth of a small, close-knit student body and the advantages of one of the world's largest cities.

CONTACT Mr. Frederic S. Rowley, Dean of Admissions, King's College, Briarcliff Manor, NY 10510, 914-944-5653.

KING'S COLLEGE
Edmonton, Alberta, Canada

Total enrollment: 318 (all UG)

Women: 54%

Application deadline: rolling

Tuition & fees: $2935

Room only: $1200

Entrance: moderately difficult

Denominational affiliation: nondenominational

GENERAL INFORMATION Independent 4-year coed college. Administratively affiliated with University of Alberta. Founded 1979. Awards B. Primary accreditation: provincial charter. Metropolitan setting; 1-acre campus. Total enrollment: 318. Faculty: 53 (24 full-time, 29 part-time); 83% of full-time faculty have doctoral degrees; graduate assistants teach a few undergraduate courses. Library holdings: 48,920 bound volumes, 256 periodical subscriptions, 1,712 records/tapes. Computer terminals/PCs available for student use: 11, located in computer lab.

UNDERGRADUATE PROFILE Fall 1989: 318 undergraduates (184 freshmen) from 6 provinces and territories and 5 foreign countries; 8% part-time; 85% province residents; 14% transfers; 54% women; 46% men; 2% blacks; 1% Native Americans; 0% Hispanics; 0% Asian Americans; 1% international students; 19% of undergraduates 25 years of age or older.

1989 FRESHMAN DATA 278 students applied for fall 1989 admission; 79% were accepted; 84% of those accepted enrolled.

ENROLLMENT PATTERNS 46% of fall 1988 freshmen returned for fall 1989 term.

FRESHMAN ADMISSIONS Option: deferred entrance. Required: high school transcript, 2 recommendations, photograph, TOEFL (for foreign students). Test scores used for admission. Application deadline: rolling. Notification date: continuous until 8/31. College's own assessment of entrance difficulty level: moderately difficult.

TRANSFER ADMISSIONS Required: high school transcript, 2 recommendations, college transcript, minimum 2.0 grade point average, photograph. Required for some: campus interview. Application deadline: rolling. Notification date: continuous until 8/31. College's own assessment of entrance difficulty level: minimally difficult.

EXPENSES (1990–91 estimated) Tuition: $2850 full-time, $285 per course part-time. Mandatory fees: $85. College room only: $1200.

FINANCIAL AID College-administered aid for all 1989–90 undergraduates: 16 need-based scholarships (average $490); 36 non-need scholarships (average $375); low-interest long-term loans from external sources (average $600); 20 part-time jobs. Supporting data: institutional form required; government form required for some. Application deadline: 3/31.

CAMPUS LIFE/STUDENT SERVICES Drama/theater group; student-run newspaper. Institution provides personal/psychological counseling.

ATHLETICS Intercollegiate sports: basketball M, W; ice hockey M; volleyball M, W.

MAJORS Biology/biological sciences B; chemistry B; English B; history B; music B; philosophy B; psychology B; social science B.

SPECIAL NOTE FROM THE COLLEGE The King's College is an independent, Christian liberal arts college located in an urban setting in one of western Canada's major cities. Christian students learn how to be "in the world, but not of the world" through an education that integrates the Christian faith with life and learning, with emphasis on the unique task of the Christian in a secular society. Although independently operated, the College has an Agreement of Affiliation with the University of Alberta, located nearby, which allows students significant interaction with that institution. At the same time, the College's small size and highly qualified faculty contribute to a caring and intellectually stimulating environment for learning and personal growth. Continued development of degree programs and plans to move to a newly built 34-acre campus in 1993 project exciting years of growth for the College and its students in the immediate future.

CONTACT Dr. Robert Day, Registrar, King's College, Edmonton, AB T5H 2M1, Canada, 403-428-0727.

LEE COLLEGE
Cleveland, Tennessee

Total enrollment: 1,535 (all UG)

Women: 54%

Application deadline: rolling

Tuition & fees: $4013

Room & board: $2700

Entrance: minimally difficult

SAT ≥ 500: N/R

ACT ≥ 21: 37%

Denominational affiliation: Church of God

GENERAL INFORMATION Independent 4-year coed college. Founded 1918. Awards B. Primary accreditation: regional. Small-town setting; 37-acre campus. Total enrollment: 1,535. Faculty: 118 (77 full-time, 41 part-time); 44% of full-time faculty have doctoral degrees; graduate assistants teach a few undergraduate courses. Library holdings: 114,000 bound volumes, 10,320 titles on microform, 857 periodical subscriptions, 15,109 records/tapes. Computer terminals/PCs available for student use: 23, located in computer center.

UNDERGRADUATE PROFILE Fall 1989: 1,535 undergraduates (369 freshmen) from 53 states and territories and 25 foreign countries; 6% part-time; 96% state residents; 14% transfers; 80% financial aid recipients; 54% women; 46% men; 2% blacks; 1% Native Americans; 3% Hispanics; 1% Asian Americans; 4% international students; 14% of undergraduates 25 years of age or older.

1989 FRESHMAN DATA 461 students applied for fall 1989 admission; 99% were accepted; 81% of those accepted enrolled.

ENROLLMENT PATTERNS 60% of fall 1988 freshmen returned for fall 1989 term. 1987–89 average: 25% of entering classes graduated; 30% of students completing a degree program went on for further study.

FRESHMAN ADMISSIONS Options: early entrance, deferred entrance. Required: high school transcript, SAT or ACT, TOEFL (for foreign students). Test scores used for counseling/placement. Application deadline: rolling. College's own assessment of entrance difficulty level: minimally difficult.

TRANSFER ADMISSIONS Required: college transcript, minimum 2.0 grade point average. Application deadline: rolling. College's own assessment of entrance difficulty level: minimally difficult.

EXPENSES (1990–91) Comprehensive fee of $6713 includes full-time tuition ($3700), mandatory fees ($313), and college room and board ($2700). College room only: $1400. Part-time tuition: $154 per semester hour.

FINANCIAL AID Fall 1989 full-time freshmen: 81% of those who applied for aid were judged to have need, 99% of those were aided; the average aided freshman received an aid package worth $3461 (28% scholarships/grants, 72% self-help) meeting 75% of need. College-administered aid for all 1989–90 undergraduates: 675 need-based scholarships (average $500); non-need scholarships; low-interest long-term loans from external sources (average $2000); SEOG; College Work-Study; part-time jobs. Supporting data: FFS, institutional form required; IRS required for some; AFSA/SAR acceptable. Priority application deadline: 4/15.

CAMPUS LIFE/STUDENT SERVICES Dress code; mandatory chapel; student-run newspaper. Institution provides health clinic, personal/psychological counseling. Social organizations: 2 local fraternities, 2 local sororities; 6% of eligible undergraduate men and 6% of eligible undergraduate women are members.

ATHLETICS Member NAIA. Intercollegiate sports: baseball/softball W(s); basketball M(s), W(s); golf M(s); soccer M(s); tennis M(s); volleyball W. Intramural sports: baseball/softball, basketball, football, racquetball, soccer, table tennis (ping pong), tennis, volleyball.

MAJORS Accounting B; biblical studies B; biology/biological sciences B; business administration/commerce/management B; business education B; chemistry B; communication B; computer information systems B; education B; elementary education B; English B; health education B; history B; mathematics B; medical technology B; modern languages B; music B; music education B; natural sciences B; physical education B; piano/organ B; psychology B; religious education B; secondary education B; secretarial studies/office management B; social science B; sociology B; theology B; voice B. Majors with highest enrollment: business administration/commerce/management, biblical studies, elementary education.

SPECIAL NOTE FROM THE COLLEGE Nestled on 37 acres in the beauty of the Southeast is Lee College. In this day of declining student populations, Lee has realized a 40% increase since 1983. This results in a student population that is alive and excited about the future. A Pentecostal/Charismatic institution, Lee is among the least expensive of the Coalition schools. In addition, Lee graduates post an exceptionally high acceptance rate into medical and other graduate schools. Combine all this with 1,600 students who live together in the shadow of the Great Smoky Mountains, and Lee becomes one of the most attractive options in higher education a Christian student can consider.

CONTACT Dr. Stanley Butler, Dean of Admissions, Lee College, Cleveland, TN 37311, 615-472-2111 or toll-free 800-LEE-9930.

LeTourneau University
Longview, Texas

Total enrollment: 773 (all UG)

Women: 17%

Application deadline: 8/15

Tuition & fees: $6802

Room & board: $3680

Entrance: moderately difficult

SAT ≥ 500: 44% V, 65% M

ACT ≥ 21: 70%

Denominational affiliation: nondenominational

GENERAL INFORMATION Independent 4-year coed college. Founded 1946. Awards A (terminal), B. Primary accreditation: regional. City setting; 162-acre campus. Total enrollment: 773. Faculty: 59 (46 full-time, 13 part-time); 43% of full-time faculty have doctoral degrees. Library holdings: 108,500 bound volumes, 29,253 titles on microform, 437 periodical subscriptions, 2,700 records/tapes. Computer terminals/PCs available for student use: 300, located in computer center, student center, library, dormitories.

UNDERGRADUATE PROFILE Fall 1989: 773 undergraduates (242 freshmen) from 52 states and territories and 24 foreign countries; 10% part-time; 28% state residents; 30% transfers; 82% financial aid recipients; 17% women; 83% men; 1% blacks; 0% Native Americans; 1% Hispanics; 1% Asian Americans; 5% international students; 18% of undergraduates 25 years of age or older.

1989 FRESHMAN DATA 311 students applied for fall 1989 admission; 97% were accepted; 80% of those accepted enrolled. 1 freshman was a National Merit Scholarship Finalist and received a National Merit Scholarship. 25% of freshmen were in top 10% of secondary school class, 95% were in top half.

ENROLLMENT PATTERNS 73% of fall 1988 freshmen returned for fall 1989 term. 1987–89 average: 48% of entering classes graduated; 7% of students completing a bachelor's program went on for further study.

FRESHMAN ADMISSIONS Options: early entrance, deferred entrance. Required: essay, high school transcript, 2 recommendations, SAT or ACT, TOEFL (for foreign students). Recommended: 3 years of high school science. Required for some: 3 years of high school math, campus interview. Test scores used for admission and counseling/placement. Application deadline: 8/15. Notification date: continuous. College's own assessment of entrance difficulty level: moderately difficult.

TRANSFER ADMISSIONS Required: essay, 2 recommendations, college transcript, minimum 2.0 grade point average. Required for some: standardized test scores, high school transcript, campus interview. Application deadline: 8/15. Notification date: continuous. College's own assessment of entrance difficulty level: moderately difficult.

EXPENSES (1990–91) Comprehensive fee of $10,482 includes full-time tuition ($6710), mandatory fees ($92), and college room and board ($3680). Part-time tuition and fees per semester (1 to 11 semester hours) range from $85 to $3065.

FINANCIAL AID Fall 1989 full-time freshmen: 88% applied for aid, 78% of those were judged to have need, 99% of those were aided; the average aided freshman received an aid package worth $7000 (54% scholarships/grants, 46% self-help) meeting 83% of need. College-administered aid for all 1989–90 undergraduates: 632 need-based scholarships (average $1070); 336 non-need scholarships (average $1066); low-interest long-term loans from college funds (average $1350), from external sources (average $2530); SEOG; College Work-Study; 190 part-time jobs. Supporting data: FAF, AFSA/SAR required; IRS required for some; FFS acceptable. Priority application deadline: 2/15.

CAMPUS LIFE/STUDENT SERVICES Dress code; mandatory chapel; drama/theater group; student-run newspaper. Institution provides health clinic, personal/psychological counseling. Social organizations: 5 local fraternities; 13% of eligible undergraduate men are members.

ATHLETICS Member NAIA. Intercollegiate sports: baseball/softball M; basketball M; cross-country running M, W; soccer M; volleyball W. Intramural sports: badminton, baseball/softball, basketball, bowling, cross-country running, field hockey, football, golf, racquetball, soccer, swimming and diving, table tennis (ping pong), tennis, track and field, volleyball, weight lifting, wrestling.

MAJORS Accounting B; aircraft and missile maintenance A; automotive technologies A; aviation technology A, B; biblical studies B; biology/biological sciences B; business administration/commerce/management B; chemistry B; computer engineering B; computer science B; computer technologies B; (pre)dentistry sequence B; drafting and design A; electrical engineering B; electrical engineering technology B; engineering (general) B; engineering technology B; English B; flight training B; history B; industrial administration B; (pre)law sequence B; marketing/retailing/merchandising B; mathematics B; mechanical engineering B; mechanical engineering technology B; medical technology B; (pre)medicine sequence B; natural sciences B; physical education B; public administration B; sports administration B; (pre)veterinary medicine sequence B; welding engineering B; welding technology B. Majors with highest enrollment: aviation technology, engineering (general), engineering technology.

SPECIAL NOTE FROM THE COLLEGE Set apart by a special "spirit of ingenuity," the LeTourneau University of today perpetuates the excellence and the inventive zeal of its heritage. Founded by industrialist R. G. LeTourneau, the world-famous inventor and designer who was responsible for more US patents than anyone other than Thomas Edison, LeTourneau University was the first evangelical Christian college to achieve professional accreditation of its engineering program by ABET (Accreditation Board for Engineering and Technology). For students contemplating a career in engineering, aviation, technology, mathematics, or computer science, LeTourneau is an excellent first choice. Students whose college plans include business, arts and sciences, or teaching certification will also want to look closely at the inventiveness and inspiration that are at the core of this university. Everyone on the LeTourneau campus is bonded by a common call to service—truly, "Faith brings us together, ingenuity sets us apart."

CONTACT Mr. Roger Kieffer, Director of Admissions, LeTourneau University, Longview, TX 75607, 214-753-0231 Ext. 240 or toll-free 800-759-8811.

MALONE COLLEGE
Canton, Ohio

Total enrollment: 1,457 (all UG)

Women: 63%

Application deadline: rolling

Tuition & fees: $7317

Room & board: $2850

Entrance: moderately difficult

SAT ≥ 500: 33% V, 64% M

ACT ≥ 21: 49%

Denominational affiliation: Evangelical Friends Church, Eastern Region

GENERAL INFORMATION Independent comprehensive coed institution. Founded 1892. Awards A (terminal), B, M. Primary accreditation: regional. City setting, with easy access to Cleveland; 78-acre campus. Total enrollment: 1,457. Faculty: 90 (53 full-time, 37 part-time); 63% of full-time faculty have doctoral degrees. Library holdings: 121,560 bound volumes, 132,103 titles on microform, 913 periodical subscriptions, 5,666 records/tapes. Computer terminals/PCs available for student use: 40, located in computer center.

UNDERGRADUATE PROFILE Fall 1989: 1,457 undergraduates (312 freshmen) from 11 states and territories and 5 foreign countries; 17% part-time; 95% state residents; 9% transfers; 69% financial aid recipients; 63% women; 37% men; 4% blacks; 1% international students; 22% of undergraduates 25 years of age or older.

1989 FRESHMAN DATA 528 students applied for fall 1989 admission; 92% were accepted; 64% of those accepted enrolled. 1 freshman was a National Merit Scholarship Finalist and received a National Merit Scholarship. 33% of freshmen were in top 10% of secondary school class, 59% were in top 25%, 83% were in top half.

ENROLLMENT PATTERNS 73% of fall 1988 freshmen returned for fall 1989 term. 1987–89 average: 61% of entering classes graduated; 24% of students completing a bachelor's program went on for further study.

FRESHMAN ADMISSIONS Options: early entrance, deferred entrance. Required: essay, high school transcript, SAT or ACT, TOEFL (for foreign students). Recommended: 3 years of high school math and science, some high school foreign language. Required for some: 2 recommendations, interview. Test scores used for counseling/placement. Application deadline: rolling. Notification date: continuous until 8/29. College's own assessment of entrance difficulty level: moderately difficult.

TRANSFER ADMISSIONS Required: 1 recommendation, college transcript, minimum 2.0 grade point average. Recommended: essay, 3 years of high school math and science, some high school foreign language. Required for some: standardized test scores, high school transcript, interview. Application deadline: rolling. Notification date: continuous until 8/29. College's own assessment of entrance difficulty level: moderately difficult.

EXPENSES (1990–91) Comprehensive fee of $10,167 includes full-time tuition ($7192), mandatory fees ($125), and college room and board ($2850). Part-time tuition: $165 per credit hour.

FINANCIAL AID Fall 1989 full-time freshmen: 98% applied for aid, 87% of those were judged to have need, 100% of those were aided; the average aided freshman received an aid package worth $5418 (54% scholarships/grants, 46% self-help) meeting 85% of need. College-administered aid for all 1989–90 undergraduates: 785 need-based scholarships (average $880); 779 non-need scholarships (average $1310); low-interest long-term loans from college funds (average $1500), from external sources (average $2457); SEOG; College Work-Study; 102 part-time jobs. Supporting data: FAF, institutional form, AFSA/SAR required; IRS, state form required for some. Application deadline: continuous to 4/15.

CAMPUS LIFE/STUDENT SERVICES Mandatory chapel; drama/theater group; student-run newspaper and radio station. Institution provides health clinic, personal/psychological counseling.

ATHLETICS Member NAIA. Intercollegiate sports: baseball/softball M(s); basketball M(s), W(s); cross-country running M(s), W(s); golf M(s); soccer M(s); tennis M(s), W(s); track and field M(s), W(s); volleyball W(s). Intramural sports: baseball/softball, basketball, bowling, cross-country running, football, golf, racquetball, skiing (cross-country), skiing (downhill), soccer, table tennis (ping pong), tennis, ultimate frisbee, volleyball, weight lifting.

MAJORS Accounting B; biology/biological sciences B; broadcasting B; business administration/commerce/management B; chemistry B; communication B; computer science B; (pre)dentistry sequence B; early childhood education A; education B; elementary education B; (pre)engineering sequence A; English B; health education B; health science B; history B; journalism B; (pre)law sequence B; liberal arts/general studies B; mathematics B; medical technology B; (pre)medicine sequence B; ministries B; music B; music education B; nursing B; physical education B; psychology B; radiological sciences B; religious education B; sacred music B; science B; science education B; secondary education B; social work B; special education B; sports medicine B; theater arts/drama B; (pre)veterinary medicine sequence B. Majors with highest enrollment: business administration/commerce/management, elementary education, ministries.

SPECIAL NOTE FROM THE COLLEGE Malone College is located in Canton, Ohio, home of the Professional Football Hall of Fame. Its location provides a varied cultural life and many employment opportunities. As a fully accredited Christian liberal arts college, Malone provides first-rate opportunities for academic excellence and spiritual development. With 29 areas of study and a new master's in education program, Malone continues to provide a high-quality education to its interdenominational student body. Many extracurricular opportunities are available, such as a strong athletics program with competition at the national level as an NAIA member. Malone is experiencing record-high enrollment, and its students continue to maintain a fine record of employment and graduate school placement. All of this and much more make Malone a distinctively different Christian liberal arts college.

CONTACT Mr. Lee J. Sommers, Director of Admissions, Malone College, Canton, OH 44709, 216-489-0800 Ext. 107 or toll-free 800-521-1146 (in-state), 800-521-8959 (out-of-state).

MASTER'S COLLEGE
Newhall, California

Total enrollment: 1,008

UG enrollment: 863 (52% W)

Application deadline: rolling

Tuition & fees: $6450

Room & board: $3690

Entrance: moderately difficult

SAT ≥ 500: 29% V, 42% M

ACT ≥ 21: 79%

Denominational affiliation: nondenominational

GENERAL INFORMATION Independent comprehensive coed institution. Founded 1927. Awards B, M. Primary accreditation: regional. City setting, with easy access to Los Angeles; 110-acre campus. Total enrollment: 1,008. Faculty: 75 (45 full-time, 30 part-time); 33% of full-time faculty have doctoral degrees; graduate assistants teach no undergraduate courses. Library holdings: 110,000 bound volumes, 202 titles on microform, 428 periodical subscriptions, 5,000 records/tapes. Computer terminals/PCs available for student use: 20, located in computer center.

UNDERGRADUATE PROFILE Fall 1989: 863 undergraduates (207 freshmen) from 38 states and territories and 15 foreign countries; 8% part-time; 97% state residents; 9% transfers; 73% financial aid recipients; 52% women; 48% men; 2% blacks; 1% Native Americans; 3% Hispanics; 3% Asian Americans; 3% international students; 10% of undergraduates 25 years of age or older.

1989 FRESHMAN DATA 332 students applied for fall 1989 admission; 95% were accepted; 66% of those accepted enrolled. 1 freshman was a National Merit Scholarship Finalist and received a National Merit Scholarship.

ENROLLMENT PATTERNS 60% of fall 1988 freshmen returned for fall 1989 term. 1987–89 average: 30% of entering classes graduated; 12% of students completing a degree program went on for further study.

FRESHMAN ADMISSIONS Option: deferred entrance. Required: essay, high school transcript, 2 years of high school foreign language, 2 recommendations, SAT or ACT, TOEFL (for foreign students). Recommended: interview, Achievement Tests, English Composition Test. Test scores used for admission. Application deadline: rolling. College's own assessment of entrance difficulty level: moderately difficult.

TRANSFER ADMISSIONS Required: essay, 2 recommendations, college transcript, minimum 2.0 grade point average. Recommended: interview. Required for some: standardized test scores, high school transcript. Application deadline: rolling.

EXPENSES (1990–91) Comprehensive fee of $10,140 includes full-time tuition ($6130), mandatory fees ($320), and college room and board ($3690). Part-time tuition: $240 per unit.

FINANCIAL AID Fall 1989 full-time freshmen: 97% applied for aid, 63% of those were judged to have need, 100% of those were aided; the average aided freshman received an aid package worth $5508 (74% scholarships/grants, 26% self-help) meeting 93% of need. College-administered aid for all 1989–90 undergraduates: 80 need-based scholarships (average $1800); 250 non-need scholarships (average $1400); SEOG; College Work-Study; part-time jobs. Supporting data: FAF, IRS, institutional form required. Application deadline: continuous to 6/30.

CAMPUS LIFE/STUDENT SERVICES Dress code; mandatory chapel; drama/theater group. Institution provides health clinic, personal/psychological counseling.

ATHLETICS Member NAIA, NLCAA. Intercollegiate sports: baseball/softball M(s); basketball M(s), W(s); cross-country running M(s), W(s); soccer M(s); volleyball W(s). Intramural sports: baseball/softball, basketball, football, volleyball.

MAJORS Behavioral sciences B; biblical studies B; biology/biological sciences B; business administration/commerce/management B; communication B; education B; elementary education B; English B; history B; home economics B; liberal arts/general studies B; mathematics B; minjstries B; music B; natural sciences B; physical education B; political science/government B; secondary education B; theology B. Majors with highest enrollment: education, biblical studies, business administration/commerce/management.

SPECIAL NOTE FROM THE COLLEGE Located in a rural country setting within an hour of white-sand beaches, ski mountains, and the cultural advantages of Los Angeles, the Master's College has a beautiful 110-acre campus in sunny southern California. Personalized scholarship and personalized discipleship are at the heart of academic and spiritual development for every student. Powerful chapels and campus ministry teams combine with vision-building opportunities that include a World Prayer Center and Summer Missions Program (designed with the eventual goal of having every student spend a summer ministering overseas before graduation). Beginning with a foundation of 18 Bible units, students can go on to 1 of 17 diverse majors, including Bible and theology, business administration, and teacher education, at a moderate cost.

CONTACT Mr. Don Gilmore, Director of Admissions, Master's College, Newhall, CA 91322, 805-259-3540 Ext. 318.

MESSIAH COLLEGE
Grantham, Pennsylvania

Total enrollment: 2,280 (all UG)

Women: 58%

Application deadline: rolling

Tuition & fees: $8070

Room & board: $3990

Entrance: moderately difficult

SAT ≥ 500: 77% V, 95% M

ACT ≥ 21: 100%

Denominational affiliation: Brethren in Christ Church

GENERAL INFORMATION Independent 4-year coed college. Founded 1909. Awards B. Primary accreditation: regional. Small-town setting; 310-acre campus. Total enrollment: 2,280. Faculty: 203 (144 full-time, 59 part-time); 66% of full-time faculty have doctoral degrees. Library holdings: 170,000 bound volumes, 5,000 titles on microform, 1,000 periodical subscriptions, 3,750 records/tapes. Computer terminals/PCs available for student use: 80, located in computer center, library.

UNDERGRADUATE PROFILE Fall 1989: 2,280 undergraduates (571 freshmen) from 39 states and territories and 21 foreign countries; 2% part-time; 51% state residents; 5% transfers; 84% financial aid recipients; 58% women; 42% men; 3% blacks; 0% Native Americans; 2% Hispanics; 2% Asian Americans; 1% international students; 3% of undergraduates 25 years of age or older.

1989 FRESHMAN DATA 1,449 students applied for fall 1989 admission; 73% were accepted; 54% of those accepted enrolled. 51% of freshmen were in top 10% of secondary school class, 86% were in top 25%, 99% were in top half.

ENROLLMENT PATTERNS 89% of fall 1988 freshmen returned for fall 1989 term. 1987–89 average: 62% of entering classes graduated; 30% of students completing a degree program went on for further study.

FRESHMAN ADMISSIONS Options: early entrance, deferred entrance. Required: essay, high school transcript, 2 recommendations, SAT or ACT. Recommended: 3 years of high school math and science. Required for some: some high school foreign language. Test scores used for admission. Application deadline: rolling. Notification date: continuous. College's own assessment of entrance difficulty level: moderately difficult.

TRANSFER ADMISSIONS Required: essay, 2 recommendations, college transcript, minimum 2.5 grade point average. Application deadline: rolling. Notification date: continuous. College's own assessment of entrance difficulty level: moderately difficult.

EXPENSES (1990–91) Comprehensive fee of $12,060 includes full-time tuition ($8000), mandatory fees ($70), and college room and board ($3990). College room only: $1950. Part-time tuition: $330 per credit.

FINANCIAL AID Fall 1989 full-time freshmen: 77% applied for aid, 81% of those were judged to have need, 99% of those were aided; the average aided freshman received an aid package worth $5049 (69% scholarships/grants, 31% self-help) meeting 76% of need. College-administered aid for all 1989–90 undergraduates: 928 need-based scholarships (average $1025); 1,300 non-need scholarships (average $1250); low-interest long-term loans from external sources (average $2500); SEOG; College Work-Study; 600 part-time jobs. Supporting data: state form required for some; FAF acceptable. Priority application deadline: 4/1.

CAMPUS LIFE Mandatory chapel; drama/theater group; student-run newspaper and radio station. Honor Society: Sigma Xi.

ATHLETICS Member NCAA (Division III). Intercollegiate sports: baseball/softball M(III); basketball M(III), W(III); cross-country running M(III), W(III); field hockey W(III); golf M(III); soccer M(III), W(III); track and field M(III), W(III); volleyball W(III); wrestling M(III). Intramural sports: baseball/softball, basketball, cross-country running, field hockey, football, golf, gymnastics, soccer, tennis, track and field, volleyball, wrestling.

MAJORS Accounting B; art/fine arts B; art history B; behavioral sciences B; biblical studies B; business administration/commerce/management B; chemistry B; civil engineering technology B; clinical psychology B; communication B; computer information systems B; computer science B; dietetics B; early childhood education B; education B; elementary education B; English B; experimental psychology B; family services B; French B; geography B; German B; history B; home economics B; humanities B; human resources B; journalism B; (pre)law sequence B; liberal arts/general studies B; marketing/retailing/merchandising B; mathematics B; medical technology B; (pre)medicine sequence B; modern languages B; music B; music education B; nursing B; pastoral studies B; physical education B; physics B; psychology B; radio and television studies B; recreation and leisure services B; religious education B; religious studies B; secondary education B; social science B; social work B; sociology B; Spanish B; speech/rhetoric/public address/debate B; sports medicine B; stringed instruments B; theology B; (pre)veterinary medicine sequence B; voice B. Majors with highest enrollment: business administration/commerce/management, computer science, education.

SPECIAL NOTE FROM THE COLLEGE Messiah College is a 4-year, residential Christian college of the arts and sciences. The size of the enrollment (2,300) provides numerous advantages, including personal contact between students and faculty. Located in Grantham, Pennsylvania, 10 miles south of Harrisburg, Messiah's 310-acre campus is easily accessible by interstate highways, Harrisburg International Airport, and train and bus lines. Messiah offers more than 50 majors, including traditional liberal arts curricula and professional and preprofessional programs in business, computer science, engineering, medicine, and nursing. Cooperative education, internships, and international service opportunities are also available at Messiah. Most of Messiah's excellent facilities have been constructed within the past 15 years, enabling the College to offer a high-quality education in an ever-changing world.

CONTACT Mr. Ron E. Long, Vice President for Admissions, Fin. Aid, and Communications, Messiah College, Grantham, PA 17027, 717-766-2511 Ext. 6000 or toll-free 800-382-1349 (in-state), 800-233-4220 (out-of-state).

MIDAMERICA NAZARENE COLLEGE
Olathe, Kansas

Total enrollment: 1,189

UG enrollment: 1,161 (51% W)

Application deadline: N/R

Tuition & fees: $5090

Room & board: $2990

Entrance: noncompetitive

SAT ≥ 500: N/R

ACT ≥ 21: 48%

Denominational affiliation: Church of the Nazarene

GENERAL INFORMATION Independent comprehensive coed institution. Founded 1966. Awards A (college transfer and terminal), B, M (in education only). Primary accreditation: regional. Small-town setting, with easy access to Kansas City; 112-acre campus. Total enrollment: 1,189. Faculty: 81 (49 full-time, 32 part-time); 37% of full-time faculty have doctoral degrees; graduate assistants teach no undergraduate courses. Library holdings: 77,272 bound volumes, 21,500 titles on microform, 405 periodical subscriptions, 1,522 records/tapes. Computer terminals/PCs available for student use: 100, located in computer center, library.

UNDERGRADUATE PROFILE Fall 1989: 1,161 undergraduates (231 freshmen) from 34 states and territories and 10 foreign countries; 17% part-time; 57% state residents; 28% transfers; 75% financial aid recipients; 51% women; 49% men; 2% blacks; 1% Native Americans; 1% Hispanics; 1% Asian Americans; 4% international students; 31% of undergraduates 25 years of age or older.

1989 FRESHMAN DATA 335 students applied for fall 1989 admission; 100% were accepted; 69% of those accepted enrolled.

ENROLLMENT PATTERNS 66% of fall 1988 freshmen returned for fall 1989 term. 1987–89 average: 34% of entering classes graduated; 38% of students completing a bachelor's program went on for further study.

FRESHMAN ADMISSIONS Open admissions. Options: early entrance, deferred entrance. Required: high school transcript, ACT, TOEFL (for foreign students). Test scores used for counseling/placement. Notification date: continuous. College's own assessment of entrance difficulty level: noncompetitive.

TRANSFER ADMISSIONS Required: standardized test scores, high school transcript, college transcript. Application deadline: rolling. Notification date: continuous.

EXPENSES (1990–91) Comprehensive fee of $8080 includes full-time tuition ($4800), mandatory fees ($290), and college room and board ($2990). Part-time tuition: $160 per semester hour.

FINANCIAL AID Fall 1989 full-time freshmen: 95% applied for aid, 97% of those were judged to have need, 100% of those were aided; the average aided freshman received an aid package worth $3430 (60% scholarships/grants, 40% self-help) meeting 40% of need. College-administered aid for all 1989–90 undergraduates: need-based scholarships; 625 non-need scholarships (average $700); low-interest long-term loans from external sources (average $2625); SEOG; College Work-Study; part-time jobs. Supporting data: FFS, IRS, institutional form, AFSA/SAR required; state form required for some; FAF acceptable. Priority application deadline: 3/1.

CAMPUS LIFE/STUDENT SERVICES Dress code; mandatory chapel; student-run newspaper. Institution provides health clinic, personal/psychological counseling.

ATHLETICS Member NAIA. Intercollegiate sports: baseball/softball M(s), W(s); basketball M(s), W(s); cross-country running M(s), W(s); football M(s); track and field M(s), W(s); volleyball W(s). Intramural sports: baseball/softball, basketball, football, track and field, volleyball, wrestling.

MAJORS Accounting B; agricultural business A, B; agricultural sciences B; biology/biological sciences B; business administration/commerce/management A, B; business education B; chemistry B; computer science B; early childhood education A, B; elementary education B; English B; history B; human development B; human resources B; international business B; liberal arts/general studies A; mathematics B; modern languages B; music B; music education B; nursing B; physical education B; physics B; psychology B; recreation and leisure services B; religious education A, B; religious studies A, B; Romance languages B; sacred music A, B; secondary education B; Spanish B; speech/rhetoric/public address/debate B. Majors with highest enrollment: human resources, business administration/commerce/management, elementary education.

SPECIAL NOTE FROM THE COLLEGE MidAmerica Nazarene College is a private, holiness college in the Wesleyan tradition. It is a coeducational, career-oriented, undergraduate college of liberal arts. New programs include management of human resources and a master's in education. The campus is located 19 miles southwest of downtown Kansas City, on 112 acres. The College has as its purpose the Christian education of individuals in a liberal arts context for personal development, service to God and humanity, and career preparation. MANC places importance on guiding the student in the development of a sense of self-worth and achievement predicated on acceptance of the inspiration of the Bible, with the life of Christian holiness as a guide.

CONTACT Mr. Dennis Troyer, Director of Admissions, MidAmerica Nazarene College, Olathe, KS 66061, 913-782-3750 Ext. 481.

MILLIGAN COLLEGE
Milligan College, Tennessee

Total enrollment: 760

UG enrollment: 733 (59% W)

Application deadline: rolling

Tuition & fees: $5742

Room & board: $2606

Entrance: moderately difficult

SAT ≥ 500: 31% V, 49% M

ACT ≥ 21: 55%

Denominational affiliation: nondenominational

GENERAL INFORMATION Independent comprehensive coed institution. Founded 1866. Awards A (terminal), B, M. Primary accreditation: regional. Rural setting; 135-acre campus. Total enrollment: 760. Faculty: 63 (46 full-time, 17 part-time); 61% of full-time faculty have doctoral degrees; graduate assistants teach no undergraduate courses. Library holdings: 154,908 bound volumes, 66,803 titles on microform, 450 periodical subscriptions, 2,468 records/tapes. Computer terminals/PCs available for student use: 29, located in computer center, classroom buildings.

UNDERGRADUATE PROFILE Fall 1989: 733 undergraduates (196 freshmen) from 35 states and territories and 5 foreign countries; 8% part-time; 29% state residents; 12% transfers; 80% financial aid recipients; 59% women; 41% men; 1% blacks; 1% Hispanics; 1% Asian Americans; 1% international students; 10% of undergraduates 25 years of age or older.

1989 FRESHMAN DATA 401 students applied for fall 1989 admission; 73% were accepted; 67% of those accepted enrolled. 21% of freshmen were in top 10% of secondary school class, 47% were in top 25%, 79% were in top half.

ENROLLMENT PATTERNS 65% of fall 1988 freshmen returned for fall 1989 term. 1987–89 average: 40% of entering classes graduated; 15% of students completing a bachelor's program went on for further study.

FRESHMAN ADMISSIONS Options: early entrance, deferred entrance. Required: high school transcript, 2 recommendations, SAT or ACT, TOEFL (for foreign students). Recommended: 3 years of high school math, 2 years of high school foreign language. Required for some: interview. Test scores used for admission. Application deadline: rolling. Notification date: continuous. College's own assessment of entrance difficulty level: moderately difficult.

TRANSFER ADMISSIONS Required: high school transcript, 2 recommendations, college transcript, minimum 2.0 grade point average. Recommended: 3 years of high school math, 2 years of high school foreign language. Required for some: interview. Application deadline: rolling. Notification date: continuous. College's own assessment of entrance difficulty level: moderately difficult.

EXPENSES (1989–90) Comprehensive fee of $8348 includes full-time tuition ($5678), mandatory fees ($64), and college room and board ($2606). College room only: $976. Part-time tuition per semester (1 to 11 semester hours) ranges from $170 to $2839.

FINANCIAL AID Fall 1989 full-time freshmen: 93% applied for aid, 96% of those were judged to have need, 95% of those were aided; the average aided freshman received an aid package worth $7084 (48% scholarships/grants, 52% self-help) meeting 75% of need. College-administered aid for all 1989–90 undergraduates: need-based scholarships (average $750); non-need scholarships (average $1200); short-term loans (average $2000); low-interest long-term loans from external sources (average $2625); SEOG; College Work-Study; part-time jobs. Supporting data: institutional form required; IRS, state form required for some; FFS, FAF, AFSA/SAR acceptable. Priority application deadline: 5/1.

CAMPUS LIFE/STUDENT SERVICES Dress code; mandatory chapel; drama/theater group; student-run newspaper. Institution provides health clinic, personal/psychological counseling.

ATHLETICS Member NAIA. Intercollegiate sports: baseball/softball M(s), W(s); basketball M(s), W(s); golf M(s); soccer M(s); tennis M(s), W(s); volleyball W(s). Intramural sports: baseball/softball, basketball, field hockey, football, table tennis (ping pong), tennis, volleyball.

MAJORS Accounting B; biblical studies B; biology/biological sciences B; business administration/commerce/management B; chemistry B; communication B; computer science B; (pre)dentistry sequence B; early childhood education B; elementary education B; English B; health education B; health services administration B; history B; humanities B; human services B; mathematics B; medical technology B; (pre)medicine sequence B; ministries B; music B; music education B; paralegal studies B; physical education B; psychology B; religious education B; sacred music B; secondary education B; secretarial studies/office management A, B; social work B; sociology B; special education B; (pre)veterinary medicine sequence B. Majors with highest enrollment: business administration/commerce/management, human services, communication.

SPECIAL NOTE FROM THE COLLEGE Milligan College combines the 3 areas of learning: God's world (taught through science), God's man (taught through the humanities), and God Himself (taught through revelation). Christ is central at Milligan College—both in its curriculum and in campus life. Milligan is a Christian liberal arts college dedicated to the integration of faith and learning in all facets of its college program. Milligan's mission is to prepare today's young people for a complicated world, and to do it in a Christian environment. Milligan's motto is "Christian education: the hope of the world!"

CONTACT Mr. Paul Bader, Director of Admissions, Milligan College, Milligan College, TN 37682, 615-929-0116 Ext. 121.

MISSISSIPPI COLLEGE
Clinton, Mississippi

Total enrollment: 4,221

UG enrollment: 2,548 (57% W)

Application deadline: rolling

Tuition & fees: $4432

Room & board: $2260

Entrance: moderately difficult

SAT ≥ 500: N/R

ACT ≥ 21: 37%

Denominational affiliation: Southern Baptist

GENERAL INFORMATION Independent comprehensive coed institution. Founded 1826. Awards B, M, D. Primary accreditation: regional. Small-town setting; 320-acre campus. Total enrollment: 4,221. Faculty: 176 (134 full-time, 42 part-time); 55% of full-time faculty have doctoral degrees; graduate assistants teach a few undergraduate courses. Library holdings: 229,473 bound volumes, 13,976 titles on microform, 821 periodical subscriptions, 9,401 records/tapes. Computer terminals/PCs available for student use: 50, located in computer center.

UNDERGRADUATE PROFILE Fall 1989: 2,548 undergraduates (352 freshmen) from 40 states and territories and 6 foreign countries; 7% part-time; 83% state residents; 15% transfers; 80% financial aid recipients; 57% women; 43% men; 8% blacks; 1% Native Americans; 1% Hispanics; 0% Asian Americans; 1% international students; 30% of undergraduates 25 years of age or older.

1989 FRESHMAN DATA 455 students applied for fall 1989 admission; 86% were accepted; 90% of those accepted enrolled. 17 freshmen were National Merit Scholarship Finalists; all received a National Merit Scholarship. 25% of freshmen were in top 10% of secondary school class, 66% were in top 25%, 89% were in top half.

ENROLLMENT PATTERNS 90% of fall 1988 freshmen returned for fall 1989 term. 1987–89 average: 75% of entering classes graduated; 41% of students completing a degree program went on for further study.

FRESHMAN ADMISSIONS Option: early entrance. Required: high school transcript, SAT or ACT, TOEFL (for foreign students). Test scores used for admission. Application deadline: rolling. Notification date: continuous. College's own assessment of entrance difficulty level: moderately difficult.

TRANSFER ADMISSIONS Required: college transcript, minimum 2.0 grade point average. Application deadline: rolling. Notification date: continuous. College's own assessment of entrance difficulty level: moderately difficult.

EXPENSES (1989–90) Comprehensive fee of $6692 includes full-time tuition ($4140), mandatory fees ($292), and college room and board ($2260). College room only: $990. Part-time tuition: $138 per credit hour.

FINANCIAL AID College-administered aid for all 1989–90 undergraduates: need-based scholarships; 550 non-need scholarships (average $2000); short-term loans (average $50); low-interest long-term loans from college funds (average $1500), from external sources (average $2500); SEOG; College Work-Study; 284 part-time jobs. Supporting data: FAF, institutional form required. Priority application deadline: 4/1.

CAMPUS LIFE/STUDENT SERVICES Dress code; mandatory chapel; drama/theater group; student-run newspaper and radio station. Institution provides health clinic, personal/psychological counseling. Social organizations: 3 local fraternities, 4 local sororities; 17% of eligible undergraduate men and 33% of eligible undergraduate women are members.

ATHLETICS Member NCAA (Division II). Intercollegiate sports: baseball/softball M(II,s), W(II); basketball M(II,s), W(I,s); cross-country running M(II,s); football M(II,s); golf M(II,s); tennis M(II,s), W(II,s); track and field M(II,s); volleyball W(II,s). Intramural sports: baseball/softball, basketball, cross-country running, football, golf, soccer, tennis, track and field, volleyball.

MAJORS Accounting B; applied art B; art education B; art/fine arts B; biblical studies B; biology/biological sciences B; business administration/commerce/management B; chemistry B; communication B; computer science B; criminal justice B; data processing B; (pre)dentistry sequence B; early childhood education B; economics B; education B; elementary education B; English B; health education B; history B; home economics B; home economics education B; interior design B; journalism B; law enforcement/police sciences B; (pre)law sequence B; marketing/retailing/merchandising B; mathematics B; medical technology B; (pre)medicine sequence B; modern languages B; music B; music education B; nursing B; nutrition B; occupational therapy B; paralegal studies B; physical education B; physical therapy B; physics B; piano/organ B; political science/government B; psychology B; public administration B; religious education B; religious studies B; retail management B; sacred music B; science education B; secretarial studies/office management B; social science B; social work B; sociology B; special education B; speech pathology and audiology B. Majors with highest enrollment: education, business administration/commerce/management, computer science.

SPECIAL NOTE FROM THE COLLEGE Mississippi College is a private, 4-year college affiliated with the Mississippi Baptist Convention. Founded in 1826, it is located 5 miles west of Jackson, in Clinton, Mississippi. Recognized as the oldest institution of higher learning in the state, it is the second-oldest Baptist college in the nation and was one of the first coeducational colleges in the country to grant degrees to women. In addition to its outstanding liberal arts program, it is recognized for its graduate school and School of Law programs. The College won the 1989 NCAA Division II national championship in football.

CONTACT Ms. Jennifer W. Trussell, Director of Admissions, Mississippi College, P.O. Box 4203, Clinton, MS 39058, 601-925-3240.

MONTREAT-ANDERSON COLLEGE
Montreat, North Carolina

Total enrollment: 414 (all UG)

Women: 43%

Application deadline: 8/20

Tuition & fees: $5250

Room & board: $3000

Entrance: minimally difficult

SAT ≥ 500: 10% V, 14% M

ACT ≥ 21: N/R

Denominational affiliation: Presbyterian

GENERAL INFORMATION Independent 4-year coed college. Founded 1916. Awards A (college transfer), B. Primary accreditation: regional. Small-town setting; 100-acre campus. Total enrollment: 414. Faculty: 43 (38 full-time, 5 part-time); 56% of full-time faculty have doctoral degrees. Library holdings: 59,182 bound volumes, 495 titles on microform, 414 periodical subscriptions, 1,546 records/tapes. Computer terminals/PCs available for student use: 30, located in computer center, student center, library, dormitories.

UNDERGRADUATE PROFILE Fall 1989: 414 undergraduates (169 freshmen) from 26 states and territories and 10 foreign countries; 3% part-time; 57% state residents; 12% transfers; 90% financial aid recipients; 43% women; 57% men; 6% blacks; 1% Native Americans; 1% Hispanics; 1% Asian Americans; 6% international students; 7% of undergraduates 25 years of age or older.

1989 FRESHMAN DATA Of the students who applied for fall 1989 admission, 80% were accepted; 52% of those accepted enrolled.

ENROLLMENT PATTERNS 70% of fall 1988 freshmen returned for fall 1989 term. 1987–89 average: 40% of entering classes graduated; 95% of students completing a college-transfer associate program went on to 4-year colleges.

FRESHMAN ADMISSIONS Options: early entrance, deferred entrance. Required: essay, high school transcript, SAT or ACT, TOEFL (for foreign students). Recommended: 3 years of high school math and science, some high school foreign language, 1 recommendation. Required for some: interview. Test scores used for admission. Application deadline: 8/20. Notification date: continuous. College's own assessment of entrance difficulty level: minimally difficult.

TRANSFER ADMISSIONS Required: essay, standardized test scores, high school transcript, college transcript. Recommended: 3 years of high school math and science, some high school foreign language, 1 recommendation, minimum 2.0 grade point average. Required for some: interview. Application deadline: 8/20. Notification date: continuous. College's own assessment of entrance difficulty level: minimally difficult.

EXPENSES (1990–91) Comprehensive fee of $8250 includes full-time tuition ($4950), mandatory fees ($300), and college room and board ($3000). Part-time tuition: $60 per semester hour.

FINANCIAL AID Fall 1989 full-time freshmen: 87% applied for aid, 82% of those were judged to have need, 100% of those were aided; the average aided freshman received an aid package worth $5772 (67% scholarships/grants, 33% self-help) meeting 85% of need. College-administered aid for all 1989–90 undergraduates: 297 need-based scholarships (average $4000); 100 non-need scholarships (average $1500); short-term loans (average $1000); low-interest long-term loans from college funds (average $1000), from external sources (average $1500); SEOG; College Work-Study; 20 part-time jobs. Supporting data: FFS, IRS, institutional form, AFSA/SAR required; state form required for some; FAF acceptable. Priority application deadline: 3/15.

CAMPUS LIFE/STUDENT SERVICES Mandatory chapel; drama/theater group; student-run newspaper. Institution provides health clinic, personal/psychological counseling.

ATHLETICS Member NJCAA. Intercollegiate sports: baseball/softball M(s), W(s); basketball M(s), W(s); soccer M(s); tennis M; volleyball W(s). Intramural sports: archery, badminton, baseball/softball, basketball, football, golf, skiing (cross-country), skiing (downhill), table tennis (ping pong), tennis, volleyball.

MAJORS Business administration/commerce/management B; child care/child and family studies B; English B; history B; international studies B; liberal arts/general studies A, B; ministries B; recreation and leisure services B; religious studies B; science A. Majors with highest enrollment: liberal arts/general studies, business administration/commerce/management, ministries.

SPECIAL NOTE FROM THE COLLEGE Montreat-Anderson College is firm in its commitment to Christian education. Its sense of Christian community is one of the most distinctive features of campus life. The small but vibrant campus creates a close-knit and personal atmosphere—an atmosphere that encourages involvement and participation from all segments of the student body. The campus is surrounded by the Blue Ridge Mountains, wooded hiking trails, mountain streams, and a mountain lake. M-AC offers students a meditative mountain setting; small, challenging classes; friendly, enthusiastic students; and a variety of degree programs plus the warmth, security, and moral structure that only a Christ-centered school can provide.

CONTACT Mr. Gary Melville, Director of Admissions, Montreat-Anderson College, Montreat, NC 28757, 704-669-8011 Ext. 22 or toll-free 800-627-1750.

MOUNT VERNON NAZARENE COLLEGE
Mount Vernon, Ohio

Total enrollment: 1,061 (all UG)

Women: 60%

Application deadline: rolling

Tuition & fees: $5490

Room & board: $2840

Entrance: moderately difficult

SAT ≥ 500: N/App

ACT ≥ 21: 40%

Denominational affiliation: Church of the Nazarene

GENERAL INFORMATION Independent 4-year coed college. Founded 1964. Awards A (college transfer and terminal), B. Primary accreditation: regional. Small-town setting, with easy access to Columbus; 210-acre campus. Total enrollment: 1,061. Faculty: 76 (48 full-time, 28 part-time); 58% of full-time faculty have doctoral degrees. Library holdings: 81,896 bound volumes, 3,600 titles on microform, 500 periodical subscriptions, 2,298 records/tapes. Computer terminals/PCs available for student use: 101, located in academic center, various offices.

UNDERGRADUATE PROFILE Fall 1989: 1,061 undergraduates (263 freshmen) from 23 states and territories and 4 foreign countries; 9% part-time; 84% state residents; 7% transfers; 85% financial aid recipients; 60% women; 40% men; 1% blacks; 0% Native Americans; 1% Hispanics; 5% of undergraduates 25 years of age or older.

1989 FRESHMAN DATA 520 students applied for fall 1989 admission; 87% were accepted; 58% of those accepted enrolled. 16% of freshmen were in top 10% of secondary school class, 37% were in top 25%, 72% were in top half.

ENROLLMENT PATTERNS 70% of fall 1988 freshmen returned for fall 1989 term. 1987–89 average: 40% of entering classes graduated; 20% of students completing a bachelor's program went on for further study.

FRESHMAN ADMISSIONS Options: early entrance, deferred entrance. Required: high school transcript, some high school foreign language, 2 recommendations, ACT, TOEFL (for foreign students). Recommended: 3 years of high school math and science, interview. Test scores used for counseling/placement. Application deadline: rolling. Notification date: continuous. College's own assessment of entrance difficulty level: moderately difficult.

TRANSFER ADMISSIONS Required: high school transcript, some high school foreign language, 2 recommendations, college transcript, minimum 2.0 grade point average. Recommended: 3 years of high school math and science, interview. Required for some: standardized test scores. Application deadline: rolling. Notification date: continuous.

EXPENSES (1990–91) Comprehensive fee of $8330 includes full-time tuition ($5194), mandatory fees ($296), and college room and board ($2840). College room only: $1600. Part-time tuition: $172 per credit hour.

FINANCIAL AID Fall 1989 full-time freshmen: 79% applied for aid, 92% of those were judged to have need, 100% of those were aided; the average aided freshman received an aid package worth $5110 (57% scholarships/grants, 43% self-help) meeting 95% of need. College-administered aid for all 1989–90 undergraduates: 88 need-based scholarships (average $4000); non-need scholarships (average $779); low-interest long-term loans from external sources (average $2000); SEOG; College Work-Study; 193 part-time jobs. Supporting data: FAF, IRS, institutional form, AFSA/SAR required; state form required for some; FFS acceptable. Priority application deadline: 4/15.

CAMPUS LIFE/STUDENT SERVICES Dress code; mandatory chapel; drama/theater group; student-run newspaper and radio station. Institution provides health clinic, personal/psychological counseling.

ATHLETICS Member NAIA. Intercollegiate sports: baseball/softball M(s), W(s); basketball M(s), W(s); golf M(s); soccer M(s); tennis M(s), W(s); volleyball W(s). Intramural sports: baseball/softball, basketball, bowling, golf, soccer, table tennis (ping pong), tennis, volleyball.

MAJORS Accounting B; art education B; art/fine arts B; biblical studies B; biology/biological sciences B; broadcasting B; business administration/commerce/management A, B; business education B; chemistry B; communication B; computer science B; computer technologies A; criminal justice B; data processing A, B; (pre)dentistry sequence B; early childhood education A, B; education B; elementary education B; (pre)engineering sequence A; English B; health science A; history B; home economics A, B; home economics education B; humanities B; human services A; (pre)law sequence B; liberal arts/general studies A; literature B; mathematics B; medical technology B; (pre)medicine sequence B; music B; music education B; natural resource management A; philosophy B; physical education B; psychology B; religious education B; religious studies B; sacred music A, B; science education B; secondary education B; secretarial studies/office management A, B; social science B; social work B; sociology B; Spanish B; theater arts/drama B; (pre)veterinary medicine sequence B. Majors with highest enrollment: business administration/commerce/management, elementary education, religious education.

SPECIAL NOTE FROM THE COLLEGE Mount Vernon Nazarene College consists of a group of people in education for Christ. A careful look uncovers a special commitment to Christ-centered education. Service to others comes alive at MVNC. Students invest themselves in ministry and mission projects within the United States and in other countries, enriching their lives and the lives of others. Apartment-style living promotes a sense of family as does a chaplaincy program, which pastors as well as preaches. A 4-1-4 academic calender allows off-campus classes midyear, such as marine biology at Padre Island, Texas. Abundant extracurricular activities contrast with MVNC's peaceful country setting, providing an opportunity for recreation as well as study and reflection.

CONTACT Mr. Ron Hyson, Director of Admissions and Enrollment Development, Mount Vernon Nazarene College, Mount Vernon, OH 43050, 614-397-7005 Ext. 235 or toll-free 800-782-2435.

NORTH PARK COLLEGE
Chicago, Illinois

Total enrollment: 1,098 (all UG)

Women: 56%

Application deadline: rolling

Tuition & fees: $9930

Room & board: $3765

Entrance: moderately difficult

SAT ≥ 500: 46% V, 65% M

ACT ≥ 21: 60%

Denominational affiliation: Evangelical Covenant Church of America

GENERAL INFORMATION Independent 4-year coed college of America. Founded 1891. Awards B. Primary accreditation: regional. Metropolitan setting; 30-acre campus. Total enrollment: 1,098. Faculty: 70 (58 full-time, 12 part-time); 60% of full-time faculty have doctoral degrees. Library holdings: 207,000 bound volumes, 3,300 titles on microform, 1,000 periodical subscriptions, 5,000 records/tapes. Computer terminals/PCs available for student use: 21, located in computer center, student center, library.

UNDERGRADUATE PROFILE Fall 1989: 1,098 undergraduates (180 freshmen) from 40 states and territories and 6 foreign countries; 8% part-time; 59% state residents; 9% transfers; 80% financial aid recipients; 56% women; 44% men; 5% blacks; 0% Native Americans; 13% Hispanics; 3% Asian Americans; 1% international students; 4% of undergraduates 25 years of age or older.

1989 FRESHMAN DATA 365 students applied for fall 1989 admission; 78% were accepted; 63% of those accepted enrolled. 5 freshmen were National Merit Scholarship Finalists; all received a National Merit Scholarship. 21% of freshmen were in top 10% of secondary school class, 51% were in top 25%, 73% were in top half.

ENROLLMENT PATTERNS 84% of fall 1988 freshmen returned for fall 1989 term. 1987–89 average: 50% of entering classes graduated; 25% of students completing a degree program went on for further study.

FRESHMAN ADMISSIONS Option: early entrance. Required: essay, high school transcript, recommendations, SAT or ACT, TOEFL (for foreign students). Recommended: 3 years of high school math and science, some high school foreign language. Required for some: campus interview. Test scores used for admission. Application deadline: rolling. Notification date: continuous. College's own assessment of entrance difficulty level: moderately difficult.

TRANSFER ADMISSIONS Required: essay, recommendations, college transcript, minimum 2.0 grade point average. Recommended: 3 years of high school math and science, some high school foreign language. Required for some: standardized test scores, high school transcript, campus interview. Application deadline: rolling. Notification date: continuous. College's own assessment of entrance difficulty level: moderately difficult.

EXPENSES (1990–91) Comprehensive fee of $13,695 includes full-time tuition ($9930) and college room and board ($3765).

FINANCIAL AID Fall 1989 full-time freshmen: 90% applied for aid, 96% of those were judged to have need, 100% of those were aided; the average aided freshman received an aid package worth $5852 (73% scholarships/grants, 27% self-help) meeting 92% of need. College-administered aid for all 1989–90 undergraduates: 600 need-based scholarships (average $3700); 110 non-need scholarships (average $1300); low-interest long-term loans from external sources (average $2250); SEOG; College Work-Study; 100 part-time jobs. Supporting data: FAF, IRS, institutional form required; state form, AFSA/SAR required for some; FFS acceptable. Priority application deadline: 8/15.

CAMPUS LIFE/STUDENT SERVICES Drama/theater group; student-run newspaper. Institution provides health clinic, personal/psychological counseling.

ATHLETICS Member NCAA (Division III). Intercollegiate sports: baseball/softball M(III), W(III); basketball M(III), W(III); cross-country running M(III), W(III); football M(III); golf M(III); soccer M(III), W; tennis M(III), W(III); track and field M(III), W(III); volleyball M(III), W(III). Intramural sports: basketball, football, ice hockey, volleyball, weight lifting.

MAJORS Accounting B; anthropology B; art education B; art/fine arts B; biblical studies B; biology/biological sciences B; business administration/commerce/management B; chemistry B; communication B; community services B; computer science B; (pre)dentistry sequence B; early childhood education B; economics B; education B; elementary education B; English B; finance/banking B; French B; German B; history B; international business B; international studies B; (pre)law sequence B; literature B; marketing/retailing/merchandising B; mathematics B; medical technology B; (pre)medicine sequence B; music B; music business B; music education B; natural sciences B; nursing B; philosophy B; physical education B; physical fitness/human movement B; physics B; political science/government B; psychology B; religious studies B; sacred music B; Scandinavian languages/studies B; science B; secondary education B; social science B; sociology B; Spanish B; speech/rhetoric/public address/debate B; sports medicine B; theology B; urban studies B; (pre)veterinary medicine sequence B; voice B. Majors with highest enrollment: business administration/commerce/management, education, psychology.

SPECIAL NOTE FROM THE COLLEGE North Park College's student body reflects considerable geographic, intellectual, ethnic, social, and religious diversity. Its faculty models Christian faith from a variety of perspectives. The College has a healthy atmosphere in which students and faculty can exchange views and learn from each other while tapping the full richness of the Christian tradition. North Park students, alumni, faculty, and staff are achievers. Students benefit from being around artists, scholars, professionals, and athletes who represent excellence. The North Park campus is based in a world-class city that has its own high standards. The result is a blend of commitment to Christ, to excellence, to the city, and to diversity.

CONTACT Mr. Randy Tumblin, Director of Admissions, North Park College, Chicago, IL 60625, 312-583-2700 or toll-free 800-888-NPC8.

NORTHWEST CHRISTIAN COLLEGE
Eugene, Oregon

Total enrollment: 216

UG enrollment: 202 (50% W)

Application deadline: rolling

Tuition & fees: $5270

Room & board: $3072

Entrance: minimally difficult

SAT ≥ 500: 20% V, 29% M

ACT ≥ 21: N/R

Denominational affiliation: interdenominational

GENERAL INFORMATION Independent comprehensive coed institution. Founded 1895. Awards A (college transfer), B, M. Primary accreditation: regional. City setting; 10-acre campus. Total enrollment: 216. Faculty: 19 (12 full-time, 7 part-time); 42% of full-time faculty have doctoral degrees; graduate assistants teach no undergraduate courses. Library holdings: 51,876 bound volumes, 551 titles on microform, 230 periodical subscriptions, 1,576 records/tapes. Computer terminals/PCs available for student use: 7, located in library.

UNDERGRADUATE PROFILE Fall 1989: 202 undergraduates (68 freshmen) from 10 states and territories and 6 foreign countries; 40% part-time; 78% state residents; 20% transfers; 85% financial aid recipients; 50% women; 50% men; 1% blacks; 0% Native Americans; 1% Hispanics; 2% Asian Americans; 5% international students; 19% of undergraduates 25 years of age or older.

1989 FRESHMAN DATA 99 students applied for fall 1989 admission; 97% were accepted; 71% of those accepted enrolled.

ENROLLMENT PATTERNS 64% of fall 1988 freshmen returned for fall 1989 term. 1987–89 average: 30% of entering classes graduated; 50% of students completing a bachelor's program went on for further study.

FRESHMAN ADMISSIONS Option: deferred entrance. Required: essay, high school transcript, 2 recommendations, SAT or ACT, TOEFL (for foreign students). Test scores used for counseling/placement. Application deadline: rolling. Notification date: continuous. College's own assessment of entrance difficulty level: minimally difficult.

TRANSFER ADMISSIONS Required: essay, 2 recommendations, college transcript. Recommended: minimum 2.0 grade point average. Application deadline: rolling. Notification date: continuous. College's own assessment of entrance difficulty level: minimally difficult.

EXPENSES (1990–91) Comprehensive fee of $8342 includes full-time tuition ($5130), mandatory fees ($140), and college room and board ($3072). Part-time tuition: $114 per quarter hour. Tuition guaranteed not to increase for student's term of enrollment.

FINANCIAL AID Fall 1989 full-time freshmen: 83% applied for aid, 86% of those were judged to have need, 100% of those were aided; the average aided freshman received an aid package worth $5097 (61% scholarships/grants, 39% self-help) meeting 81% of need. College-administered aid for all 1989–90 undergraduates: 87 need-based scholarships (average $961); 51 non-need scholarships (average $729); low-interest long-term loans from external sources (average $2993); SEOG; College Work-Study; 47 part-time jobs. Supporting data: FFS, FAF, institutional form, AFSA/SAR acceptable. Priority application deadline: 4/15.

CAMPUS LIFE/STUDENT SERVICES Mandatory chapel; student-run newspaper. Institution provides health clinic, personal/psychological counseling.

ATHLETICS Intercollegiate sport: basketball M. Intramural sports: baseball/softball, basketball, football, racquetball, volleyball.

MAJORS Biblical studies A, B; business administration/commerce/management B; communication B; interdisciplinary studies B; liberal arts/general studies A; ministries B; pastoral studies B; religious studies A, B; sacred music B; theology B. Majors with highest enrollment: ministries, biblical studies, pastoral studies.

SPECIAL NOTE FROM THE COLLEGE Northwest Christian College has helped thousands of students move toward competence in their chosen career while developing enduring Christian values and a deeper faith. Whatever career a student pursues, he or she has a unique, God-given ministry. Whether a student becomes a pastor, a teacher, a business manager, or a physician, God can use him or her to extend the kingdom of Jesus Christ. NCC integrates Christian faith with the world of academics. An NCC education challenges each student to grow as a total person. It stretches minds without neglecting hearts and souls. It touches the intellect, will, and imagination of each student. It inspires a vision of responsible and exciting Christian service and embraces all of life.

CONTACT Dr. Richard Busic, Vice President for Admissions and Development, Northwest Christian College, Eugene, OR 97401, 503-343-1641.

NORTHWESTERN COLLEGE
Orange City, Iowa

Total enrollment: 1,064

UG enrollment: 1,049 (55% W)

Application deadline: rolling

Tuition & fees: $7400

Room & board: $2700

Entrance: moderately difficult

SAT ≥ 500: N/R

ACT ≥ 21: 59%

Denominational affiliation: Reformed Church in America

GENERAL INFORMATION Independent comprehensive coed institution. Founded 1882. Awards A (terminal), B, M. Primary accreditation: regional. Rural setting; 40-acre campus. Total enrollment: 1,064. Faculty: 88 (52 full-time, 36 part-time); 70% of full-time faculty have doctoral degrees; graduate assistants teach no undergraduate courses. Library holdings: 90,000 bound volumes, 509 periodical subscriptions, 2,700 records/tapes. Computer terminals/PCs available for student use: 50, located in computer center, classrooms.

UNDERGRADUATE PROFILE Fall 1989: 1,049 undergraduates (348 freshmen) from 26 states and territories and 12 foreign countries; 5% part-time; 70% state residents; 5% transfers; 95% financial aid recipients; 55% women; 45% men; 2% blacks; 0% Native Americans; 0% Hispanics; 4% international students.

1989 FRESHMAN DATA 691 students applied for fall 1989 admission; 89% were accepted; 57% of those accepted enrolled. 3 freshmen were National Merit Scholarship Finalists; all received a National Merit Scholarship. 24% of freshmen were in top 10% of secondary school class, 55% were in top 25%, 84% were in top half.

ENROLLMENT PATTERNS 85% of fall 1988 freshmen returned for fall 1989 term. 1987–89 average: 48% of entering classes graduated; 15% of students completing a bachelor's program went on for further study.

FRESHMAN ADMISSIONS Option: deferred entrance. Required: high school transcript, 1 recommendation, SAT or ACT, TOEFL (for foreign students). Recommended: 3 years of high school math and science, interview. Test scores used for admission. Application deadline: rolling. Notification date: continuous until 8/30. College's own assessment of entrance difficulty level: moderately difficult.

TRANSFER ADMISSIONS Required: 1 recommendation, college transcript, minimum 2.0 grade point average. Recommended: interview. Application deadline: rolling. Notification date: continuous until 8/30.

EXPENSES (1990–91 estimated) Comprehensive fee of $10,100 includes full-time tuition ($7400) and college room and board ($2700). College room only: $1125. Part-time tuition per semester (1 to 11 credit hours) ranges from $150 to $3300.

FINANCIAL AID Fall 1989 full-time freshmen: 94% applied for aid, 95% of those were judged to have need, 100% of those were aided; the average aided freshman received an aid package worth $6597 (67% scholarships/grants, 33% self-help) meeting 98% of need. College-administered aid for all 1989–90 undergraduates: need-based scholarships; non-need scholarships; low-interest long-term loans from college funds (average $1200); SEOG; College Work-Study; 200 part-time jobs. Supporting data: institutional form required; AFSA/SAR required for some; FFS, FAF acceptable. Priority application deadline: 7/15.

CAMPUS LIFE/STUDENT SERVICES Mandatory chapel; drama/theater group; student-run newspaper and radio station. Institution provides health clinic, personal/psychological counseling.

ATHLETICS Member NAIA. Intercollegiate sports: baseball/softball M(s), W(s); basketball M(s), W(s); cross-country running M(s), W(s); football M(s); golf M(s), W(s); tennis M(s), W(s); track and field M(s), W(s); volleyball W(s); wrestling M(s). Intramural sports: badminton, baseball/softball, basketball, bowling, cross-country running, football, golf, racquetball, soccer, table tennis (ping pong), tennis, ultimate frisbee, volleyball.

MAJORS Accounting B; art education B; biology/biological sciences B; business administration/commerce/management B; business education B; chemistry B; communication B; computer science B; criminal justice B; (pre)dentistry sequence B; early childhood education B; economics B; education B; elementary education B; English B; French B; history B; humanities B; (pre)law sequence B; literature B; mathematics B; medical technology B; (pre)medicine sequence B; music B; music education B; natural sciences B; philosophy B; physical education B; physics B; political science/government B; psychology B; recreation and leisure services B; religious studies B; secondary education B; secretarial studies/office management A; social work B; sociology B; Spanish B; special education B; theater arts/drama B; theology B; (pre)veterinary medicine sequence B. Majors with highest enrollment: business administration/commerce/management, physical education, elementary education.

SPECIAL NOTE FROM THE COLLEGE Northwestern College of Iowa's newest facilities—built since 1981—reflect the College's purpose. The Learning Resource Center, with computer and audiovisual equipment, and the Business/Education Center, housing the College's 2 largest departments, are important resources for the academic program. Christ Chapel and DeWitt Music Hall, winners of numerous design awards, demonstrate the importance of worship and the arts. The Rowenhorst Student Center enhances campus life through its art gallery, theater, game room, and fitness center. But off-campus experiences are also important. Internships involve students in the workplace, and an extensive service-project program provides opportunities for ministry locally and throughout the world. All of these help Northwestern develop well-rounded Christians for today's society.

CONTACT Mr. Ronald K. DeJong, Director of Admissions, Northwestern College, Orange City, IA 51041, 712-737-4821 Ext. 137.

NORTHWESTERN COLLEGE
St. Paul, Minnesota

Total enrollment: 1,036 (all UG)

Women: 57%

Application deadline: rolling

Tuition & fees: $8310

Room & board: $2595

Entrance: moderately difficult

SAT ≥ 500: N/R

ACT ≥ 21: 52%

Denominational affiliation: interdenominational

GENERAL INFORMATION Independent 4-year coed college. Founded 1902. Awards A (college transfer and terminal), B. Primary accreditation: regional. Metropolitan setting; 95-acre campus. Total enrollment: 1,036. Faculty: 82 (55 full-time, 27 part-time); 36% of full-time faculty have doctoral degrees. Library holdings: 75,000 bound volumes, 44,000 titles on microform, 550 periodical subscriptions, 4,500 records/tapes. Computer terminals/PCs available for student use: 40, located in computer center, classrooms.

UNDERGRADUATE PROFILE Fall 1989: 1,036 undergraduates (290 freshmen) from 35 states and territories and 13 foreign countries; 6% part-time; 67% state residents; 10% transfers; 69% financial aid recipients; 57% women; 43% men; 1% blacks; 0% Native Americans; 0% Hispanics; 0% Asian Americans; 2% international students; 8% of undergraduates 25 years of age or older.

1989 FRESHMAN DATA 426 students applied for fall 1989 admission; 99% were accepted; 69% of those accepted enrolled. 5 freshmen were National Merit Scholarship Finalists. 17% of freshmen were in top 10% of secondary school class, 44% were in top 25%, 69% were in top half.

ENROLLMENT PATTERNS 73% of fall 1988 freshmen returned for fall 1989 term. 1987–89 average: 35% of entering classes graduated; 21% of students completing a college-transfer associate program went on to 4-year colleges; 17% of students completing a bachelor's program went on for further study.

FRESHMAN ADMISSIONS Options: early entrance, deferred entrance. Required: essay, high school transcript, 2 recommendations, SAT or ACT, TOEFL (for foreign students), PSAT. Recommended: 2 years of high school foreign language. Required for some: campus interview. Test scores used for counseling/placement. Application deadline: rolling. Notification date: continuous until 8/15. College's own assessment of entrance difficulty level: moderately difficult.

TRANSFER ADMISSIONS Required: essay, high school transcript, 2 recommendations, college transcript. Recommended: 2 years of high school foreign language, minimum 2.0 grade point average. Required for some: standardized test scores, campus interview. Application deadline: rolling. Notification date: continuous until 8/15. College's own assessment of entrance difficulty level: moderately difficult.

EXPENSES (1990–91) Comprehensive fee of $10,905 includes full-time tuition ($8310) and college room and board ($2595). College room only: $1500. Part-time tuition: $231 per credit.

FINANCIAL AID Fall 1989 full-time freshmen: 95% applied for aid, 100% of those were judged to have need, 100% of those were aided; the average aided freshman received an aid package worth $6539 (74% scholarships/grants, 26% self-help) meeting 80% of need. College-administered aid for all 1989–90 undergraduates: 596 need-based scholarships (average $1434); 644 non-need scholarships (average $778); low-interest long-term loans from external sources (average $2355); SEOG; College Work-Study; 153 part-time jobs. Supporting data: IRS, AFSA/SAR required; institutional form required for some; FFS, FAF acceptable. Priority application deadline: 3/1.

CAMPUS LIFE/STUDENT SERVICES Dress code; mandatory chapel; drama/theater group; student-run newspaper and radio station. Institution provides health clinic, personal/psychological counseling.

ATHLETICS Intercollegiate sports: baseball/softball M, W; basketball M, W; cross-country running M, W; football M; soccer M; track and field M, W; volleyball W; wrestling M. Intramural sports: badminton, baseball/softball, basketball, bowling, football, ice hockey, racquetball, sailing, skiing (cross-country), soccer, table tennis (ping pong), tennis, volleyball.

MAJORS Accounting A, B; agricultural business A; art/fine arts B; biblical studies A, B; broadcasting A, B; business administration/commerce/management A, B; commercial art A, B; communication B; computer information systems A, B; education B; elementary education B; (pre)engineering sequence A; English B; history B; human resources B; journalism B; legal secretarial studies A; liberal arts/general studies A; literature B; marketing/retailing/merchandising B; mathematics B; ministries B; music A, B; music education B; pastoral studies B; physical education B; psychology B; radio and television studies A, B; religious education B; science A; secondary education B; secretarial studies/office management A, B; social science B; speech/rhetoric/public address/debate B; sports administration B; theater arts/drama B; theology B. Majors with highest enrollment: biblical studies, elementary education, business administration/commerce/management.

SPECIAL NOTE FROM THE COLLEGE Northwestern College is the only private, nondenominational Christian liberal arts college in the state of Minnesota. Northwestern students have 2 majors. Every bachelor's degree program requires 45 credits of Bible-related courses in addition to those obtained from 1 of 28 additional majors. The warm, friendly campus; challenging academic programs; and superb facilities offer each student the environment to develop as an individual both academically and spiritually.

CONTACT Mr. Ralph D. Anderson, Dean of Admissions, Northwestern College, St. Paul, MN 55113, 612-631-5111.

NORTHWEST NAZARENE COLLEGE
Nampa, Idaho

Total enrollment: 1,133

UG enrollment: 1,081 (54% W)

Application deadline: 9/20

Tuition & fees: $6510

Room & board: $2490

Entrance: moderately difficult

SAT ≥ 500: N/R

ACT ≥ 21: 48%

Denominational affiliation: Church of the Nazarene

GENERAL INFORMATION Independent comprehensive coed institution. Founded 1913. Awards A (college transfer and terminal), B, M. Primary accreditation: regional. Small-town setting; 65-acre campus. Total enrollment: 1,133. Faculty: 85 (81 full-time, 4 part-time); graduate assistants teach no undergraduate courses.

UNDERGRADUATE PROFILE Fall 1989: 1,081 undergraduates (263 freshmen) from 30 states and territories and 18 foreign countries; 8% part-time; 42% state residents; 9% transfers; 97% financial aid recipients; 54% women; 46% men; 1% blacks; 1% Native Americans; 2% Hispanics; 1% Asian Americans; 2% international students; 13% of undergraduates 25 years of age or older.

1989 FRESHMAN DATA 462 students applied for fall 1989 admission; 94% were accepted; 66% of those accepted enrolled. 1 freshman was a National Merit Scholarship Finalist. 22% of freshmen were in top 10% of secondary school class, 43% were in top 25%, 78% were in top half.

ENROLLMENT PATTERNS 61% of fall 1988 freshmen returned for fall 1989 term. 1987–89 average: 30% of entering classes graduated; 25% of students completing a bachelor's program went on for further study.

FRESHMAN ADMISSIONS Options: early entrance, deferred entrance. Required: high school transcript, recommendations, TOEFL (for foreign students). Recommended: SAT or ACT, WPCT. Test scores used for counseling/placement. Application deadline: 9/20. Notification date: continuous. College's own assessment of entrance difficulty level: moderately difficult.

TRANSFER ADMISSIONS Required: recommendations, college transcript. Required for some: standardized test scores, high school transcript. Application deadline: 9/20. Notification date:

continuous. College's own assessment of entrance difficulty level: moderately difficult.

EXPENSES (1990–91) Comprehensive fee of $9000 includes full-time tuition ($6216), mandatory fees ($294), and college room and board ($2490). College room only: $1500. Part-time tuition: $159 per credit.

FINANCIAL AID Fall 1989 full-time freshmen: 78% applied for aid, 90% of those were judged to have need, 98% of those were aided; the average aided freshman received an aid package worth $5744 (61% scholarships/grants, 39% self-help) meeting 82% of need. College-administered aid for all 1989–90 undergraduates: need-based scholarships; non-need scholarships; low-interest long-term loans from external sources (average $2500); SEOG; College Work-Study; 347 part-time jobs. Supporting data: FAF, IRS, institutional form, AFSA/SAR required; FFS acceptable. Priority application deadline: 3/1.

CAMPUS LIFE/STUDENT SERVICES Mandatory chapel; drama/theater group; student-run newspaper. Institution provides health clinic, personal/psychological counseling.

ATHLETICS Member NAIA. Intercollegiate sports: baseball/softball M(s); basketball M(s), W(s); soccer M(s); track and field M(s), W(s); volleyball W(s). Intramural sports: archery, badminton, baseball/softball, basketball, bowling, cross-country running, football, gymnastics, racquetball, skiing (cross-country), skiing (downhill), soccer, swimming and diving, table tennis (ping pong), track and field, volleyball, weight lifting.

MAJORS Accounting B; applied art A, B; art education B; art/fine arts A, B; biology/biological sciences B; broadcasting A; business administration/commerce/management A, B; business education B; chemical engineering technology A; chemistry A, B; computer information systems B; computer programming A; computer science B; data processing A; (pre)dentistry sequence B; elementary education B; engineering physics B; (pre)engineering sequence A; English B; family services A; graphic arts A; health education B; health science A; history B; home economics A, B; home economics education B; international studies B; (pre)law sequence B; mathematics B; medical technology B; (pre)medicine sequence B; ministries B; music B; music education B; pastoral studies B; philosophy B; physical education B; physics B; psychology B; recreation and leisure services B; religious education A, B; religious studies B; science education B; secondary education B; secretarial studies/office management A, B; social science B; social work A, B; special education B; speech pathology and audiology B; speech/rhetoric/public address/debate B; (pre)veterinary medicine sequence B. Majors with highest enrollment: business administration/commerce/management, elementary education, religious studies.

SPECIAL NOTE FROM THE COLLEGE Northwest Nazarene College is committed to providing its students with a familiarity with the major fields of knowledge, an effective foundation in and a working grasp of one field, a balance in the development of their powers, and encouragement to Christian commitment. Rick Heib, a NASA astronaut and 1977 graduate, said: "The solid academic preparation is important and the personal involvement of the faculty with students is something crucial to scholastic development. . . . I think of NNC experiences, ranging from music, athletics, and student body activities to community involvement, all in the overall framework of putting others ahead of oneself."

CONTACT Mr. Terrence A. Blom, Admissions and Financial Aid Officer, Northwest Nazarene College, Nampa, ID 83686, 208-467-8496 or toll-free 800-NNC-4-YOU (out-of-state).

NYACK COLLEGE
Nyack, New York

Total enrollment: 814

UG enrollment: 540 (56% W)

Application deadline: 8/15

Tuition & fees: $6380

Room & board: $3080

Entrance: minimally difficult

SAT ≥ 500: 24% V, 29% M

ACT ≥ 21: 20%

Denominational affiliation: The Christian and Missionary Alliance

GENERAL INFORMATION Independent comprehensive coed institution. Founded 1882. Awards A (college transfer), B, M. Primary accreditation: regional. Small-town setting, with easy access to New York City; 64-acre campus. Total enrollment: 814. Faculty: 77 (44 full-time, 33 part-time); 70% of full-time faculty have doctoral degrees; graduate assistants teach no undergraduate courses. Library holdings: 77,000 bound volumes, 420 titles on microform, 614 periodical subscriptions. Computer terminals/PCs available for student use: 10, located in computer center.

UNDERGRADUATE PROFILE Fall 1989: 540 undergraduates (194 freshmen) from 31 states and territories and 3 foreign countries; 12% part-time; 52% state residents; 15% transfers; 68% financial aid recipients; 56% women; 44% men; 7% blacks; 1% Native Americans; 5% Hispanics; 9% Asian Americans; 1% international students; 19% of undergraduates 25 years of age or older.

1989 FRESHMAN DATA 559 students applied for fall 1989 admission; 63% were accepted; 55% of those accepted enrolled.

ENROLLMENT PATTERNS 72% of fall 1988 freshmen returned for fall 1989 term. 1987–89 average: 44% of entering classes graduated; 65% of students completing a bachelor's program went on for further study.

FRESHMAN ADMISSIONS Options: early entrance, deferred entrance. Required: essay, high school transcript, 3 recommendations, TOEFL (for foreign students). Recommended: 3 years of high school math and science, some high school foreign language. Required for some: interview, SAT or ACT. Test scores used for admission. Application deadline: 8/15. Notification date: continuous. College's own assessment of entrance difficulty level: minimally difficult.

TRANSFER ADMISSIONS Required: essay, 3 recommendations, college transcript, minimum 2.0 grade point average. Recommended: some high school foreign language. Required for some: standardized test scores, high school transcript, interview. Application deadline: 8/15. Notification date: continuous. College's own assessment of entrance difficulty level: moderately difficult.

EXPENSES (1990–91) Comprehensive fee of $9460 includes full-time tuition ($6100), mandatory fees ($280), and college room and board ($3080). College room only: $1320. Part-time tuition: $257 per credit hour. Part-time mandatory fees per semester (1 to 11 credit hours) range from $30 to $50.

FINANCIAL AID College-administered aid for all 1989–90 undergraduates: need-based scholarships; 110 non-need scholarships (average $530); low-interest long-term loans from external sources (average $1200); SEOG; College Work-Study; 200 part-time jobs. Supporting data: FAF, IRS, institutional form, AFSA/SAR required; state form required for some; FFS acceptable. Priority application deadline: 5/15.

CAMPUS LIFE/STUDENT SERVICES Dress code; mandatory chapel; drama/theater group; student-run newspaper and radio station. Institution provides health clinic, personal/psychological counseling.

ATHLETICS Member NAIA. Intercollegiate sports: baseball/softball M(s), W(s); basketball M(s), W(s); soccer M(s); tennis M, W; volleyball W. Intramural sports: baseball/softball, basketball, football, soccer, volleyball.

MAJORS Adult and continuing education B; biblical studies B; business administration/commerce/management B; early childhood education A; education A; elementary education B; English B; history B; interdisciplinary studies B; liberal arts/general studies A; ministries B; music B; music education B; nursing A; pastoral studies B; philosophy B; piano/organ B; psychology B; religious education B; religious studies B; sacred music B; social science B; voice B. Majors with highest enrollment: psychology, education, biblical studies.

SPECIAL NOTE FROM THE COLLEGE Beautifully situated in a suburban community on the Hudson River, Nyack College partakes of the rich cultural and ethnic diversity of Metropolitan New York. An excellent school of music and a bustling seminary located on the campus enrich the College atmosphere. Founded in 1882 as a college for missionaries and ministers, Nyack has a long tradition of providing education that blends scholarship and service. Though today's curriculum is more diverse, ranging from business to missiology, a sound education and a thorough grounding in the faith still characterize the Nyack graduate.

CONTACT Mr. Timothy D. Crouch, Director of Admissions, Nyack College, Nyack, NY 10960, 914-358-1710 Ext. 200.

OLIVET NAZARENE UNIVERSITY
Kankakee, Illinois

Total enrollment: 1,875

UG enrollment: 1,595 (55% W)

Application deadline: 8/1

Tuition & fees: $5548

Room & board: $3078

Entrance: minimally difficult

SAT ≥ 500: N/App

ACT ≥ 21: 39%

Denominational affiliation: Church of the Nazarene

GENERAL INFORMATION Independent comprehensive coed institution. Founded 1907. Awards A (college transfer and terminal), B, M. Primary accreditation: regional. Small-town setting, with easy access to Chicago; 160-acre campus. Total enrollment: 1,875. Faculty: 115 (95 full-time, 20 part-time); 42% of full-time faculty have doctoral degrees; graduate assistants teach no undergraduate courses. Library holdings: 147,400 bound volumes, 38,800 titles on microform, 850 periodical subscriptions, 4,800 records/tapes. Computer terminals/PCs available for student use: 300, located in computer center, library, various departments.

UNDERGRADUATE PROFILE Fall 1989: 1,595 undergraduates (622 freshmen) from 36 states and territories and 11 foreign countries; 8% part-time; 44% state residents; 20% transfers; 80% financial aid recipients; 55% women; 45% men; 4% blacks; 0% Native Americans; 1% Hispanics; 1% Asian Americans; 4% international students; 10% of undergraduates 25 years of age or older.

1989 FRESHMAN DATA 717 students applied for fall 1989 admission; 99% were accepted; 88% of those accepted enrolled. 20% of freshmen were in top 10% of secondary school class, 40% were in top 25%, 71% were in top half.

ENROLLMENT PATTERNS 67% of fall 1988 freshmen returned for fall 1989 term. 1987–89 average: 40% of entering classes graduated; 10% of students completing a bachelor's program went on for further study.

FRESHMAN ADMISSIONS Options: early entrance, deferred entrance. Required: high school transcript, 3 recommendations, ACT, TOEFL (for foreign students). Recommended: interview. Test scores used for counseling/placement. Application deadline: 8/1. Notification date: continuous. College's own assessment of entrance difficulty level: minimally difficult.

TRANSFER ADMISSIONS Required: 3 recommendations, college transcript, minimum 2.0 grade point average. Recommended: interview. Required for some: high school transcript. Application deadline: 8/1. Notification date: continuous. College's own assessment of entrance difficulty level: minimally difficult.

EXPENSES (1989–90) Comprehensive fee of $8626 includes full-time tuition ($5412), mandatory fees ($136), and college room and board ($3078). Part-time tuition: $226 per semester hour. Part-time mandatory fees per semester (1 to 11 semester hours) range from $10 to $68.

FINANCIAL AID Fall 1989 full-time freshmen: 78% applied for aid, 84% of those were judged to have need, 100% of those were aided; the average aided freshman received an aid package worth $6617 (57% scholarships/grants, 43% self-help) meeting 80% of need. College-administered aid for all 1989–90 undergraduates: need-based scholarships; non-need scholarships (average $591); low-interest long-term loans from external sources (average $1000); SEOG; College Work-Study; 400 part-time jobs. Supporting data: FAF, institutional form, AFSA/SAR required; IRS, state form required for some; FFS acceptable. Priority application deadline: 8/1.

CAMPUS LIFE/STUDENT SERVICES Dress code; mandatory chapel. Institution provides health clinic, personal/psychological counseling.

ATHLETICS Member NAIA. Intercollegiate sports: baseball/softball M(s), W(s); basketball M(s), W(s); cross-country running M(s), W(s); football M(s); golf M; soccer M; tennis M, W; volleyball W; wrestling M(s). Intramural sports: baseball/softball, basketball, cross-country running, football, golf, soccer, tennis, volleyball, wrestling.

MAJORS Accounting B; anthropology B; art education B; art/fine arts B; biblical studies B; biochemistry B; biology/biological sciences B; biophysics B; botany/plant sciences B; broadcasting B; business administration/commerce/management B; business economics B; business education B; chemistry B; child care/child and family studies B; communication B; computer information systems B; computer science B; criminal justice B; (pre)dentistry sequence B; dietetics A, B; early childhood education B; earth science B; economics B; education B; elementary education B; engineering physics B; engineering sciences B; English B; family services B; fashion merchandising B; finance/banking B; food sciences B; food services management B; geochemistry B; geology B; geophysics B; history B; home economics B; home economics education B; interdisciplinary studies B; journalism B; (pre)law sequence B; liberal arts/general studies B; literature B; marketing/retailing/merchandising B; mathematics B; medical technology B; (pre)medicine sequence B; ministries A, B; modern languages B; music B; music education B; natural sciences B; nursing B; pastoral studies B; philosophy B; physical education B; physical sciences A, B; physical therapy B; piano/organ B; psychology B; radio and television studies B; religious education B; religious studies B; Romance languages B; sacred music B; science B; science education B; secondary education B; secretarial studies/office management A, B; social science B; social work A, B; sociology A, B; speech/rhetoric/public address/debate B; stringed instruments B; teacher aide studies A; textiles and clothing B; theology B; (pre)veterinary medicine sequence B; voice B; wind and percussion instruments B; zoology B. Majors with highest enrollment: business administration/commerce/management, education, nursing.

SPECIAL NOTE FROM THE COLLEGE Olivet Nazarene University, 60 miles south of Chicago's Loop, offers students a high-quality liberal arts education based on Christian values. The scenic 160-acre campus includes a planetarium, a 35,000-watt FM radio station, and a new 4,000-seat convocation/athletic center. There are 29 major buildings. Five years after graduation, 85% of Olivet's alumni report employment in an area related to their college major. Internships are available in most majors. Four choirs, a concert band, a symphony orchestra, and other ensembles involve 400 students. Ten spiritual life organizations provide opportunities for service and ministry both on and off campus. Olivet specializes in campus visits as its best recruitment feature. Prospective students are welcome.

CONTACT Mr. John Mongerson, Director of Admissions, Olivet Nazarene University, Kankakee, IL 60901, 815-939-5203.

PALM BEACH ATLANTIC COLLEGE
West Palm Beach, Florida

Total enrollment: 1,375 (all UG)

Women: 53%

Application deadline: 8/1

Tuition & fees: $4960

Room & board: $2650

Entrance: moderately difficult

Denominational affiliation: Southern Baptist

GENERAL INFORMATION Independent 4-year coed college. Founded 1968. Awards B. Primary accreditation: regional. City setting, with easy access to Miami; 21-acre campus. Total enrollment: 1,375. Faculty: 98 (43 full-time, 55 part-time); 74% of full-time faculty have doctoral degrees.

UNDERGRADUATE PROFILE Fall 1989: 1,375 undergraduates (350 freshmen) from 35 states and territories and 23 foreign countries; 20% part-time; 70% state residents; 35% transfers; 75% financial aid recipients; 53% women; 47% men; 10% blacks; 1% Native Americans; 5% Hispanics; 2% Asian Americans.

1989 FRESHMAN DATA 850 students applied for fall 1989 admission; 65% were accepted; 64% of those accepted enrolled.

FRESHMAN ADMISSIONS Options: early entrance, deferred entrance. Required: essay, high school transcript, 2 recommendations, SAT or ACT, TOEFL (for foreign students). Recommended: 3 years of high school math and science, some high school foreign language, interview. Test scores used for counseling/placement. Application deadline: 8/1. Notification date: continuous. College's own assessment of entrance difficulty level: moderately difficult.

TRANSFER ADMISSIONS Required: essay, 2 recommendations, college transcript, minimum 2.0 grade point average.

Recommended: 3 years of high school math and science, some high school foreign language, interview, minimum 3.0 grade point average. Application deadline: 8/1. Notification date: continuous. College's own assessment of entrance difficulty level: moderately difficult.

EXPENSES (1989–90) Comprehensive fee of $7610 includes full-time tuition ($4960) and college room and board ($2650). College room only: $1300. Part-time tuition: $155 per credit hour.

FINANCIAL AID Fall 1989 full-time freshmen: 90% applied for aid, 70% of those were judged to have need, 100% of those were aided; the average aided freshman received an aid package worth $576 meeting 90% of need. College-administered aid for all 1989–90 undergraduates: need-based scholarships; non-need scholarships; low-interest long-term loans from external sources; SEOG; College Work-Study. Supporting data: IRS required; institutional form required for some; FFS, FAF, AFSA/SAR acceptable. Priority application deadline: 5/1.

CAMPUS LIFE/STUDENT SERVICES Dress code; mandatory chapel; drama/theater group; student-run newspaper. Institution provides health clinic, personal/psychological counseling.

ATHLETICS Intercollegiate sports: baseball/softball M, W; basketball M; soccer M; volleyball W. Intramural sports: baseball/softball, basketball, bowling, football, racquetball, table tennis (ping pong), tennis, volleyball.

MAJORS Accounting B; biology/biological sciences B; business administration/commerce/management B; (pre)dentistry sequence B; education B; elementary education B; English B; history B; (pre)law sequence B; mathematics B; (pre)medicine sequence B; music B; psychology B; religious studies B; science B; speech/rhetoric/public address/debate B. Majors with highest enrollment: business administration/commerce/management, elementary education, psychology.

SPECIAL NOTE FROM THE COLLEGE Palm Beach Atlantic College is a 4-year, coeducational, liberal arts Christian college affiliated with the Baptist denomination. PBAC attracts students who desire the benefits of a college committed to academic excellence within a Christian environment. The campus is an attractive mixture of the old and new and is in the early stages of a $100-million expansion program. It has built upon a rich heritage, adapting to the needs of students and faculty. Located in the fastest-growing city in the country and one of the fastest-growing counties in the nation, it is ideally situated on beautiful Lake Worth, 1 mile from Palm Beach and the Atlantic Ocean. PBAC provides educational opportunities through a scholarship program to many deserving students who might not otherwise be able to attend college.

CONTACT Mr. Tim Dickerson, Director of Admissions, Palm Beach Atlantic College, West Palm Beach, FL 33402, 407-835-4309.

POINT LOMA NAZARENE COLLEGE
San Diego, California

Total enrollment: 2,221

UG enrollment: 1,837 (57% W)

Application deadline: rolling

Tuition & fees: $7221

Room & board: $3390

Entrance: moderately difficult

SAT ≥ 500: 16% V, 25% M

ACT ≥ 21: 28%

Denominational affiliation: Church of the Nazarene

GENERAL INFORMATION Independent comprehensive coed institution. Founded 1902. Awards B, M. Primary accreditation: regional. Metropolitan setting; 88-acre campus. Total enrollment: 2,221. Faculty: 204 (92 full-time, 112 part-time); 60% of full-time faculty have doctoral degrees; graduate assistants teach no undergraduate courses. Library holdings: 150,000 bound volumes, 27,000 titles on microform, 488 periodical subscriptions. Computer terminals/PCs available for student use: 30, located in computer center.

UNDERGRADUATE PROFILE Fall 1989: 1,837 undergraduates (501 freshmen) from 36 states and territories and 40 foreign countries; 6% part-time; 82% state residents; 10% transfers; 63% financial aid recipients; 57% women; 43% men; 2% blacks; 1% Native Americans; 5% Hispanics; 4% Asian Americans; 5% international students; 8% of undergraduates 25 years of age or older.

1989 FRESHMAN DATA 832 students applied for fall 1989 admission; 95% were accepted; 63% of those accepted enrolled. 12% of freshmen were in top 10% of secondary school class, 29% were in top 25%, 63% were in top half.

ENROLLMENT PATTERNS 75% of fall 1988 freshmen returned for fall 1989 term. 1987–89 average: 26% of entering classes graduated; 25% of students completing a degree program went on for further study.

FRESHMAN ADMISSIONS Options: early entrance, deferred entrance. Required: high school transcript, 2 years of high school foreign language, 2 recommendations, SAT or ACT, TOEFL (for foreign students). Recommended: 3 years of high school math and science. Required for some: campus interview. Test scores used for counseling/placement. Application deadline: rolling. Notification date: continuous. College's own assessment of entrance difficulty level: moderately difficult.

TRANSFER ADMISSIONS Required: standardized test scores, 2 years of high school foreign language, 2 recommendations, college transcript, minimum 2.0 grade point average. Required for some: high school transcript, campus interview. Application deadline: rolling. Notification date: continuous. College's own assessment of entrance difficulty level: moderately difficult.

EXPENSES (1990–91 estimated) Comprehensive fee of $10,611 includes full-time tuition ($7104), mandatory fees ($117), and college room and board ($3390). College room only: $1530. Part-time tuition: $148 per unit.

FINANCIAL AID Fall 1989 full-time freshmen: 80% applied for aid, 75% of those were judged to have need, 100% of those were aided; the average aided freshman received an aid package meeting 70% of need. College-administered aid for all 1989–90 undergraduates: need-based scholarships; non-need scholarships; low-interest long-term loans from external sources (average $1500); SEOG; College Work-Study; 100 part-time jobs. Supporting data: FAF, institutional form, AFSA/SAR required. Priority application deadline: 4/10.

CAMPUS LIFE/STUDENT SERVICES Mandatory chapel; drama/theater group; student-run newspaper. Institution provides health clinic, personal/psychological counseling. Social organizations: local fraternities, local sororities.

ATHLETICS Member NAIA. Intercollegiate sports: baseball/softball M(s); basketball M(s), W(s); cross-country running M(s), W(s); golf M(s); soccer M(s); tennis M(s), W(s); track and field M(s), W(s); volleyball W(s). Intramural sports: badminton, basketball, bowling, cross-country running, football, golf, racquetball, sailing, soccer, swimming and diving, table tennis (ping pong), tennis, track and field, ultimate frisbee, volleyball, water polo, weight lifting.

MAJORS Accounting B; art education B; art/fine arts B; biblical studies B; biochemistry B; biology/biological sciences B; business administration/commerce/management B; business education B; chemistry B; child psychology/child development B; communication B; computer information systems B; computer science B; (pre)dentistry sequence B; early childhood education B; economics B; engineering physics B; English B; graphic arts B; history B; home economics B; home economics education B; journalism B; (pre)law sequence B; liberal arts/general studies B; literature B; mathematics B; (pre)medicine sequence B; modern languages B; music B; music business B; music education B; nursing B; pastoral studies B; philosophy B; physical education B; physical fitness/human movement B; physics B; piano/organ B; political science/government B; psychology B; religious education B; religious studies B; sacred music B; secretarial studies/office management B; social science B; sociology B; Spanish B; speech therapy B; stringed instruments B; studio art B; theater arts/drama B; theology B; (pre)veterinary medicine sequence B; voice B; wind and percussion instruments B. Majors with highest enrollment: business administration/commerce/management, liberal arts/general studies, nursing.

SPECIAL NOTE FROM THE COLLEGE Point Loma Nazarene College is an 88-year-old Christian liberal arts college located in a semitropical, residential setting resting on the crest of historic Point Loma. Collegians enjoy a clear view westward overlooking the Pacific Ocean and eastward across downtown San Diego, where many cultural and employment advantages are available to them. Point Loma offers a wide variety of academic programs, continually modified to meet changing needs. The 17 academic programs offer 42 majors plus many subspecialties, credentials, and certificates. The 2,200 students come from 36 states and 40 countries. At Point Loma Nazarene, students strive for 3 lofty goals: spiritual development, academic excellence, and social and personal enhancement.

CONTACT Mr. Bill Young, Director of Admissions, Point Loma Nazarene College, San Diego, CA 92106, 619-221-2225.

REDEEMER COLLEGE
Ancaster, Ontario, Canada

Total enrollment: 373 (all UG)

Women: 61%

Application deadline: 8/15

Tuition & fees: $6043

Room & board: $2958

Entrance: moderately difficult

SAT ≥ 500: N/R

ACT ≥ 21: 90%

Denominational affiliation: interdenominational

GENERAL INFORMATION Independent 4-year coed college. Founded 1980. Awards B. Primary accreditation: provincial charter. Small-town setting, with easy access to Toronto; 78-acre campus. Total enrollment: 373. Faculty: 57 (34 full-time, 23 part-time); 71% of full-time faculty have doctoral degrees; graduate assistants teach a few undergraduate courses. Library holdings: 82,219 bound volumes, 229 periodical subscriptions, 537 records/tapes. Computer terminals/PCs available for student use: 20, located in computer center, dormitories.

UNDERGRADUATE PROFILE Fall 1989: 373 undergraduates (144 freshmen) from 8 provinces and territories and 5 foreign countries; 8% part-time; 96% province residents; 2% transfers; 90% financial aid recipients; 61% women; 39% men; 2% blacks; 1% Native Americans; 1% Hispanics; 0% Asian Americans; 2% international students; 8% of undergraduates 25 years of age or older.

1989 FRESHMAN DATA 202 students applied for fall 1989 admission; 95% were accepted; 75% of those accepted enrolled.

ENROLLMENT PATTERNS 78% of fall 1988 freshmen returned for fall 1989 term. 1987–89 average: 42% of entering classes graduated; 25% of students completing a degree program went on for further study.

FRESHMAN ADMISSIONS Preference given to Christians. Option: deferred entrance. Required: high school transcript, 4 years of high school math and science, 4 years of high school foreign language, 2 recommendations, pastoral reference, TOEFL (for foreign students). Required for some: essay, interview, SAT or ACT, Achievement Tests, English Composition Test. Test scores used for counseling/placement. Application deadline: 8/15. College's own assessment of entrance difficulty level: moderately difficult; very difficult for education programs.

TRANSFER ADMISSIONS Required: high school transcript, 4 years of high school math and science, 4 years of high school foreign language, 2 recommendations, college transcript, pastoral reference. Recommended: minimum 2.0 grade point average. Required for some: essay, standardized test scores, interview, minimum 3.0 grade point average. College's own assessment of entrance difficulty level: moderately difficult.

EXPENSES (1990–91 estimated) Comprehensive fee of $9001 includes full-time tuition ($5830), mandatory fees ($213), and college room and board ($2958). Part-time tuition: $728 per course.

FINANCIAL AID College-administered aid for all 1989–90 undergraduates: 266 need-based scholarships (average $2986); 147 non-need scholarships (average $1673); short-term loans (average $4032); 200 part-time jobs. Supporting data: government form required; institutional form required for some; FFS acceptable. Priority application deadline: 5/15.

CAMPUS LIFE/STUDENT SERVICES Drama/theater group; student-run newspaper. Institution provides personal/psychological counseling.

ATHLETICS Intercollegiate sports: badminton M, W; cross-country running M, W; ice hockey M, W; soccer M, W; volleyball M, W. Intramural sports: archery, badminton, baseball/softball, basketball, bowling, ice hockey, racquetball, skiing (cross-country), skiing (downhill), soccer, squash, swimming and diving, volleyball.

MAJORS Accounting B; art/fine arts B; behavioral sciences B; biblical languages B; biblical studies B; biology/biological sciences B; botany/plant sciences B; business administration/commerce/management B; classics B; clinical psychology B; (pre)dentistry sequence B; education B; elementary education B; English B; French B; history B; humanities B; (pre)law sequence B; liberal arts/general studies B; literature B; mathematics B; (pre)medicine sequence B; modern languages B; music B; natural sciences B; philosophy B; physical education B; political science/government B; psychology B; religious studies B; Romance languages B; science B; secondary education B; sociology B; theater arts/drama B; theology B; (pre)veterinary medicine sequence B. Majors with highest enrollment: education, psychology, English.

SPECIAL NOTE FROM THE COLLEGE Students at Redeemer College enjoy a Canadian Christian university that offers 20 majors, state-of-the-art facilities, town house–style residences, a vibrant Christian community, a location just minutes from Toronto and Niagara Falls, and a Canadian Christian perspective on issues of national and international significance. Redeemer College prepares its students for life, for a career, and for graduate work. Students grow spiritually and explore the relation of faith, learning, and living. The skills they develop are always in demand in the marketplace—a mind trained to think, imagine, and express itself.

CONTACT Mr. Mark Van Beveren, Admissions Director, Redeemer College, Ancaster, ON L9G 3N6, Canada, 416-648-2131 or toll-free 800-263-6467 (in-province).

ROBERTS WESLEYAN COLLEGE
Rochester, New York

Total enrollment: 824 (all UG)

Women: 64%

Application deadline: rolling

Tuition & fees: $8082

Room & board: $2826

Entrance: moderately difficult

SAT ≥ 500: 64% V, 68% M

ACT ≥ 21: 64%

Denominational affiliation: Free Methodist Church of North America

GENERAL INFORMATION Independent 4-year coed college. Founded 1866. Awards A (terminal), B. Primary accreditation: regional. Metropolitan setting; 75-acre campus. Total enrollment: 824. Faculty: 66 (47 full-time, 19 part-time); 47% of full-time faculty have doctoral degrees. Library holdings: 94,372 bound volumes, 510 titles on microform, 631 periodical subscriptions, 2,424 records/tapes. Computer terminals/PCs available for student use: 47, located in computer center, library.

UNDERGRADUATE PROFILE Fall 1989: 824 undergraduates (163 freshmen) from 21 states and territories and 11 foreign countries; 4% part-time; 85% state residents; 20% transfers; 85% financial aid recipients; 64% women; 36% men; 6% blacks; 1% Native Americans; 3% Hispanics; 1% Asian Americans; 8% international students; 22% of undergraduates 25 years of age or older.

1989 FRESHMAN DATA 307 students applied for fall 1989 admission; 89% were accepted; 60% of those accepted enrolled. 22% of freshmen were in top 10% of secondary school class, 49% were in top 25%, 73% were in top half.

ENROLLMENT PATTERNS 70% of fall 1988 freshmen returned for fall 1989 term. 1987–89 average: 51% of entering classes graduated; 10% of students completing a bachelor's program went on for further study.

FRESHMAN ADMISSIONS Options: early entrance, deferred entrance. Required: essay, high school transcript, 1 recommendation, SAT or ACT, TOEFL (for foreign students). Recommended: 3 years of high school math and science, 3 years of high school foreign language, campus interview. Test scores used for counseling/placement. Application deadline: rolling. College's own assessment of entrance difficulty level: moderately difficult.

TRANSFER ADMISSIONS Required: essay, high school transcript, 1 recommendation, college transcript, minimum 2.0 grade point average. Recommended: 3 years of high school math and science, 3 years of high school foreign language, campus interview. Application deadline: rolling. College's own assessment of entrance difficulty level: moderately difficult.

EXPENSES (1990–91) Comprehensive fee of $10,908 includes full-time tuition ($7890), mandatory fees ($192), and college room and board ($2826). College room only: $1166. Part-time tuition: $135 per semester hour.

FINANCIAL AID Fall 1989 full-time freshmen: 97% applied for aid, 94% of those were judged to have need, 100% of those were aided; the average aided freshman received an aid package worth $9587 (70% scholarships/grants, 30% self-help) meeting 93% of need. College-administered aid for all 1989–90 undergraduates: 390 need-based scholarships; non-need scholarships; low-interest long-term loans from college funds (average $1000), from external sources (average $2930); SEOG; College Work-Study; 275 part-time jobs. Supporting data: FAF, institutional form required; IRS, state form required for some; FFS, AFSA/SAR acceptable. Priority application deadline: 7/15.

CAMPUS LIFE/STUDENT SERVICES Dress code; mandatory chapel; drama/theater group; student-run newspaper. Institution provides health clinic, personal/psychological counseling.

ATHLETICS Member NCAA, NAIA. Intercollegiate sports: baseball/softball M, W(s); basketball M(s), W(s); cross-country running M(s), W(s); soccer M(s), W(s); track and field M(s), W(s). Intramural sports: baseball/softball, basketball, racquetball, soccer, table tennis (ping pong), tennis, volleyball.

MAJORS Accounting B; art education B; art/fine arts B; biology/biological sciences B; business administration/commerce/management B; chemistry B; communication B; computer science B; criminal justice B; (pre)dentistry sequence B; education B; elementary education B; English B; gerontology B; graphic arts B; history B; humanities B; human resources B; mathematics B; medical technology B; ministries B; music A, B; music education B; natural sciences A; nursing B; physical sciences A; physics B; piano/organ A, B; psychology B; religious studies B; science B; secondary education B; social science B; social work B; sociology B; studio art B; voice A, B. Majors with highest enrollment: nursing, education, business administration/commerce/management.

SPECIAL NOTE FROM THE COLLEGE Roberts Wesleyan College offers the ideal setting for a contemporary liberal arts education. The modern 75-acre suburban campus encourages contemplative study and a relaxed, but vital, life-style. The thriving urban center of Rochester, just a few minutes away, offers numerous cultural and recreational opportunities for students. Rochester's vigorous economy also provides valuable internship, job, and career placement opportunities. The College's broadly based curriculum of more than 35 majors includes such traditional programs as nursing, social work, and music and such contemporary courses of study as gerontology, communication, computer science, and criminal justice. Roberts is honoring its 120-year commitment to address society's ever-changing needs through high-quality, accredited educational programs in the Christian tradition.

CONTACT Mr. Barry M. Smith, Director of Admissions, Roberts Wesleyan College, Rochester, NY 14624, 716-594-9471 Ext. 410.

SEATTLE PACIFIC UNIVERSITY
Seattle, Washington

Total enrollment: 3,435

UG enrollment: 2,444 (61% W)

Application deadline: 9/1

Tuition & fees: $9000

Room & board: $3432

Entrance: moderately difficult

SAT ≥ 500: 42% V, 53% M

ACT ≥ 21: N/R

Denominational affiliation: Free Methodist

GENERAL INFORMATION Independent comprehensive coed institution. Founded 1891. Awards B, M. Primary accreditation: regional. Metropolitan setting; 35-acre campus. Total enrollment: 3,435. Faculty: 240 (130 full-time, 110 part-time); 70% of full-time faculty have doctoral degrees; graduate assistants teach no undergraduate courses. Library holdings: 140,000 bound volumes, 300,000 titles on microform, 1,350 periodical subscriptions, 4,000 records/tapes. Computer terminals/PCs available for student use: 92, located in 2 labs and the media center.

UNDERGRADUATE PROFILE Fall 1989: 2,444 undergraduates (460 freshmen) from 34 states and territories and 42 foreign countries; 17% part-time; 74% state residents; 37% transfers; 65% financial aid recipients; 61% women; 39% men; 1% blacks; 1% Native Americans; 1% Hispanics; 4% Asian Americans; 5% international students; 21% of undergraduates 25 years of age or older.

1989 FRESHMAN DATA 978 students applied for fall 1989 admission; 88% were accepted; 54% of those accepted enrolled.

ENROLLMENT PATTERNS 67% of fall 1988 freshmen returned for fall 1989 term. 1987–89 average: 34% of entering classes graduated.

FRESHMAN ADMISSIONS Options: early entrance, early decision, deferred entrance. Required: essay, high school transcript, 1 recommendation, minimum 2.5 grade point average, SAT or ACT, TOEFL (for foreign students), WPCT. Recommended: 3 years of high school math and science, some high school foreign language. Test scores used for counseling/placement. Application deadlines: 9/1, 12/1 for early decision. Notification date: continuous. College's own assessment of entrance difficulty level: moderately difficult.

TRANSFER ADMISSIONS Required: essay, high school transcript, 1 recommendation, college transcript, minimum 2.0 grade point average. Recommended: 3 years of high school math

and science, some high school foreign language. Required for some: standardized test scores. Application deadline: 9/1. Notification date: continuous. College's own assessment of entrance difficulty level: moderately difficult.

EXPENSES (1989–90) Comprehensive fee of $12,432 includes full-time tuition ($9000) and college room and board ($3432). Part-time tuition per credit: $140 for the first 8 credits, $250 for the next 3 credits.

FINANCIAL AID Fall 1989 full-time freshmen: 75% applied for aid, 69% of those were judged to have need, 100% of those were aided; the average aided freshman received an aid package meeting 100% of need. College-administered aid for all 1989–90 undergraduates: 1,166 need-based scholarships (average $2619); 606 non-need scholarships (average $2415); short-term loans (average $307); low-interest long-term loans from external sources (average $3036); SEOG; College Work-Study; 215 part-time jobs. Supporting data: FAF required; IRS, AFSA/SAR required for some; FFS acceptable. Priority application deadline: 3/1.

CAMPUS LIFE/STUDENT SERVICES Mandatory chapel; drama/theater group; student-run newspaper. Institution provides health clinic, personal/psychological counseling.

ATHLETICS Member NCAA (Division II). Intercollegiate sports: basketball M(II,s), W(II,s); crew M, W; cross-country running M(II,s), W(II,s); gymnastics W(II,s); soccer M(II,s); tennis M(II), W(II); track and field M(II), W(II,s); volleyball W(II,s). Intramural sports: badminton, baseball/softball, basketball, bowling, crew, cross-country running, football, golf, lacrosse, racquetball, skiing (cross-country), skiing (downhill), soccer, swimming and diving, table tennis (ping pong), tennis, track and field, ultimate frisbee, volleyball, weight lifting, wrestling.

MAJORS Accounting B; anthropology B; art education B; art/fine arts B; biblical languages B; biblical studies B; biology/biological sciences B; business administration/commerce/management B; chemistry B; communication B; computer science B; ecology/environmental studies B; economics B; education B; educational media B; electrical engineering B; engineering sciences B; English B; European studies B; finance/banking B; history B; home economics B; home economics education B; interdisciplinary studies B; liberal arts/general studies B; linguistics B; marine biology B; marketing/retailing/merchandising B; mathematics B; ministries B; music B; music education B; nursing B; nutrition B; philosophy B; physical education B; physical fitness/human movement B; physics B; political science/government B; psychology B; reading education B; recreation and leisure services B; religious education B; religious studies B; Russian B; sacred music B; secondary education B; social science B; sociology B; special education B; textiles and clothing B; theater arts/drama B; urban studies B. Majors with highest enrollment: computer science, business administration/commerce/management, psychology.

SPECIAL NOTE FROM THE COLLEGE Seattle Pacific University will soon mark a century of academic inquiry and Christian service. Located in Seattle, which has been rated by _Money_ magazine as "the most livable city in America," Seattle Pacific's 35-acre main campus lies on residential Queen Anne Hill, just minutes from the heart of the city. SPU students succeed in life for many reasons. The University has an unwavering commitment to educational excellence and offers 56 undergraduate majors and 12 areas of graduate specialization. More than 3,400 students enjoy personalized attention from professors who are teachers and role models as well as serious scholars and researchers (75% of the teaching faculty hold doctoral degrees). The student-faculty ratio if 17:1. Through internships, a new chapel program that emphasizes worship, Urban Plunge, Urban Involvement, and travel programs, SPU students are supported, encouraged, and educated for effective Christian living.

CONTACT Ms. Jan Walton, Associate Director of Admissions, Seattle Pacific University, Seattle, WA 98119, 206-281-2021 or toll-free 800-366-3344.

SIMPSON COLLEGE
Redding, California

Total enrollment: 206

UG enrollment: 198 (47% W)

Application deadline: rolling

Tuition & fees: $5672

Room & board: $3300

Entrance: minimally difficult

SAT ≥ 500: 28% V, 28% M

ACT ≥ 21: 37%

Denominational affiliation: The Christian and Missionary Alliance

GENERAL INFORMATION Independent comprehensive coed institution. Founded 1921. Awards A (terminal), B, M. Primary accreditation: regional and AABC. City setting; 60-acre campus. Total enrollment: 206. Faculty: 27 (21 full-time, 6 part-time); 48% of full-time faculty have doctoral degrees; graduate assistants teach no undergraduate courses. Library holdings: 53,000 bound volumes, 29 titles on microform, 332 periodical subscriptions, 1,848 records/tapes. Computer terminals/PCs available for student use: 8, located in computer center.

UNDERGRADUATE PROFILE Fall 1989: 198 undergraduates (60 freshmen) from 18 states and territories and 3 foreign countries; 10% part-time; 76% state residents; 55% transfers; 77% financial aid recipients; 47% women; 53% men; 2% blacks; 1% Native Americans; 2% Hispanics; 14% Asian Americans; 2% international students; 33% of undergraduates 25 years of age or older.

1989 FRESHMAN DATA 98 students applied for fall 1989 admission; 83% were accepted; 74% of those accepted enrolled.

ENROLLMENT PATTERNS 69% of fall 1988 freshmen returned for fall 1989 term.

FRESHMAN ADMISSIONS Options: early entrance, deferred entrance. Required: essay, high school transcript, 2 recommendations, medical history from physician, SAT or ACT, TOEFL (for foreign students). Recommended: 3 years of high school math and science, some high school foreign language, interview. Test scores used for counseling/placement. Application deadline: rolling. Notification date: continuous. College's own assessment of entrance difficulty level: minimally difficult.

TRANSFER ADMISSIONS Required: essay, standardized test scores, high school transcript, 2 recommendations, college transcript, minimum 2.0 grade point average, medical history from physician. Recommended: 3 years of high school math and science, some high school foreign language, interview, minimum 3.0 grade point average. Application deadline: rolling. Notification date: continuous. College's own assessment of entrance difficulty level: minimally difficult.

EXPENSES (1989–90) Comprehensive fee of $8972 includes full-time tuition ($5500), mandatory fees ($172), and college room and board ($3300). Part-time tuition and fees per semester (1 to 11 credits) range from $329 to $2690.

FINANCIAL AID College-administered aid for all 1989–90 undergraduates: 28 need-based scholarships (average $836); 117 non-need scholarships (average $1519); low-interest long-term loans from college funds (average $1555), from external sources (average $2932); SEOG; College Work-Study; 35 part-time jobs. Supporting data: FAF, institutional form, AFSA/SAR required; IRS, state form required for some; FFS acceptable. Priority application deadline: 3/31.

CAMPUS LIFE/STUDENT SERVICES Dress code; mandatory chapel; drama/theater group; student-run newspaper. Institution provides personal/psychological counseling. Social organizations: men's and women's associations; 100% of eligible undergraduate men and 100% of eligible undergraduate women are members.

ATHLETICS Intercollegiate sports: basketball M(s), W(s); soccer M(s); volleyball M(s), W(s). Intramural sports: baseball/softball, basketball, cross-country running, football, volleyball.

MAJORS Archaeology B; biblical studies A, B; business administration/commerce/management B; communication B; education B; elementary education B; English B; history B; international studies B; liberal arts/general studies B; ministries B; music B; pastoral studies B; psychology A, B; religious education B; sacred music B; secondary education B. Majors with highest enrollment: biblical studies, elementary education, ministries.

SPECIAL NOTE FROM THE COLLEGE Simpson College is a Christian college offering baccalaureate and graduate programs. Its mission is to provide leadership education for the Church of Jesus Christ, preparing students for both lay and ministerial vocations. The undergraduate division is designed to build an educational foundation upon which professional majors can be based. This foundation integrates a biblical interpretation of knowledge with the broad liberal studies curriculum to develop a Christian world view. The major program offerings fall into 3 general tracts of professional ministry studies: lay professions, ministry, and liberal arts. The graduate program offers professional programs in Bible and theology and education.

CONTACT Mr. Greg Collord, Director of Admissions, Simpson College, Redding, CA 96003, 916-243-1991.

SIOUX FALLS COLLEGE
Sioux Falls, South Dakota

Total enrollment: 962

UG enrollment: 909 (60% W)

Application deadline: rolling

Tuition & fees: $6210

Room & board: $2575

Entrance: moderately difficult

SAT ≥ 500: 14% V, 8% M

ACT ≥ 21: 56%

Denominational affiliation: American Baptist

GENERAL INFORMATION Independent comprehensive coed institution. Founded 1883. Awards A (college transfer), B, M. Primary accreditation: regional. City setting; 14-acre campus. Total enrollment: 962. Faculty: 66 (40 full-time, 26 part-time); 60% of full-time faculty have doctoral degrees; graduate assistants teach no undergraduate courses. Library holdings: 80,000 bound volumes, 450 periodical subscriptions, 4,600 records/tapes. Computer terminals/PCs available for student use: 25, located in computer center, library.

UNDERGRADUATE PROFILE Fall 1989: 909 undergraduates (257 freshmen) from 4 states and territories and 4 foreign countries; 34% part-time; 54% state residents; 1% transfers; 93% financial aid recipients; 60% women; 40% men; 1% blacks; 1% Native Americans; 1% Hispanics; 1% Asian Americans; 1% international students; 40% of undergraduates 25 years of age or older.

1989 FRESHMAN DATA 420 students applied for fall 1989 admission; 93% were accepted; 66% of those accepted enrolled. 1 freshman was a National Merit Scholarship Finalist and received a National Merit Scholarship. 10% of freshmen were in top 10% of secondary school class, 30% were in top 25%, 65% were in top half.

ENROLLMENT PATTERNS 58% of fall 1988 freshmen returned for fall 1989 term. 1987–89 average: 63% of entering classes graduated; 75% of students completing a college-transfer associate program went on to 4-year colleges; 15% of students completing a bachelor's program went on for further study.

FRESHMAN ADMISSIONS Options: early entrance, deferred entrance. Required: high school transcript, SAT or ACT, TOEFL (for foreign students). Recommended: essay, 3 years of high school math and science, 1 year of high school foreign language. Required for some: 2 recommendations, interview. Test scores used for admission and counseling/placement. Application deadline: rolling. College's own assessment of entrance difficulty level: moderately difficult.

TRANSFER ADMISSIONS Required: high school transcript, college transcript, minimum 2.0 grade point average. Recommended: essay, standardized test scores, 3 years of high school math and science, 1 year of high school foreign language. Required for some: 2 recommendations, interview. Application deadline: rolling.

EXPENSES (1990–91) Comprehensive fee of $8785 includes full-time tuition ($6210) and college room and board ($2575). College room only: $1125. Part-time tuition per semester hour: $168 for the first 7 semester hours, $290 for the next 4 semester hours.

FINANCIAL AID Fall 1989 full-time freshmen: 94% applied for aid, 88% of those were judged to have need, 100% of those were aided; the average aided freshman received an aid package worth $6800 (47% scholarships/grants, 53% self-help) meeting 92% of need. College-administered aid for all 1989–90 undergraduates: need-based scholarships; 300 non-need scholarships; low-interest long-term loans from external sources (average $3825); SEOG; College Work-Study; 20 part-time jobs. Supporting data: FFS, institutional form, AFSA/SAR required; IRS, state form required for some; FAF acceptable. Priority application deadline: 4/1.

CAMPUS LIFE/STUDENT SERVICES Drama/theater group; student-run newspaper and radio station. Institution provides health clinic, personal/psychological counseling, women's center.

ATHLETICS Member NAIA. Intercollegiate sports: basketball M(s), W(s); football M(s); tennis M(s), W(s); track and field M(s), W(s); volleyball W(s). Intramural sports: badminton, baseball/softball, basketball, football, racquetball, soccer, table tennis (ping pong), tennis, volleyball.

MAJORS Accounting B; applied art B; applied mathematics B; art education B; biology/biological sciences B; business administration/commerce/management A, B; chemistry B; child psychology/child development A; commercial art B; communication B; computer information systems B; computer science B; (pre)dentistry sequence B; early childhood education A; education B; elementary education B; (pre)engineering sequence A; English B; health education B; history B; humanities A; interdisciplinary studies A, B; management information systems B; mathematics B; medical technology B; (pre)medicine sequence B; music B; music business B; music education B; physical education B; physical fitness/human movement B; psychology B; public relations B; radio and television studies B; recreational facilities management B; religious studies A, B; secondary education B; social science A, B; social work B; sociology B; speech/rhetoric/public address/debate B; theater arts/drama A, B; (pre)veterinary medicine sequence B. Majors with highest enrollment: business administration/commerce/management, elementary education, physical education.

SPECIAL NOTE FROM THE COLLEGE Sioux Falls College is a 4-year Christian liberal arts college affiliated with the American Baptist Churches. In an environment that both challenges and supports, students are encouraged to develop knowledge and wisdom for discerning truth and meeting human needs, to build a value system in keeping with Christ's teachings, to achieve emotional maturity, to pursue physical fitness, and to gain interpersonal skills. Students develop close, caring relationships with professors in and out of the classroom. Beyond the classroom, there are numerous cocurricular activities important to a college education. Sioux Falls is large enough to provide many opportunities for involvement and small enough to encourage participation.

CONTACT Mr. John P. French, Director of Admissions, Sioux Falls College, Sioux Falls, SD 57105, 605-331-6600.

SOUTHERN CALIFORNIA COLLEGE
Costa Mesa, California

Total enrollment: 898

UG enrollment: 830 (51% W)

Application deadline: 7/31

Tuition & fees: $6360

Room & board: $3100

Entrance: moderately difficult

SAT ≥ 500: 35% V, 41% M

ACT ≥ 21: N/R

Denominational affiliation: Assemblies of God

GENERAL INFORMATION Independent comprehensive coed institution. Founded 1920. Awards B, M. Primary accreditation: regional. City setting, with easy access to Los Angeles; 40-acre campus. Total enrollment: 898. Faculty: 81 (41 full-time, 40 part-time); 70% of full-time faculty have doctoral degrees; graduate assistants teach no undergraduate courses. Library holdings: 91,800 bound volumes, 4,852 titles on microform, 680 periodical subscriptions, 3,238 records/tapes. Computer terminals/PCs available for student use: 37, located in computer center, library.

UNDERGRADUATE PROFILE Fall 1989: 830 undergraduates (133 freshmen) from 28 states and territories and 28 foreign countries; 15% part-time; 76% state residents; 14% transfers; 80% financial aid recipients; 51% women; 49% men; 2% blacks; 1% Native Americans; 8% Hispanics; 3% Asian Americans; 2% international students; 30% of undergraduates 25 years of age or older.

1989 FRESHMAN DATA 266 students applied for fall 1989 admission; 83% were accepted; 60% of those accepted enrolled. 13% of freshmen were in top 10% of secondary school class, 35% were in top 25%, 59% were in top half.

ENROLLMENT PATTERNS 70% of fall 1988 freshmen returned for fall 1989 term. 1987–89 average: 35% of entering classes graduated.

FRESHMAN ADMISSIONS Preference given to Christians. Option: deferred entrance. Required: essay, high school transcript, 2 recommendations, SAT or ACT, TOEFL (for foreign students). Recommended: 3 years of high school math and science. Required for some: campus interview. Test scores used for counseling/placement. Application deadline: 7/31.

Notification date: continuous until 8/31. College's own assessment of entrance difficulty level: moderately difficult.

TRANSFER ADMISSIONS Required: essay, 2 recommendations, college transcript, minimum 2.0 grade point average. Required for some: standardized test scores, high school transcript, campus interview. Application deadline: 7/31. Notification date: continuous until 8/31. College's own assessment of entrance difficulty level: moderately difficult.

EXPENSES (1989–90) Comprehensive fee of $9460 includes full-time tuition ($6170), mandatory fees ($190), and college room and board ($3100). College room only: $1500. Part-time tuition: $250 per credit.

FINANCIAL AID College-administered aid for all 1989–90 undergraduates: need-based scholarships; non-need scholarships; short-term loans; low-interest long-term loans from college funds, from external sources; SEOG; College Work-Study; part-time jobs. Supporting data: FAF, state form, institutional form, AFSA/SAR required; IRS required for some. Priority application deadline: 3/2.

CAMPUS LIFE/STUDENT SERVICES Mandatory chapel; drama/theater group; student-run newspaper. Institution provides personal/psychological counseling.

ATHLETICS Member NAIA. Intercollegiate sports: baseball/softball M(s), W(s); basketball M(s), W(s); cross-country running M(s), W(s); soccer M(s); tennis M; volleyball W(s). Intramural sports: badminton, baseball/softball, basketball, football, golf, racquetball, table tennis (ping pong), tennis, volleyball, weight lifting.

MAJORS Accounting B; anthropology B; biblical studies B; biology/biological sciences B; broadcasting B; business administration/commerce/management B; chemistry B; communication B; education B; elementary education B; English B; finance/banking B; history B; humanities B; journalism B; (pre)law sequence B; marketing/retailing/merchandising B; mathematics B; (pre)medicine sequence B; ministries B; music B; music education B; pastoral studies B; physical education B; political science/government B; psychology B; radio and television studies B; religious education B; religious studies B; science B; secondary education B; social science B; sociology B; speech/rhetoric/public address/debate B; theater arts/drama B; (pre)veterinary medicine sequence B. Majors with highest enrollment: social science, business administration/commerce/management, humanities.

SPECIAL NOTE FROM THE COLLEGE Southern California College is a private, Christian, liberal arts college that believes its evangelical, Pentecostal community offers a unique opportunity for academic achievement, spiritual foundation, and personal development. SCC is considered a leader in helping students develop values and integrity that will enhance their life. It is accredited by the Western Association of Schools and Colleges and is also approved by the California Commission on Teacher Credentialing for 9 different credentials. The campus is ideally located in the Costa Mesa/Newport Beach area of Orange County, where corporate, business, and recreational activities provide students with countless jobs, internships, and leisure opportunities that maximize the superb climate and SCC's proximity to the beach.

CONTACT Mr. Richard Hardy, Assistant Dean for Enrollment Management, Southern California College, Costa Mesa, CA 92626, 714-556-3610 Ext. 217 or toll-free 800-722-6279.

SOUTHERN NAZARENE UNIVERSITY
Bethany, Oklahoma

Total enrollment: 1,402

UG enrollment: 1,254 (55% W)

Application deadline: rolling

Tuition & fees: $3696

Room & board: $2822

Entrance: noncompetitive

SAT ≥ 500: N/R

ACT ≥ 21: 42%

Denominational affiliation: Church of the Nazarene

GENERAL INFORMATION Independent comprehensive coed institution. Founded 1899. Awards A (college transfer and terminal), B, M. Primary accreditation: regional. Small-town setting, with easy access to Oklahoma City; 40-acre campus. Total enrollment: 1,402. Faculty: 103 (66 full-time, 37 part-time); 44% of full-time faculty have doctoral degrees; graduate assistants teach a few undergraduate courses. Library holdings: 108,200 bound volumes, 163,746 titles on microform, 610 periodical subscriptions, 2,927 records/tapes. Computer terminals/PCs available for student use: 55, located in computer center, library, academic classrooms.

UNDERGRADUATE PROFILE Fall 1989: 1,254 undergraduates (427 freshmen) from 31 states and territories and 22 foreign countries; 16% part-time; 65% state residents; 8% transfers; 72% financial aid recipients; 55% women; 45% men; 5% blacks; 1% Native Americans; 1% Hispanics; 1% Asian Americans; 5% international students; 21% of undergraduates 25 years of age or older.

1989 FRESHMAN DATA 460 students applied for fall 1989 admission; 98% were accepted; 95% of those accepted enrolled. 8% of freshmen were in top 10% of secondary school class, 25% were in top 25%, 40% were in top half.

ENROLLMENT PATTERNS 70% of fall 1988 freshmen returned for fall 1989 term. 1987–89 average: 35% of students completing a bachelor's program went on for further study.

FRESHMAN ADMISSIONS Open admissions. Option: early entrance. Required: high school transcript, 2 recommendations, SAT or ACT, TOEFL (for foreign students). Test scores used for counseling/placement. Application deadline: rolling. College's own assessment of entrance difficulty level: noncompetitive.

TRANSFER ADMISSIONS Required: college transcript. Recommended: minimum 2.0 grade point average. Application deadline: rolling. College's own assessment of entrance difficulty level: minimally difficult.

EXPENSES (1989–90) Comprehensive fee of $6518 includes full-time tuition ($3456), mandatory fees ($240), and college room and board ($2822). College room only: $1354. Part-time tuition: $144 per credit hour. Tuition prepayment plan available.

FINANCIAL AID Fall 1989 full-time freshmen: 84% applied for aid, 95% of those were judged to have need, 100% of those were aided; the average aided freshman received an aid package worth $4975 (53% scholarships/grants, 47% self-help) meeting 77% of need. College-administered aid for all 1989–90 undergraduates: 933 need-based scholarships; non-need scholarships (average $1510); low-interest long-term loans from college funds (average $1200), from external sources (average $2700); SEOG; College Work-Study; 196 part-time jobs. Supporting data: FFS required; IRS required for some; FAF, state form, AFSA/SAR acceptable. Priority application deadline: 5/30.

CAMPUS LIFE/STUDENT SERVICES Dress code; mandatory chapel; drama/theater group; student-run newspaper. Institution provides health clinic, personal/psychological counseling.

ATHLETICS Member NAIA. Intercollegiate sports: basketball M(s), W(s); soccer M(s); volleyball W(s). Intramural sports: baseball/softball, basketball, bowling, football, racquetball, sailing, swimming and diving, table tennis (ping pong), tennis, volleyball, weight lifting.

MAJORS Accounting B; adult and continuing education B; applied mathematics B; art education B; art/fine arts B; behavioral sciences B; biblical languages B; biblical studies B; biology/biological sciences B; business administration/commerce/management A, B; business economics B; business education A; chemistry B; child care/child and family studies A, B; child psychology/child development B; commercial art A; communication B; computer information systems B; computer programming B; computer science A, B; criminal justice B; data processing B; (pre)dentistry sequence B; early childhood education B; economics B; education B; elementary education B; (pre)engineering sequence A; English B; family services B; fashion merchandising A, B; flight training B; gerontology B; health education B; health science A; history B; home economics B; home economics education B; human resources B; information science B; interior design A, B; international studies B; journalism B; laboratory technologies A; (pre)law sequence B; liberal arts/general studies B; literature B; management information systems B; marketing/retailing/merchandising A, B; mathematics B; medical laboratory technology A; medical technology B; (pre)medicine sequence B; ministries B; modern languages B; music B; music education B; natural sciences B; nursing B; occupational therapy A; pastoral studies B; pharmacy/pharmaceutical sciences A; philosophy B; physical education B; physical therapy A; physics B; piano/organ B; political science/government B; psychology B; reading education B; recreation and leisure services B; religious education B; religious studies B; sacred music B; science B; secondary education B; secretarial studies/office management A, B; social science B; sociology B; Spanish B; speech/rhetoric/public address/debate B; theology B; (pre)veterinary medicine sequence B; voice B; zoology B. Majors with highest enrollment: business administration/commerce/management, education, religious studies.

SPECIAL NOTE FROM THE COLLEGE Southern Nazarene University offers its students a reputation of excellence that spans a century. A distinctly targeted curriculum provides a myriad of opportunities for vocational preparation. Evidence of the level of quality to be found at Southern Nazarene University includes a 90% acceptance rate of premedical students into medical colleges; a national championship in computer business assimilation competition (CASBEL); 2 national sports championships in a decade (the only NAIA school to ever achieve that); and alumni around the world placed in leadership roles in business, the church, and innumerable professions. Southern's unusual freshman orientation brings new students and their parents together with returning student and faculty mentors. Activities encourage building relationships and getting acquainted with university life. An extended orientation involves students throughout the first semester in small contact groups. The University provides high-quality experience at a reasonable price.

CONTACT Mr. Jeff Sexton, Director of Student Recruitment, Southern Nazarene University, Bethany, OK 73008, 405-789-6400 Ext. 6320.

SPRING ARBOR COLLEGE
Spring Arbor, Michigan

Total enrollment: 807 (all UG)

Women: 58%

Application deadline: rolling

Tuition & fees: $7246

Room & board: $2783

Entrance: minimally difficult

SAT ≥ 500: N/R

ACT ≥ 21: 38%

Denominational affiliation: Free Methodist

GENERAL INFORMATION Independent 4-year coed college. Founded 1873. Awards A (college transfer), B. Primary accreditation: regional. Rural setting; 70-acre campus. Total enrollment: 807. Faculty: 86 (59 full-time, 27 part-time); 44% of full-time faculty have doctoral degrees. Library holdings: 85,089 bound volumes, 26,498 titles on microform, 358 periodical subscriptions, 3,320 records/tapes. Computer terminals/PCs available for student use: 25, located in computer center, student center.

UNDERGRADUATE PROFILE Fall 1989: 807 undergraduates (159 freshmen) from 23 states and territories and 5 foreign countries; 21% part-time; 88% state residents; 11% transfers; 90% financial aid recipients; 58% women; 42% men; 3% blacks; 0% Native Americans; 0% Hispanics; 2% international students.

1989 FRESHMAN DATA 282 students applied for fall 1989 admission; 94% were accepted; 60% of those accepted enrolled. 1 freshman was a National Merit Scholarship Finalist and received a National Merit Scholarship. 17% of freshmen were in top 10% of secondary school class, 38% were in top 25%, 71% were in top half.

ENROLLMENT PATTERNS 75% of fall 1988 freshmen returned for fall 1989 term. 1987–89 average: 36% of entering classes graduated; 9% of students completing a bachelor's program went on for further study.

FRESHMAN ADMISSIONS Options: early entrance, deferred entrance. Required: high school transcript, SAT or ACT, TOEFL (for foreign students). Recommended: essay, 2 years of high school foreign language, 1 recommendation, interview, guidance counselor's evaluation form. Test scores used for admission.

Application deadline: rolling. Notification date: continuous. College's own assessment of entrance difficulty level: minimally difficult.

TRANSFER ADMISSIONS Required: college transcript, minimum 2.0 grade point average. Recommended: essay, 1 recommendation, interview. Required for some: standardized test scores, high school transcript. Application deadline: rolling. Notification date: continuous.

EXPENSES (1990–91) Comprehensive fee of $10,029 includes full-time tuition ($7190), mandatory fees ($56), and college room and board ($2783). College room only: $1148. Part-time tuition per credit: $132 for the first 8 credits, $250 for the next 3 credits. Tuition prepayment plan available.

FINANCIAL AID Fall 1989 full-time freshmen: 88% applied for aid, 69% of those were judged to have need, 90% of those were aided. College-administered aid for all 1989–90 undergraduates: need-based scholarships; 800 non-need scholarships (average $850); short-term loans; low-interest long-term loans from college funds, from external sources (average $2000); SEOG; College Work-Study; 290 part-time jobs. Supporting data: FAF required; IRS, institutional form required for some. Priority application deadline: 2/15.

CAMPUS LIFE/STUDENT SERVICES Mandatory chapel; student-run newspaper and radio station. Institution provides health clinic, personal/psychological counseling.

ATHLETICS Member NAIA. Intercollegiate sports: baseball/softball M(s), W(s); basketball M(s), W(s); cross-country running M(s), W(s); golf M(s); soccer M(s), W(s); tennis M(s), W(s); track and field M(s), W(s); volleyball W(s). Intramural sports: baseball/softball, basketball, football, soccer, volleyball.

MAJORS Art/fine arts B; biology/biological sciences B; business administration/commerce/management B; business economics B; chemistry B; communication B; computer science B; early childhood education B; education B; elementary education B; English B; French B; history B; liberal arts/general studies A; mathematics B; ministries B; music B; music education B; philosophy B; physical education B; physics B; piano/organ B; psychology B; recreation and leisure services B; religious studies B; sacred music B; secondary education B; social science B; social work B; sociology B; Spanish B; speech/rhetoric/public address/debate B; sports administration B; voice B; wind and percussion instruments B. Majors with highest enrollment: elementary education, business administration/commerce/management, communication.

SPECIAL NOTE FROM THE COLLEGE Spring Arbor College invites students to an adventure in learning and living. Its Discovery course helps freshmen adjust to the many new challenges they will face academically, socially, spiritually, and personally. "Whole person" advising continues throughout the college years. Students are challenged to learn and grow through hands-on experience with excellent equipment and facilities, including student-run AM and FM radio stations, highly specialized science equipment, and a new all-weather track. Students also have the opportunity to experience the people, traditions, sights, smells, and sounds of another part of the world through Spring Arbor College's cross-cultural requirement. Recent destinations have been Guatemala, the Dominican Republic, Jamaica, Israel, England, France, Africa, Mexico, and Germany.

CONTACT Mr. Terry L. Valentine, Director of Enrollment Services, Spring Arbor College, Spring Arbor, MI 49283, 517-750-1200 Ext. 401 or toll-free 800-748-0011.

STERLING COLLEGE
Sterling, Kansas

Total enrollment: 457 (all UG)

Women: 46%

Application deadline: rolling

Tuition & fees: $6250

Room & board: $2800

Entrance: minimally difficult

SAT ≥ 500: 16% V, 28% M

ACT ≥ 21: 57%

Denominational affiliation: Presbyterian

GENERAL INFORMATION Independent 4-year coed college. Founded 1887. Awards B. Primary accreditation: regional. Small-town setting; 46-acre campus. Total enrollment: 457. Faculty: 44 (34 full-time, 10 part-time); 48% of full-time faculty have doctoral degrees. Library holdings: 84,000 bound volumes, 1,200 titles on microform, 450 periodical subscriptions, 1,000 records/tapes. Computer terminals/PCs available for student use: 15, located in computer center.

UNDERGRADUATE PROFILE Fall 1989: 457 undergraduates (157 freshmen) from 20 states and territories and 4 foreign countries; 6% part-time; 40% state residents; 13% transfers; 87% financial aid recipients; 46% women; 54% men; 12% blacks; 1% Native Americans; 5% Hispanics; 1% Asian Americans; 2% international students; 2% of undergraduates 25 years of age or older.

1989 FRESHMAN DATA 461 students applied for fall 1989 admission; 96% were accepted; 36% of those accepted enrolled. 10% of freshmen were in top 10% of secondary school class, 41% were in top 25%, 74% were in top half.

ENROLLMENT PATTERNS 47% of fall 1988 freshmen returned for fall 1989 term. 1987–89 average: 29% of entering classes graduated; 10% of students completing a degree program went on for further study.

FRESHMAN ADMISSIONS Options: early entrance, deferred entrance. Required: high school transcript, SAT or ACT, TOEFL (for foreign students). Recommended: 3 years of high school math and science, some high school foreign language. Test scores used for admission and counseling/placement. Application deadline: rolling. Notification date: continuous. College's own assessment of entrance difficulty level: minimally difficult.

TRANSFER ADMISSIONS Required: college transcript, minimum 2.0 grade point average. Application deadline: rolling. Notification date: continuous. College's own assessment of entrance difficulty level: minimally difficult.

EXPENSES (1990–91) Comprehensive fee of $9050 includes full-time tuition ($6150), mandatory fees ($100), and college room and board ($2800). Part-time tuition per credit hour: $130 for the first 6 credit hours, $175 for the next 5 credit hours.

FINANCIAL AID College-administered aid for all 1989–90 undergraduates: need-based scholarships; non-need scholarships (average $750); low-interest long-term loans from external sources (average $2000); SEOG; College Work-Study; part-time jobs. Supporting data: FFS, IRS, AFSA/SAR required; FAF acceptable. Priority application deadline: 4/21.

CAMPUS LIFE/STUDENT SERVICES Mandatory chapel; drama/theater group; student-run newspaper. Institution provides health clinic, personal/psychological counseling.

ATHLETICS Member NAIA. Intercollegiate sports: baseball/softball M(s), W(s); basketball M(s), W(s); cross-country running M(s), W(s); football M(s); soccer M(s); tennis M(s), W(s); track and field M(s), W(s); volleyball W(s). Intramural sports: baseball/softball, basketball, soccer, table tennis (ping pong), tennis, track and field, ultimate frisbee, volleyball.

MAJORS Accounting B; art education B; art/fine arts B; behavioral sciences B; biology/biological sciences B; business administration/commerce/management B; business education B; chemistry B; child care/child and family studies B; communication B; computer science B; (pre)dentistry sequence B; education B; elementary education B; English B; history B; home economics B; home economics education B; (pre)law sequence B; liberal arts/general studies B; mathematics B; (pre)medicine sequence B; music B; music business B; music education B; natural sciences B; nutrition B; philosophy B; physical education B; piano/organ B; political science/government B; psychology B; religious education B; religious studies B; secondary education B; sociology B; special education B; speech/rhetoric/public address/debate B; theater arts/drama B; (pre)veterinary medicine sequence B; voice B. Majors with highest enrollment: education, behavioral sciences, business administration/commerce/management.

SPECIAL NOTE FROM THE COLLEGE Sterling College is a place that cares about its students—cares about how they deal with finding God's will for their life; about their hurts and disappointments; and about whether they understand chemistry, history, and literary criticism. Its students care not just about themselves but about the whole world and have a view that reaches beyond the campus. Because we live in a fascinating and diverse but difficult world, Sterling College believes the world needs trained professionals and needs the love of Christ.

CONTACT Mr. Dennis Dutton, Director of Admissions, Sterling College, Sterling, KS 67579, 316-278-2173 Ext. 275.

TABOR COLLEGE
Hillsboro, Kansas

Total enrollment: 436 (all UG)

Women: 45%

Application deadline: rolling

Tuition & fees: $5590

Room & board: $2750

Entrance: moderately difficult

SAT ≥ 500: N/R

ACT ≥ 21: 41%

Denominational affiliation: Mennonite Brethren

GENERAL INFORMATION Independent 4-year coed college. Founded 1908. Awards A (college transfer and terminal), B. Primary accreditation: regional. Small-town setting; 26-acre campus. Total enrollment: 436. Faculty: 46 (31 full-time, 15 part-time); 55% of full-time faculty have doctoral degrees. Library holdings: 70,000 bound volumes, 450 periodical subscriptions, 2,000 records/tapes. Computer terminals/PCs available for student use: 30, located in administration/business building.

UNDERGRADUATE PROFILE Fall 1989: 436 undergraduates (129 freshmen) from 30 states and territories and 4 foreign countries; 8% part-time; 54% state residents; 7% transfers; 75% financial aid recipients; 45% women; 55% men; 4% blacks; 1% Native Americans; 1% Hispanics; 1% Asian Americans; 1% international students; 11% of undergraduates 25 years of age or older.

1989 FRESHMAN DATA 327 students applied for fall 1989 admission; 46% were accepted; 86% of those accepted enrolled. 21% of freshmen were in top 10% of secondary school class, 77% were in top half.

ENROLLMENT PATTERNS 60% of fall 1988 freshmen returned for fall 1989 term. 1987–89 average: 46% of entering classes graduated; 14% of students completing a bachelor's program went on for further study.

FRESHMAN ADMISSIONS Required: essay, high school transcript, 2 recommendations, SAT or ACT, TOEFL (for foreign students). Test scores used for admission and counseling/placement. Application deadline: rolling. Notification date: continuous. College's own assessment of entrance difficulty level: moderately difficult.

TRANSFER ADMISSIONS Required: essay, standardized test scores, high school transcript, 2 recommendations, college transcript, minimum 2.0 grade point average. Recommended: minimum 3.0 grade point average. Application deadline: rolling. Notification date: continuous.

EXPENSES (1989–90) Comprehensive fee of $8340 includes full-time tuition ($5420), mandatory fees ($170), and college room and board ($2750). College room only: $1100. Part-time tuition and fees per semester (1 to 11 hours) range from $115 to $2258.

FINANCIAL AID Fall 1989 full-time freshmen: 94% applied for aid, 83% of those were judged to have need, 100% of those were aided; the average aided freshman received an aid package worth $5983 (66% scholarships/grants, 34% self-help) meeting 80% of need. College-administered aid for all 1989–90 undergraduates: need-based scholarships; non-need scholarships; low-interest long-term loans from college funds (average $233), from external sources (average $1100); SEOG; College Work-Study; 84 part-time jobs. Supporting data: FFS, IRS required; FAF, AFSA/SAR acceptable. Priority application deadline: 6/30.

CAMPUS LIFE/STUDENT SERVICES Mandatory chapel; student-run newspaper. Institution provides personal/psychological counseling.

ATHLETICS Member NAIA. Intercollegiate sports: baseball/softball M(s), W(s); basketball M(s), W(s); cross-country running M, W; football M(s); soccer M(s); tennis M(s), W(s); track and field M(s), W(s); volleyball W(s). Intramural sports: baseball/softball, basketball, football, racquetball, soccer, table tennis (ping pong), tennis, track and field, ultimate frisbee, volleyball, weight lifting.

MAJORS Accounting B; actuarial science B; agricultural business B; applied mathematics B; biblical studies A, B; biology/biological sciences B; business administration/commerce/management B; business education B; chemistry B; computer science A, B; (pre)dentistry sequence B; education B; elementary education B; (pre)engineering sequence A; English B; environmental biology B; health education B; history B; humanities B; international studies B; (pre)law sequence B; legal secretarial studies B; mathematics B; medical secretarial studies B; medical technology B; (pre)medicine sequence B; ministries B; music B; music education B; natural sciences B; philosophy B; physical education B; piano/organ B; psychology B; religious studies A, B; science B; science education B; secondary education B; secretarial studies/office management A, B; social science B; social work B; sociology B; special education B; voice B. Majors with highest enrollment: business administration/commerce/management, elementary education, physical education.

SPECIAL NOTE FROM THE COLLEGE Tabor's religious heritage places utmost importance on a voluntary, adult commitment to follow Christ. This includes a life of personal devotion and outer witness, serious corporate biblical study, and service to others, which is the foundation of Tabor's mission statement. The academic program, therefore, is designed to develop servants of Christ for all walks of life. This occurs in a Christian learning community, which emphasizes fellowship and mutual accountability. Themes of stewardship and service infuse the College's majors. The student development program stresses personal growth, self-discipline, acceptance of responsibility, and the development of decision-making skills. Tabor provides global travel/service experiences each Interterm and structured opportunities to serve others for Christ through a variety of local ministries.

CONTACT Ms. Mary Ellen Kuehl, Interim Director of Admissions, Tabor College, Hillsboro, KS 67063, 316-947-3121.

TAYLOR UNIVERSITY
Upland, Indiana

Total enrollment: 1,708 (all UG)

Women: 55%

Application deadline: rolling

Tuition & fees: $8183

Room & board: $3142

Entrance: moderately difficult

SAT ≥ 500: 46% V, 70% M

ACT ≥ 21: N/R

Denominational affiliation: interdenominational

GENERAL INFORMATION Independent 4-year coed college. Founded 1846. Awards A (terminal), B. Primary accreditation: regional. Rural setting, with easy access to Indianapolis; 250-acre campus. Total enrollment: 1,708. Faculty: 132 (98 full-time, 34 part-time); 66% of full-time faculty have doctoral degrees. Library holdings: 150,000 bound volumes, 10,000 titles on microform, 750 periodical subscriptions, 3,700 records/tapes. Computer terminals/PCs available for student use: 192, located in computer center, library, dormitories, computer lab.

UNDERGRADUATE PROFILE Fall 1989: 1,708 undergraduates (406 freshmen) from 42 states and territories and 17 foreign countries; 3% part-time; 37% state residents; 3% transfers; 65% financial aid recipients; 55% women; 45% men; 1% blacks; 1% international students.

1989 FRESHMAN DATA 1,691 students applied for fall 1989 admission; 77% were accepted; 31% of those accepted enrolled. 35% of freshmen were in top 10% of secondary school class, 67% were in top 25%, 99% were in top half.

ENROLLMENT PATTERNS 97% of fall 1988 freshmen returned for fall 1989 term. 1987–89 average: 75% of entering classes graduated; 16% of students completing a bachelor's program went on for further study.

FRESHMAN ADMISSIONS Options: early entrance, deferred entrance. Required: essay, high school transcript, recommendations, SAT or ACT. Recommended: some high school foreign language, interview. Required for some: TOEFL (for foreign students). Test scores used for admission. Application deadline: rolling. Notification date: continuous. College's own assessment of entrance difficulty level: moderately difficult.

TRANSFER ADMISSIONS Required: essay, high school transcript, recommendations, college transcript, minimum 2.5 grade point average. Recommended: standardized test scores. Application deadline: rolling. Notification date: continuous.

EXPENSES (1989–90) Comprehensive fee of $11,325 includes full-time tuition ($8007), mandatory fees ($176), and college room and board ($3142). College room only: $1554. Part-time tuition per credit hour: $233 for the first 7 credit hours, $295 for the next 4 credit hours.

FINANCIAL AID Fall 1989 full-time freshmen: 75% applied for aid, 81% of those were judged to have need, 100% of those were aided; the average aided freshman received an aid package worth $6512 (71% scholarships/grants, 29% self-help) meeting 100% of need. College-administered aid for all 1989–90 undergraduates: 1,240 need-based scholarships; non-need scholarships (average $850); short-term loans (average $60); low-interest long-term loans from college funds (average $1500), from external sources (average $1200); SEOG; College Work-Study; 250 part-time jobs. Supporting data: FAF, IRS required. Application deadline: 3/1.

CAMPUS LIFE/STUDENT SERVICES Dress code; mandatory chapel; drama/theater group; student-run newspaper and radio station. Institution provides health clinic, personal/psychological counseling.

ATHLETICS Member NAIA. Intercollegiate sports: baseball/softball M, W; basketball M, W; cross-country running M, W; football M; golf M; soccer M; tennis M, W; track and field M, W; volleyball W. Intramural sports: badminton, baseball/softball, basketball, cross-country running, equestrian sports, football, golf, racquetball, soccer, table tennis (ping pong), tennis, track and field, volleyball.

MAJORS Accounting B; art education B; art/fine arts B; biblical studies B; biology/biological sciences B; business administration/commerce/management A, B; chemistry B; communication B; computer science B; (pre)dentistry sequence B; early childhood education A; economics B; education B; elementary education B; engineering (general) B; English B; French B; history B; (pre)law sequence B; mathematics B; (pre)medicine sequence B; modern languages B; music B; music education B; natural sciences B; philosophy B; physical education B; physics B; political science/government B; psychology B; recreation and leisure services B; religious education B; religious studies B; sacred music B; science education B; secondary education B; social science B; social work B; sociology B; Spanish B; speech/rhetoric/public address/debate B; systems science A; theater arts/drama B; theology B; (pre)veterinary medicine sequence B; voice B. Majors with highest enrollment: business administration/commerce/management, education, psychology.

SPECIAL NOTE FROM THE COLLEGE At Taylor University, a tradition of engaging the world through scholarship, leadership, and Christian commitment flourishes. On its campus in America's heartland, a global perspective on Christ and His world crystallizes into a growing, sharing, intellectual community. Students find their best and use it, identify their potential and develop it, live their faith and share it. Taylor's tradition is to help students become world Christians.

CONTACT Mr. Herb Frye, Dean of Admissions, Taylor University, Upland, IN 46989, 317-998-5206 or toll-free 800-882-2345 (in-state), 800-882-3456 (out-of-state).

TREVECCA NAZARENE COLLEGE
Nashville, Tennessee

Total enrollment: 1,436

UG enrollment: 964 (54% W)

Application deadline: rolling

Tuition & fees: $4870

Room & board: $2500

Entrance: noncompetitive

SAT ≥ 500: N/App

ACT ≥ 21: 33%

Denominational affiliation: Nazarene

GENERAL INFORMATION Independent comprehensive coed institution. Founded 1901. Awards A (terminal), B, M. Primary accreditation: regional. Metropolitan setting; 80-acre campus. Total enrollment: 1,436. Faculty: 131 (59 full-time, 72 part-time); 50% of full-time faculty have doctoral degrees; graduate assistants teach no undergraduate courses. Library holdings: 85,500 bound volumes, 82,300 titles on microform, 482 periodical subscriptions, 1,908 records/tapes. Computer terminals/PCs available for student use: 30, located in computer center, library.

UNDERGRADUATE PROFILE Fall 1989: 964 undergraduates (292 freshmen) from 46 states and territories and 5 foreign countries; 12% part-time; 45% state residents; 20% transfers; 81% financial aid recipients; 54% women; 46% men; 5% blacks; 0% Native Americans; 1% Hispanics; 2% international students.

1989 FRESHMAN DATA 406 students applied for fall 1989 admission; 100% were accepted; 72% of those accepted enrolled.

ENROLLMENT PATTERNS 64% of fall 1988 freshmen returned for fall 1989 term. 1987–89 average: 49% of entering classes graduated; 23% of students completing a bachelor's program went on for further study.

FRESHMAN ADMISSIONS Open admissions. Options: early entrance, deferred entrance. Required: high school transcript, medical history, ACT, TOEFL (for foreign students). Required for some: recommendations. Test scores used for counseling/placement. Application deadline: rolling. College's own assessment of entrance difficulty level: noncompetitive.

TRANSFER ADMISSIONS Required: college transcript, medical history. Required for some: recommendations. Application deadline: rolling. College's own assessment of entrance difficulty level: noncompetitive.

EXPENSES (1990–91) Comprehensive fee of $7370 includes full-time tuition ($4590), mandatory fees ($280), and college room and board ($2500). College room only: $1100. Part-time tuition: $153 per semester hour.

FINANCIAL AID Fall 1989 full-time freshmen: 87% applied for aid, 72% of those were judged to have need, 100% of those were aided; the average aided freshman received an aid package worth $5154 (39% scholarships/grants, 61% self-help) meeting 92% of need. College-administered aid for all 1989–90 undergraduates: need-based scholarships; 401 non-need scholarships (average $875); short-term loans; low-interest long-term loans from external sources (average $2000); SEOG; College Work-Study; 221 part-time jobs. Supporting data: FFS required; FAF acceptable. Priority application deadline: 4/15.

CAMPUS LIFE/STUDENT SERVICES Dress code; mandatory chapel. Institution provides health clinic, personal/psychological counseling.

ATHLETICS Member NAIA. Intercollegiate sports: baseball/softball M(s); basketball M(s); tennis M(s), W(s); volleyball W(s). Intramural sports: badminton, baseball/softball, basketball, bowling, football, gymnastics, racquetball, swimming and diving, tennis, volleyball, weight lifting, wrestling.

MAJORS Accounting B; behavioral sciences B; biology/biological sciences B; broadcasting A, B; business administration/commerce/management B; business education B; chemistry B; child care/child and family studies A; communication B; computer information systems A, B; computer science A, B; early childhood education B; education B; elementary education B; (pre)engineering sequence A; English B; health education B; history B; humanities B; human resources B; (pre)law sequence B; liberal arts/general studies A; mathematics B; medical assistant technologies A; medical secretarial studies A; medical technology B; (pre)medicine sequence B; ministries A, B; music B; music business B; music education B; natural sciences B; pastoral studies B; philosophy B; physical education B; physical fitness/human movement B; physical therapy A; physician's assistant studies B; psychology B; radio and television studies A, B; religious education B; religious studies A, B; sacred music B; science education B; secondary education B; secretarial studies/office management A, B; social science B; social work B; special education B; speech/rhetoric/public address/debate B; theater arts/drama B; theology B. Majors with highest enrollment: business administration/commerce/management, education, religious studies.

SPECIAL NOTE FROM THE COLLEGE Trevecca Nazarene's goal is to prepare students for Christian service in all areas of life by providing an education that integrates faith and learning. The College seeks to combine the best in liberal arts as "preparation for life" and the best in career education as "preparation to earn a living." It also provides many opportunities for spiritual growth through chapel services, student organizations, convocations and revivals, and visiting lecturers. In addition, students are actively involved with the Nashville community through local churches and service clubs, which reflects Trevecca's service-oriented philosophy.

CONTACT Dr. Melvin Welch, Director of Admissions, Trevecca Nazarene College, Nashville, TN 37210, 615-248-1320.

TRINITY CHRISTIAN COLLEGE
Palos Heights, Illinois

Total enrollment: 534 (all UG)

Women: 64%

Application deadline: 8/15

Tuition & fees: $6890

Room & board: $2910

Entrance: moderately difficult

SAT ≥ 500: N/R

ACT ≥ 21: 48%

Denominational affiliation: Christian Reformed Church

GENERAL INFORMATION Independent 4-year coed college. Founded 1959. Awards B. Primary accreditation: regional. Small-town setting, with easy access to Chicago; 53-acre campus. Total enrollment: 534. Faculty: 65 (40 full-time, 25 part-time); 52% of full-time faculty have doctoral degrees. Library holdings: 55,000 bound volumes, 30,000 titles on microform, 325 periodical subscriptions, 600 records/tapes. Computer terminals/PCs available for student use: 35, located in computer center.

UNDERGRADUATE PROFILE Fall 1989: 534 undergraduates (134 freshmen) from 20 states and territories and 2 foreign countries; 10% part-time; 71% state residents; 16% transfers; 78% financial aid recipients; 64% women; 36% men; 10% blacks; 0% Native Americans; 2% Hispanics; 1% Asian Americans; 1% international students; 10% of undergraduates 25 years of age or older.

1989 FRESHMAN DATA 370 students applied for fall 1989 admission; 98% were accepted; 37% of those accepted enrolled.

ENROLLMENT PATTERNS 70% of fall 1988 freshmen returned for fall 1989 term. 1987–89 average: 39% of entering classes graduated; 20% of students completing a degree program went on for further study.

FRESHMAN ADMISSIONS Options: early entrance, deferred entrance. Required: essay, high school transcript. Recommended: 3 years of high school math and science, some high school foreign language, ACT, TOEFL (for foreign students). Required for some: recommendations, interview. Test scores used for admission. Application deadline: 8/15. Notification date: continuous until

8/15. College's own assessment of entrance difficulty level: moderately difficult.

TRANSFER ADMISSIONS Required: essay, college transcript. Recommended: standardized test scores, high school transcript, some high school foreign language, minimum 2.0 grade point average. Required for some: recommendations, interview. Application deadline: rolling. College's own assessment of entrance difficulty level: moderately difficult.

EXPENSES (1990–91 estimated) Comprehensive fee of $9800 includes full-time tuition ($6890) and college room and board ($2910). College room only: $1255. Part-time tuition: $235 per credit.

FINANCIAL AID Fall 1989 full-time freshmen: 70% applied for aid, 80% of those were judged to have need, 100% of those were aided; the average aided freshman received an aid package worth $6243 (49% scholarships/grants, 51% self-help) meeting 94% of need. College-administered aid for all 1989–90 undergraduates: 97 need-based scholarships (average $630); 418 non-need scholarships (average $1110); low-interest long-term loans from external sources (average $2451); SEOG; College Work-Study; 125 part-time jobs. Supporting data: FAF required; state form required for some; FFS, IRS, AFSA/SAR acceptable. Priority application deadline: 2/15.

CAMPUS LIFE/STUDENT SERVICES Student-run newspaper. Institution provides personal/psychological counseling.

ATHLETICS Intercollegiate sports: baseball/softball M, W; basketball M, W; golf M, W; soccer M; track and field M, W; volleyball W. Intramural sports: badminton, baseball/softball, basketball, bowling, cross-country running, field hockey, football, racquetball, skiing (cross-country), soccer, tennis, ultimate frisbee, volleyball, weight lifting.

MAJORS Accounting B; art/fine arts B; biology/biological sciences B; business administration/commerce/management B; business education B; chemistry B; computer science B; (pre)dentistry sequence B; education B; elementary education B; English B; history B; industrial arts B; mathematics B; medical technology B; (pre)medicine sequence B; music B; music education B; nursing B; painting/drawing B; philosophy B; physical education B; piano/organ B; psychology B; religious education B; religious studies B; science education B; secondary education B; sociology B; theology B; (pre)veterinary medicine sequence B; Western civilization and culture B. Major with highest enrollment: business administration/commerce/management.

SPECIAL NOTE FROM THE COLLEGE Trinity Christian College is located in Palos Heights, a suburb southwest of Chicago. Its proximity to the city offers students access to cultural, educational, and employment opportunities through the College-wide internship program and the Chicago Metropolitan Studies Program. Trinity offers majors in 21 areas of study; in addition, there are 25 minor programs available. The nursing program is fully accredited by the National League for Nursing. Trinity graduates enjoy the benefits of a solid, Christian, liberal arts education. They have an excellent acceptance rate into graduate programs in business, education, science, and medicine, as well as great success in career placement.

CONTACT Mr. Jon F. Bontekoe, Director of Admissions and Financial Aid, Trinity Christian College, Palos Heights, IL 60463, 708-597-3000 Ext. 307 or toll-free 800-748-0085.

TRINITY COLLEGE
Deerfield, Illinois

Total enrollment: 849 (all UG)

Women: 47%

Application deadline: rolling

Tuition & fees: $8130

Room & board: $3690

Entrance: moderately difficult

SAT ≥ 500: N/R

ACT ≥ 21: 50%

Denominational affiliation: Evangelical Free Church of America

GENERAL INFORMATION Independent 4-year coed college. Founded 1897. Awards B. Primary accreditation: regional. Small-town setting, with easy access to Chicago; 80-acre campus. Total enrollment: 849. Faculty: 58 (28 full-time, 30 part-time); 57% of full-time faculty have doctoral degrees. Library holdings: 205,000 bound volumes, 63,875 titles on microform, 1,700 periodical subscriptions, 4,352 records/tapes. Computer terminals/PCs available for student use: 25, located in computer center, library.

UNDERGRADUATE PROFILE Fall 1989: 849 undergraduates (355 freshmen) from 28 states and territories and 3 foreign countries; 12% part-time; 48% state residents; 39% transfers; 87% financial aid recipients; 47% women; 53% men; 4% blacks; 0% Native Americans; 2% Hispanics; 4% Asian Americans; 5% international students; 13% of undergraduates 25 years of age or older.

1989 FRESHMAN DATA 762 students applied for fall 1989 admission; 75% were accepted; 62% of those accepted enrolled. 1 freshman was a National Merit Scholarship Finalist. 12% of freshmen were in top 10% of secondary school class, 80% were in top half.

ENROLLMENT PATTERNS 70% of fall 1988 freshmen returned for fall 1989 term. 1987–89 average: 47% of entering classes graduated; 40% of students completing a degree program went on for further study.

FRESHMAN ADMISSIONS Required: essay, high school transcript, 1 recommendation, SAT or ACT, TOEFL (for foreign students). Recommended: 3 years of high school math and science. Test scores used for admission. Application deadline: rolling. College's own assessment of entrance difficulty level: moderately difficult.

TRANSFER ADMISSIONS Required: essay, high school transcript, 1 recommendation, college transcript, minimum 2.0 grade point average. Recommended: 3 years of high school math and science. Application deadline: rolling. College's own assessment of entrance difficulty level: moderately difficult.

EXPENSES (1990–91) Comprehensive fee of $11,820 includes full-time tuition ($8000), mandatory fees ($130), and college room and board ($3690). College room only: $1680 (minimum). Part-time tuition: $330 per hour.

FINANCIAL AID College-administered aid for all 1989–90 undergraduates: need-based scholarships (average $300); non-need scholarships (average $750); low-interest long-term loans from college funds (average $900), from external sources (average $2000); SEOG; College Work-Study; part-time jobs. Supporting data: FAF, AFSA/SAR required; FFS acceptable. Priority application deadline: 5/1.

CAMPUS LIFE/STUDENT SERVICES Mandatory chapel; drama/theater group; student-run newspaper. Institution provides personal/psychological counseling.

ATHLETICS Member NAIA. Intercollegiate sports: baseball/softball M(s), W(s); basketball M(s), W(s); football M(s); golf M(s); soccer M(s), W; tennis M(s), W(s); volleyball M, W(s); wrestling M. Intramural sports: baseball/softball, basketball, football, racquetball, soccer, table tennis (ping pong), tennis.

MAJORS Biblical studies B; biology/biological sciences B; business administration/commerce/management B; chemistry B; communication B; computer information systems B; computer science B; economics B; education B; elementary education B; English B; history B; humanities B; liberal arts/general studies B; mathematics B; ministries B; music B; music education B; philosophy B; physical education B; psychology B; social science B; sociology B. Majors with highest enrollment: elementary education, business administration/commerce/management, psychology.

SPECIAL NOTE FROM THE COLLEGE Trinity College, committed to a Christian liberal arts education, is located on Chicago's North Shore. Students are trained to make their profession of choice their mission field. They are challenged to honestly examine their faith and to discover personal answers to the "whys" and "hows" of believing and how their commitment to Christ relates to their academics, life-style, and professional goals. Students acquire book knowledge but also have opportunities to gain practical experience. Activities and internship programs provide chances for students to develop leadership, organizational, and communication skills, as well as gain valuable experience in their major. Trinity students discover challenging academics, an enlightening spiritual life, and lots of fun. They enjoy Chicago, a city with continuous energy, and, most important, build lifelong friendships with Christians from all over the country.

CONTACT Mr. Brian Medaglia, Director of Admissions, Trinity College, Deerfield, IL 60015, 708-948-8980 Ext. 214 or toll-free 800-822-3225 (out-of-state).

TRINITY WESTERN UNIVERSITY
Langley, British Columbia, Canada

Total enrollment: 1,300

UG enrollment: 1,276 (50% W)

Application deadline: rolling

Tuition & fees: $5525

Room & board: $3760

Entrance: moderately difficult

SAT ≥ 500: 95% V, 85% M

ACT ≥ 21: 48%

Denominational affiliation: Evangelical Free Church of America

GENERAL INFORMATION Independent comprehensive coed institution. Founded 1962. Awards B, M. Primary accreditation: provincial charter. Small-town setting, with easy access to Vancouver; 110-acre campus. Total enrollment: 1,300. Faculty: 76 (41 full-time, 35 part-time); 70% of full-time faculty have doctoral degrees; graduate assistants teach no undergraduate courses. Library holdings: 75,172 bound volumes, 82,569 titles on microform, 573 periodical subscriptions, 221 records/tapes. Computer terminals/PCs available for student use: 36, located in computer center, library.

UNDERGRADUATE PROFILE Fall 1989: 1,276 undergraduates (475 freshmen) from 22 provinces and territories and 23 foreign countries; 16% part-time; 62% province residents; 10% transfers; 52% financial aid recipients; 50% women; 50% men; 3% blacks; 1% Native Americans; 0% Hispanics; 0% Asian Americans; 7% international students; 16% of undergraduates 25 years of age or older.

1989 FRESHMAN DATA 1,009 students applied for fall 1989 admission; 81% were accepted; 58% of those accepted enrolled. 2 freshmen were National Merit Scholarship Finalists; 1 received a National Merit Scholarship. 20% of freshmen were in top 10% of secondary school class, 60% were in top half.

ENROLLMENT PATTERNS 62% of fall 1988 freshmen returned for fall 1989 term. 1987–89 average: 30% of entering classes graduated; 20% of students completing a college-transfer associate program went on to 4-year colleges; 31% of students completing a degree program went on for further study.

FRESHMAN ADMISSIONS Options: early entrance, deferred entrance. Required: essay, high school transcript, 2 recommendations, TOEFL (for foreign students). Recommended: 3 years of high school math and science, some high school foreign language. Required for some: interview, SAT or ACT. Test scores used for admission. Standardized test score cutoffs for U.S. applicants: 950 on SAT (verbal and math combined), 18 on ACT (composite). Application deadline: rolling. College's own assessment of entrance difficulty level: moderately difficult; very difficult for aviation technology program.

TRANSFER ADMISSIONS Required: essay, high school transcript, 2 recommendations, college transcript. Recommended: 3 years of high school math and science, some high school foreign language, minimum 2.0 grade point average. Required for some: standardized test scores, interview. Application deadline: rolling. College's own assessment of entrance difficulty level: moderately difficult.

EXPENSES (1990–91) Comprehensive fee of $9285 includes full-time tuition ($5350), mandatory fees ($175), and college room and board ($3760). Part-time tuition: $182 per semester hour. (All figures are in Canadian dollars.).

FINANCIAL AID College-administered aid for all 1989–90 undergraduates: 300 need-based scholarships (average $650); 150 non-need scholarships (average $500); low-interest long-term loans from external sources (average $1800); 42 part-time jobs. Supporting data: institutional form required; government form required for some; FFS, FAF, IRS, AFSA/SAR acceptable. Priority application deadline: 6/1.

CAMPUS LIFE/STUDENT SERVICES Drama/theater group; student-run newspaper. Institution provides health clinic, personal/psychological counseling. Social organizations: social clubs.

ATHLETICS Intercollegiate sports: basketball M, W; rugby M; soccer M; volleyball M, W. Intramural sports: badminton, basketball, football, ice hockey, table tennis (ping pong), tennis, ultimate frisbee, volleyball.

MAJORS Applied mathematics B; art/fine arts B; biblical studies B; biology/biological sciences B; business administration/commerce/management B; chemistry B; communication B; computer science B; (pre)dentistry sequence B; education B; elementary education B; English B; flight training B; geography B; history B; humanities B; human services B; (pre)law sequence B; liberal arts/general studies B; linguistics B; mathematics B; (pre)medicine sequence B; music B; natural sciences B; philosophy B; physical education B; psychology B; religious studies B; science B; secondary education B; social science B; theater arts/drama B; (pre)veterinary medicine sequence B. Majors with highest enrollment: psychology, business administration/commerce/management, education.

SPECIAL NOTE FROM THE COLLEGE Trinity Western is set on a wooded 100-acre campus. Its students enjoy the solitude of a rural environment and have easy access to the beautiful urban center of Vancouver, just 20 miles away. Trinity is committed to the development of godly Christian leaders—men and women who will take their education and skills into the marketplace and work for the cause of Christ. The whole-student approach to education provides an environment that challenges students to develop intellectually, socially, physically, and spiritually.

CONTACT Mr. Kirk Kauffeldt, Associate Director of Admissions, Trinity Western University, Langley, BC V3A 6H4, Canada, 604-888-7511 Ext. 2016.

WARNER PACIFIC COLLEGE
Portland, Oregon

Total enrollment: 450

UG enrollment: 448 (49% W)

Application deadline: rolling

Tuition & fees: $7044

Room & board: $3188

Entrance: moderately difficult

SAT ≥ 500: 24% V, 33% M

ACT ≥ 21: N/R

Denominational affiliation: Church of God

GENERAL INFORMATION Independent comprehensive coed institution. Founded 1937. Awards A (college transfer and terminal), B, M. Primary accreditation: regional. Metropolitan setting; 15-acre campus. Total enrollment: 450. Faculty: 51 (27 full-time, 24 part-time); 55% of full-time faculty have doctoral degrees; graduate assistants teach no undergraduate courses. Library holdings: 60,000 bound volumes, 250 periodical subscriptions, 1,500 records/tapes. Computer terminals/PCs available for student use: 10, located in computer center, library.

UNDERGRADUATE PROFILE Fall 1989: 448 undergraduates (50 freshmen) from 31 states and territories and 14 foreign countries; 9% part-time; 49% state residents; 17% transfers; 83% financial aid recipients; 49% women; 51% men; 3% blacks; 2% Native Americans; 1% Hispanics; 3% Asian Americans; 5% international students; 30% of undergraduates 25 years of age or older.

1989 FRESHMAN DATA 89 students applied for fall 1989 admission; 61% were accepted; 93% of those accepted enrolled.

ENROLLMENT PATTERNS 69% of fall 1988 freshmen returned for fall 1989 term. 1987–89 average: 40% of entering classes graduated; 14% of students completing a bachelor's program went on for further study.

FRESHMAN ADMISSIONS Option: deferred entrance. Required: high school transcript, 2 recommendations, SAT or ACT, TOEFL (for foreign students). Test scores used for admission and counseling/placement. Application deadline: rolling. Notification date: continuous. College's own assessment of entrance difficulty level: moderately difficult.

TRANSFER ADMISSIONS Required: standardized test scores, 2 recommendations, college transcript, minimum 2.0 grade point average. Required for some: high school transcript. Application deadline: rolling. Notification date: continuous.

EXPENSES (1990–91) Comprehensive fee of $10,232 includes full-time tuition ($6800), mandatory fees ($244), and college room and board ($3188). College room only: $1300. Part-time tuition per semester hour: $212 for the first 5 semester hours, $262 for the next 6 semester hours.

FINANCIAL AID Fall 1989 full-time freshmen: 100% applied for aid, 88% of those were judged to have need, 100% of those were aided; the average aided freshman received an aid package worth $6714 (57% scholarships/grants, 43% self-help) meeting 95% of need. College-administered aid for all 1989–90 undergraduates: 310 need-based scholarships (average $1468); non-need scholarships (average $724); low-interest long-term loans from external sources (average $800); SEOG; College Work-Study; 50 part-time jobs. Supporting data: FAF, AFSA/SAR required; IRS required for some; FFS acceptable. Priority application deadline: 4/1.

CAMPUS LIFE/STUDENT SERVICES Dress code; mandatory chapel; drama/theater group; student-run newspaper. Institution provides legal services, health clinic, personal/psychological counseling.

ATHLETICS Member NAIA. Intercollegiate sports: baseball/softball M, W; basketball M(s), W(s); soccer M(s); volleyball W(s). Intramural sports: badminton, baseball/softball, basketball, football, skiing (cross-country), skiing (downhill), soccer, table tennis (ping pong), tennis, track and field, volleyball.

MAJORS American studies B; biblical studies A, B; biology/biological sciences B; business administration/commerce/management B; English B; history B; human development B; liberal arts/general studies A, B; mathematics A, B; ministries A, B; music B; music education B; pastoral studies B; physical education B; psychology B; religious education A, B; religious studies B; science B; science education B; secondary education B; social science A, B; social work B; sociology B; theology B.

SPECIAL NOTE FROM THE COLLEGE Warner Pacific College is shaped by an assumption that there must be a strong and reinforcing relationship between faith, learning, and life. Faculty members are selected for their ability to teach; for evidence of thoughtful personal, spiritual, and professional growth; and for being expert in their subject area. There is a conviction that students are expected to develop servant leadership and a global perspective by staffing and managing the Bethlehem Inn, an overnight shelter for homeless families, and through international experiences such as the exchange program with Kiev Pedagogical Language Institute in the Soviet Union. Well-trained residence and counseling staffs help students resolve normal difficulties. All students benefit from the Academic Support Center. Warner Pacific is located 15 minutes from downtown Portland, Oregon, and less than 2 hours by car from Mt. Hood ski slopes and Pacific Ocean beaches.

CONTACT Mrs. Janice Settlemyre, Administrative Assistant, Admissions, Warner Pacific College, Portland, OR 97215, 503-775-4366 Ext. 510.

WARNER SOUTHERN COLLEGE
Lake Wales, Florida

Total enrollment: 423 (all UG)

Women: 57%

Application deadline: rolling

Tuition & fees: $4850

Room & board: $2740

Entrance: minimally difficult

SAT ≥ 500: 13% V, 29% M

ACT ≥ 21: 16%

Denominational affiliation: Church of God

GENERAL INFORMATION Independent 4-year coed college. Founded 1968. Awards A (college transfer and terminal), B. Primary accreditation: regional. Rural setting, with easy access to Tampa; 350-acre campus. Total enrollment: 423. Faculty: 31 (23 full-time, 8 part-time); 47% of full-time faculty have doctoral degrees. Library holdings: 66,000 bound volumes, 6,200 titles on microform, 5,500 periodical subscriptions, 3,320 records/tapes. Computer terminals/PCs available for student use: 21, located in computer center.

UNDERGRADUATE PROFILE Fall 1989: 423 undergraduates (97 freshmen) from 27 states and territories and 6 foreign countries; 16% part-time; 58% state residents; 15% transfers; 82% financial aid recipients; 57% women; 43% men; 7% blacks; 1% Native Americans; 1% Hispanics; 1% Asian Americans; 3% international students; 32% of undergraduates 25 years of age or older.

1989 FRESHMAN DATA 391 students applied for fall 1989 admission; 69% were accepted; 36% of those accepted enrolled. 12% of freshmen were in top 10% of secondary school class, 41% were in top 25%, 86% were in top half.

ENROLLMENT PATTERNS 58% of fall 1988 freshmen returned for fall 1989 term. 1987–89 average: 46% of entering classes graduated; 20% of students completing a bachelor's program went on for further study.

FRESHMAN ADMISSIONS Preference given to Christians. Options: early entrance, deferred entrance. Required: essay, high school transcript, 1 recommendation, SAT or ACT. Required for some: interview. Test scores used for admission and counseling/placement. Application deadline: rolling. Notification date: continuous. College's own assessment of entrance difficulty level: minimally difficult.

TRANSFER ADMISSIONS Required: essay, standardized test scores, 1 recommendation, college transcript, minimum 2.0 grade point average. Required for some: interview. Application deadline: rolling. Notification date: continuous.

EXPENSES (1989–90) Comprehensive fee of $7590 includes full-time tuition ($4610), mandatory fees ($240), and college room and board ($2740). College room only: $1150. Part-time tuition per semester hour: $100 for the first 7 semester hours, $135 for the next 4 semester hours.

FINANCIAL AID Fall 1989 full-time freshmen: 96% applied for aid, 88% of those were judged to have need, 100% of those were aided; the average aided freshman received an aid package worth $3426 (49% scholarships/grants, 51% self-help) meeting 56% of need. College-administered aid for all 1989–90 undergraduates: 50 need-based scholarships (average $725); 124 non-need scholarships (average $613); low-interest long-term loans from external sources (average $2800); SEOG; College Work-Study; 58 part-time jobs. Supporting data: FFS, IRS, AFSA/SAR required for some; FAF acceptable. Priority application deadline: 4/1.

CAMPUS LIFE/STUDENT SERVICES Dress code; mandatory chapel; drama/theater group; student-run newspaper and radio station. Institution provides health clinic, personal/psychological counseling.

ATHLETICS Member NAIA. Intercollegiate sports: baseball/softball M, W; basketball M, W; soccer M; volleyball W. Intramural sports: baseball/softball, basketball, football, racquetball, table tennis (ping pong), tennis, volleyball.

MAJORS Accounting B; biblical studies A, B; biology/biological sciences B; business administration/commerce/management A, B; communication B; early childhood education B; elementary education B; English B; international studies B; ministries A, B; music A, B; music education B; pastoral studies B; physical education B; psychology B; religious education A, B; religious studies A, B; science education B; secondary education B; secretarial studies/office management A; social science B; sociology B; speech/rhetoric/public address/debate B; theology B. Majors with highest enrollment: elementary education, business administration/commerce/management, pastoral studies.

SPECIAL NOTE FROM THE COLLEGE Warner Southern College is located in beautiful central Florida just a few miles south of Walt Disney World on Lake Caloosa. Warner Southern offers a rich atmosphere of concern for each student and is committed to serving students in every area of their lives. It is an accredited 4-year Christian college in the liberal arts tradition, offering a broad scope of majors in which students are able to excel. Students develop a close bond with their professors because of the low student-faculty ratio and with fellow students because of the friendly atmosphere. Students often remark that they enjoy the size of the classes and the spiritual atmosphere that exists on campus.

CONTACT Mr. Greg Hird, Director of Admissions, Warner Southern College, Lake Wales, FL 33853, 813-638-2109.

WESTMONT COLLEGE
Santa Barbara, California

Total enrollment: 1,256 (all UG)

Women: 59%

Application deadline: 3/1

Tuition & fees: $11,530

Room & board: $4650

Entrance: moderately difficult

SAT ≥ 500: 45% V, 68% M

ACT ≥ 21: 71%

Denominational affiliation: interdenominational/ nondenominational

GENERAL INFORMATION Independent-religious 4-year coed college. Founded 1940. Awards B. Primary accreditation: regional. City setting; 133-acre campus. Total enrollment: 1,256. Faculty: 109 (66 full-time, 43 part-time); 67% of full-time faculty have doctoral degrees. Library holdings: 142,423 bound volumes, 18,407 titles on microform, 700 periodical subscriptions, 4,414 records/tapes. Computer terminals/PCs available for student use: 35, located in library.

UNDERGRADUATE PROFILE Fall 1989: 1,256 undergraduates (338 freshmen) from 39 states and territories and 17 foreign countries; 1% part-time; 67% state residents; 20% transfers; 76% financial aid recipients; 59% women; 41% men; 1% blacks; 2% Native Americans; 3% Hispanics; 2% Asian Americans; 2% international students; 0% of undergraduates 25 years of age or older.

1989 FRESHMAN DATA 942 students applied for fall 1989 admission; 76% were accepted; 47% of those accepted enrolled. 36% of freshmen were in top 10% of secondary school class, 69% were in top 25%, 93% were in top half.

ENROLLMENT PATTERNS 81% of fall 1988 freshmen returned for fall 1989 term. 1987–89 average: 50% of entering classes graduated; 45% of students completing a degree program went on for further study.

FRESHMAN ADMISSIONS Options: early entrance, deferred entrance. Required: essay, high school transcript, SAT or ACT, TOEFL (for foreign students). Recommended: 3 years of high school math and science, 2 years of high school foreign language, recommendations, interview, English Composition Test (with essay). Test scores used for admission. Application deadline: 3/1. Notification date: continuous until 6/1. College's own assessment of entrance difficulty level: moderately difficult.

TRANSFER ADMISSIONS Required: essay, high school transcript, college transcript, minimum 2.0 grade point average, minimum 2.5 grade point average for transfers from 2-year colleges. Recommended: 3 years of high school math and science, some high school foreign language, recommendations, interview. Required for some: standardized test scores. Application deadline: 3/1. Notification date: continuous until 6/1. College's own assessment of entrance difficulty level: moderately difficult.

EXPENSES (1989–90) Comprehensive fee of $16,180 includes full-time tuition ($10,900), mandatory fees ($630), and college room and board ($4650). College room only: $2676. Part-time tuition: $440 per unit.

FINANCIAL AID Fall 1989 full-time freshmen: 85% applied for aid, 83% of those were judged to have need, 100% of those were aided; the average aided freshman received an aid package meeting 92% of need. College-administered aid for all 1989–90 undergraduates: 586 need-based scholarships (average $3000); non-need scholarships (average $2500); short-term loans (average $100); low-interest long-term loans from college funds (average $3000), from external sources (average $2500); SEOG; College Work-Study; 250 part-time jobs. Supporting data: IRS, institutional form, AFSA/SAR required; state form required for some; FFS, FAF acceptable. Priority application deadline: 3/1.

CAMPUS LIFE/STUDENT SERVICES Mandatory chapel; drama/theater group; student-run newspaper. Institution provides legal services, health clinic, personal/psychological counseling.

ATHLETICS Member NAIA. Intercollegiate sports: baseball/ softball M(s); basketball M(s); cross-country running M(s), W(s); soccer M(s), W(s); tennis M(s), W(s); track and field M(s), W(s); volleyball W(s). Intramural sports: badminton, baseball/softball, basketball, cross-country running, football, golf, racquetball, soccer, swimming and diving, table tennis (ping pong), tennis, ultimate frisbee, volleyball, water polo.

MAJORS Art/fine arts B; behavioral sciences B; biology/ biological sciences B; business economics B; chemistry B; communication B; computer science B; (pre)dentistry sequence B; economics B; education B; elementary education B; engineering (general) B; engineering physics B; English B; French B; history B; (pre)law sequence B; liberal arts/general studies B; literature B; mathematics B; (pre)medicine sequence B; ministries B; modern languages B; music B; natural sciences B; philosophy B; physical education B; physical sciences B; physics B; political science/government B; psychology B; religious studies B; secondary education B; social science B; sociology B; Spanish B; theater arts/drama B; (pre)veterinary medicine sequence B. Majors with highest enrollment: business economics, English, liberal arts/general studies.

SPECIAL NOTE FROM THE COLLEGE Westmont's mission is to provide a program uncompromised in its commitment to a high-quality liberal arts education and integrated with enthusiastic, evangelical Christian faith. Close interaction between students and faculty is a Westmont hallmark. Opportunities beyond the classroom include cross-cultural studies in Western and Eastern Europe, Africa, Costa Rica, and the Holy Lands. Semester study programs are available in San Francisco and Washington, DC, as well as at 1 of the 12 other member colleges of the Christian College Consortium.

CONTACT Mr. David A. Morley, Director of Admissions, Westmont College, Santa Barbara, CA 93108, 805-565-6200.

WHEATON COLLEGE
Wheaton, Illinois

Total enrollment: 2,548

UG enrollment: 2,282 (53% W)

Application deadline: 2/15

Tuition & fees: $8836

Room & board: $3640

Entrance: very difficult

SAT ≥ 500: 72% V, 91% M

ACT ≥ 21: 95%

Denominational affiliation: nondenominational

GENERAL INFORMATION Independent comprehensive coed institution. Founded 1860. Awards B, M. Primary accreditation: regional. Small-town setting, with easy access to Chicago; 80-acre campus. Total enrollment: 2,548. Faculty: 246 (147 full-time, 99 part-time); 80% of full-time faculty have doctoral degrees; graduate assistants teach no undergraduate courses. Library holdings: 323,754 bound volumes, 310,000 titles on microform, 2,199 periodical subscriptions, 9,000 records/tapes. Computer terminals/PCs available for student use: 100, located in computer center, library, computer labs.

UNDERGRADUATE PROFILE Fall 1989: 2,282 undergraduates (539 freshmen) from 48 states and territories and 7 foreign countries; 3% part-time; 23% state residents; 10% transfers; 42% financial aid recipients; 53% women; 47% men; 1% blacks; 1% Hispanics; 4% Asian Americans; 1% international students; 2% of undergraduates 25 years of age or older.

1989 FRESHMAN DATA 1,182 students applied for fall 1989 admission; 78% were accepted; 59% of those accepted enrolled. 22 freshmen were National Merit Scholarship Finalists; all received a National Merit Scholarship. 51% of freshmen were in top 10% of secondary school class, 81% were in top 25%, 97% were in top half.

ENROLLMENT PATTERNS 93% of fall 1988 freshmen returned for fall 1989 term. 1987–89 average: 76% of entering classes graduated; 20% of students completing a degree program went on for further study.

FRESHMAN ADMISSIONS Preference given to Christians. Options: early action, deferred entrance. Required: essay, high school transcript, 3 recommendations, interview, SAT or ACT, TOEFL (for foreign students). Recommended: 3 years of high school math and science, 2 years of high school foreign language, Achievement Tests, English Composition Test. Test scores used for admission. Application deadlines: 2/15, 12/1 for early action. Notification dates: continuous until 4/15, 2/15 for early action. College's own assessment of entrance difficulty level: very difficult.

TRANSFER ADMISSIONS Required: essay, standardized test scores, high school transcript, 3 recommendations, interview, college transcript, minimum 3.0 grade point average. Recommended: 3 years of high school math and science, 2 years of high school foreign language. Application deadline: 3/1. Notification date: continuous until 5/1. College's own assessment of entrance difficulty level: moderately difficult.

EXPENSES (1990–91) Comprehensive fee of $12,476 includes full-time tuition ($8836) and college room and board ($3640). College room only: $2110. Part-time tuition: $370 per hour.

FINANCIAL AID Fall 1989 full-time freshmen: 85% applied for aid, 78% of those were judged to have need, 100% of those were aided; the average aided freshman received an aid package worth $4739 (70% scholarships/grants, 30% self-help) meeting 100% of need. College-administered aid for all 1989–90 undergraduates: 977 need-based scholarships (average $3921); 137 non-need scholarships (average $1000); low-interest long-term loans from college funds (average $1006), from external sources (average $2667); SEOG; College Work-Study; part-time jobs. Supporting data: FAF, IRS required. Priority application deadline: 3/15.

CAMPUS LIFE/STUDENT SERVICES Dress code; mandatory chapel; drama/theater group; student-run newspaper and radio station. Institution provides health clinic, personal/psychological counseling.

ATHLETICS Member NCAA (Division III). Intercollegiate sports: baseball/softball M(III), W(III); basketball M(III), W(III); cross-country running M(III), W(III); football M(III); golf M(III); soccer M(III), W(III); swimming and diving M(III), W(III); tennis M(III), W(III); track and field M(III), W(III); volleyball W(III); wrestling M(III). Intramural sports: badminton, baseball/softball, basketball, field hockey, football, ice hockey, lacrosse, skiing (cross-country), soccer, volleyball, weight lifting.

MAJORS Archaeology B; art education B; art/fine arts B; art history B; biblical languages B; biblical studies B; biology/biological sciences B; broadcasting B; business economics B; chemistry B; classics B; communication B; computer science B; (pre)dentistry sequence B; economics B; elementary education B; French B; geology B; German B; history B; interdisciplinary studies B; journalism B; (pre)law sequence B; literature B; mathematics B; (pre)medicine sequence B; modern languages B; music B; music business B; music education B; music history B; philosophy B; physical education B; physics B; piano/organ B; political science/government B; psychology B; religious education B; religious studies B; science education B; secondary education B; sociology B; Spanish B; speech/rhetoric/public address/debate B; stringed instruments B; studio art B; theater arts/drama B; voice B; wind and percussion instruments B. Majors with highest enrollment: business economics, literature, communication.

SPECIAL NOTE FROM THE COLLEGE Convinced that "all truth is God's truth," Wheaton College pursues the integration of biblical Christianity with life in the 20th century. The education at Wheaton is one of high quality and distinction. Approximately 2,200 gifted students foster a climate for learning charged with creative thinking, exhaustive study, and training of high caliber. Combine this with a distinguished and dedicated faculty known for its outstanding teaching and scholarship, and the result is a college committed to an exceptional education "For Christ and His kingdom."

CONTACT Mr. Daniel Crabtree, Director of Admissions, Wheaton College, Wheaton, IL 60187, 708-260-5011 or toll-free 800-222-2419 (out-of-state).

WHITWORTH COLLEGE
Spokane, Washington

Total enrollment: 1,788

UG enrollment: 1,237 (61% W)

Application deadline: 3/1

Tuition & fees: $9090

Room & board: $3425

Entrance: moderately difficult

SAT ≥ 500: 35% V, 48% M

ACT ≥ 21: 63%

Denominational affiliation: Presbyterian

GENERAL INFORMATION Independent comprehensive coed institution. Founded 1890. Awards B, M. Primary accreditation: regional. City setting; 200-acre campus. Total enrollment: 1,788. Faculty: 92 (79 full-time, 13 part-time); 70% of full-time faculty have doctoral degrees; graduate assistants teach a few undergraduate courses. Library holdings: 141,000 bound volumes, 54,250 titles on microform, 810 periodical subscriptions, 1,528 records/tapes. Computer terminals/PCs available for student use: 90, located in computer center, labs.

UNDERGRADUATE PROFILE Fall 1989: 1,237 undergraduates (299 freshmen) from 31 states and territories and 17 foreign countries; 18% part-time; 57% state residents; 25% transfers; 83% financial aid recipients; 61% women; 39% men; 1% blacks; 1% Native Americans; 1% Hispanics; 3% Asian Americans; 3% international students; 15% of undergraduates 25 years of age or older.

1989 FRESHMAN DATA 866 students applied for fall 1989 admission; 87% were accepted; 40% of those accepted enrolled. 28% of freshmen were in top 10% of secondary school class, 57% were in top 25%, 87% were in top half.

ENROLLMENT PATTERNS 75% of fall 1988 freshmen returned for fall 1989 term. 1987–89 average: 41% of entering classes graduated; 35% of students completing a degree program went on for further study.

FRESHMAN ADMISSIONS Options: early decision, deferred entrance. Required: essay, high school transcript, SAT or ACT, TOEFL (for foreign students), WPCT. Recommended: 3 years of high school math and science, some high school foreign language. Required for some: recommendations, interview. Test scores used for admission. Application deadlines: 3/1, 11/30 for early decision. Notification dates: 4/1, 12/15 for early decision. College's own assessment of entrance difficulty level: moderately difficult.

TRANSFER ADMISSIONS Required: essay, college transcript, minimum 2.0 grade point average. Recommended: 3 years of high school math and science, some high school foreign language. Required for some: standardized test scores, high school transcript, recommendations, interview. Application deadline: 4/1. Notification date: continuous until 8/1. College's own assessment of entrance difficulty level: moderately difficult.

EXPENSES (1989–90) Comprehensive fee of $12,515 includes full-time tuition ($8975), mandatory fees ($115), and college room and board ($3425). Part-time tuition per semester (1 to 3 courses) ranges from $650 to $3900 for daytime classes, $300 per course for evening classes.

FINANCIAL AID Fall 1989 full-time freshmen: 95% applied for aid, 88% of those were judged to have need, 100% of those were aided; the average aided freshman received an aid package worth $9491 (46% scholarships/grants, 54% self-help). College-administered aid for all 1989–90 undergraduates: 924 need-based scholarships (average $2325); 97 non-need scholarships (average $1318); low-interest long-term loans from college funds (average $923), from external sources (average $3262); SEOG; College Work-Study; 350 part-time jobs. Supporting data: FAF, institutional form required; IRS required for some; FFS, AFSA/SAR acceptable. Priority application deadline: 2/15.

CAMPUS LIFE/STUDENT SERVICES Drama/theater group; student-run newspaper and radio station. Institution provides health clinic, personal/psychological counseling.

ATHLETICS Member NAIA. Intercollegiate sports: baseball/ softball M; basketball M, W; cross-country running M, W; football M; soccer M, W; swimming and diving M, W; tennis M, W; track and field M, W; volleyball W. Intramural sports: baseball/softball, basketball, equestrian sports, football, rugby, skiing (cross-country), skiing (downhill), table tennis (ping pong), volleyball, water polo.

MAJORS Accounting B; American studies B; art education B; art/fine arts B; art history B; arts administration B; biology/ biological sciences B; business administration/commerce/ management B; chemistry B; communication B; computer science B; creative writing B; (pre)dentistry sequence B; elementary education B; English B; French B; health education B; history B; international business B; international studies B; journalism B; (pre)law sequence B; literature B; mathematics B; (pre)medicine sequence B; music B; music education B; nursing B; peace studies B; philosophy B; physical education B; physics B; political science/ government B; psychology B; religious studies B; secondary education B; sociology B; Spanish B; speech/rhetoric/public address/debate B; studio art B; theater arts/drama B; (pre)veterinary medicine sequence B. Majors with highest enrollment: business administration/commerce/management, elementary education, English.

SPECIAL NOTE FROM THE COLLEGE For a century, Whitworth has dedicated itself to a blend of educational components: rigorous academics, teaching by Christian scholars, deep Christian roots, active residential life, and a commitment to fostering an understanding of other cultures within the nation and the world. Study tours and exchanges provide opportunities for students to visit such countries as France, Germany, Spain, and Thailand. Internships to allow students to gain experience and build contacts in the professional community are encouraged. Whitworth has a clear mission to prepare students for a career and for a life that will be lived to honor God.

CONTACT Mr. John W. Reed, Director of Admissions, Whitworth College, Spokane, WA 99251, 509-466-3212 Ext. 4348 or toll-free 800-533-4668.

WILLIAM JENNINGS BRYAN COLLEGE
Dayton, Tennessee

Total enrollment: 551 (all UG)

Women: 59%

Application deadline: rolling

Tuition & fees: $5270

Room & board: $3200

Entrance: moderately difficult

SAT ≥ 500: 30% V, 36% M

ACT ≥ 21: 52%

Denominational affiliation: interdenominational

GENERAL INFORMATION Independent 4-year coed college. Founded 1930. Awards A (terminal), B. Primary accreditation: regional. Small-town setting; 100-acre campus. Total enrollment: 551. Faculty: 45 (27 full-time, 18 part-time); 68% of full-time faculty have doctoral degrees. Library holdings: 58,968 bound volumes, 280 titles on microform, 350 periodical subscriptions, 3,250 records/tapes. Computer terminals/PCs available for student use: 100, located in computer center, library, dormitories.

UNDERGRADUATE PROFILE Fall 1989: 551 undergraduates (117 freshmen) from 30 states and territories and 11 foreign countries; 29% part-time; 28% state residents; 9% transfers; 85% financial aid recipients; 59% women; 41% men; 2% blacks; 0% Native Americans; 1% Hispanics; 1% Asian Americans; 3% international students; 7% of undergraduates 25 years of age or older.

1989 FRESHMAN DATA 241 students applied for fall 1989 admission; 75% were accepted; 65% of those accepted enrolled.

ENROLLMENT PATTERNS 71% of fall 1988 freshmen returned for fall 1989 term. 1987–89 average: 28% of entering classes graduated.

FRESHMAN ADMISSIONS Options: early entrance, deferred entrance. Required: high school transcript, 3 recommendations, SAT or ACT, TOEFL (for foreign students). Required for some: interview. Test scores used for counseling/placement. Application deadline: rolling. College's own assessment of entrance difficulty level: moderately difficult.

TRANSFER ADMISSIONS Required: high school transcript, 3 recommendations, college transcript, minimum 2.0 grade point average. Required for some: interview. Application deadline: rolling. College's own assessment of entrance difficulty level: moderately difficult.

EXPENSES (1989–90) Comprehensive fee of $8470 includes full-time tuition ($5100), mandatory fees ($170), and college room and board ($3200). College room only: $1400. Part-time tuition: $200 per semester hour.

FINANCIAL AID Fall 1989 full-time freshmen: 92% applied for aid, 79% of those were judged to have need, 100% of those were aided; the average aided freshman received an aid package worth $4600 meeting 95% of need. College-administered aid for all 1989–90 undergraduates: 113 need-based scholarships; 215 non-need scholarships; short-term loans (average $2000); low-interest long-term loans from external sources (average $2400); SEOG; College Work-Study; 90 part-time jobs. Supporting data: FFS, IRS, institutional form required; state form required for some; FAF, AFSA/SAR acceptable. Priority application deadline: 5/1.

CAMPUS LIFE/STUDENT SERVICES Dress code; mandatory chapel; drama/theater group; student-run newspaper. Institution provides health clinic, personal/psychological counseling.

ATHLETICS Member NAIA. Intercollegiate sports: basketball M(s), W(s); soccer M(s); volleyball W(s). Intramural sports: baseball/softball, basketball, football, soccer, tennis, track and field, volleyball.

MAJORS Accounting B; biblical studies B; biology/biological sciences B; business administration/commerce/management A, B; business education B; communication B; elementary education B; English B; history B; mathematics B; music B; music education B; psychology B; religious education B; science education B. Majors with highest enrollment: business administration/commerce/management, psychology, elementary education.

SPECIAL NOTE FROM THE COLLEGE William Jennings Bryan College's mission is to educate servants of Christ for today's world. The College offers the Residence Hall of Tomorrow, an innovative computer network that allows students to access a variety of software programs from the computer in their room. A major in communication arts was initiated in September 1990. More than two thirds of all students at Bryan participate in voluntary Practical Christian Involvement programs. Bryan emphasizes a firm biblical basis within a high-quality academic program.

CONTACT Mrs. Mildred Arnold, Admissions Office Manager, William Jennings Bryan College, Dayton, TN 37321, 615-775-2041 Ext. 204 or toll-free 800-332-7926 (out-of-state).

AMERICAN STUDIES PROGRAM

Students at each of the colleges listed in this guide are eligible and invited to apply for participation in the Christian College Coalition's American Studies Program (ASP), which serves as a Washington campus for the Coalition member colleges.

The American Studies Program, which began in September 1976, provides a variety of work-study opportunities for students from CCC institutions. Based on the principle of integrating faith, learning, and living, students spend time in Washington, D.C., earning academic credit by serving as interns and participating in a contemporary issue-oriented seminar program.

The American Studies Program is designed for juniors and seniors with a wide range of academic majors and vocational interests. Because of its unique location in the nation's capital, the ASP is viewed as a special way of challenging students to consider the meaning of proclaiming the Lordship of Jesus Christ in all areas of life, including career choices, public policy issues, and personal relationships.

During the fall and spring terms, students participating in the American Studies Program are engaged in two principal activities: working as unpaid interns in their intended vocational fields and studying public policy issues in seminar classes. Over 1,200 students have been placed in internships in Congressional offices, executive agencies, legal offices, lobbying and research groups, Christian ministries, social service agencies, cultural institutions, and other businesses throughout Washington; 300 offices have served as internship sites since the Program began.

The Program has had a life-changing impact on its participants, as related by alumni:

I loved the Program because it challenged me to look deeper into beliefs I already had and to explore beliefs I'd never considered, substantiating them through Scripture and faith. Additionally, the responsibilities expected of me on the Program, combined with the job skills I learned in the internship, provided a smoother transition from college to the workplace. (Sharlene Case, spring 1987)

The Program has been enlightening in a variety of ways. Through the internship, I've learned how to be a Christian in a professional setting. In the seminars, I've learned how to apply my Christian faith to the urgent public policy issues of our times. (Keith Williams, fall 1987)

Additional information on the American Studies Program is available from the academic dean's office at any of the colleges listed in this guide or by writing to:

American Studies Program
Christian College Coalition
329 Eighth Street, NE
Washington, D.C. 20002

AU SABLE INSTITUTE OF ENVIRONMENTAL STUDIES

Students from the colleges listed in this guide are eligible for participation in the programs at Au Sable Institute of Environmental Studies. This institution is located in the beautiful northwoods country of Michigan's Lower Peninsula.

Activities at the Institute fall into three main categories: the environmental education center, where over 4,000 kindergarten to twelfth grade students experience and learn about the natural world; retreats and conferences for college, church, and organizational groups; and the college program, in which Coalition college students participate.

The college program focuses on providing an education that will enable students to be knowledgeable caretakers of the environment. Courses cover different aspects of environmental studies, ecology, and stewardship and provide ecological information and experience in both field and laboratory techniques. Vocational certificates for water resources analyst, land resources analyst, environmental analyst, and naturalist are available to those who have completed the required courses and demonstrated proficiency in specific techniques. Students receive their certificate after they get their bachelor's degree.

The college program was designed to support and serve Christian liberal arts colleges. It provides course work that normally is not available at the student's home campus. Classes are small and individualized, and teaching excellence is emphasized.

The campus includes an earth-sheltered classroom and laboratory building, a dining hall, a lodge, an environmental learning center, various recreational facilities, and living accommodations ranging from rustic to modern. With ready access to diverse land and water resources, the Institute is particularly suited to its goals.

Students who seek certification, as well as those who simply wish to take a course at the Institute, enroll through their home college in one or more of the four sessions. January and May terms are 3 weeks long and coincide with periods when many colleges are not meeting for regular classes. Two 5-week summer sessions begin in early June and end by mid-August.

Au Sable financial aid is available to students recommended by their home college. For students at thirty CCC colleges directly affiliated with the Institute, financial aid recommendations go through a designated faculty representative. At other Coalition schools, financial assistance is administered by the Christian College Coalition and the Institute.

For those students interested in teaching or natural history interpretation, Au Sable offers paid internships as part of its environmental education center program. Internships provide students with direct teaching experience in diverse situations.

Additional information on opportunities at Au Sable is available from the academic dean's office at any of the colleges listed in this guide, from the Christian College Coalition, or by contacting:

Au Sable Institute
7526 Sunset Trail, NE
Mancelona, Michigan 49659
616-587-8686

LATIN AMERICAN STUDIES PROGRAM

An opportunity to live and learn in Latin America is available to students from Coalition member colleges through the Latin American Studies Program (LASP). Located in San José, Costa Rica, the Program is committed to helping students examine and live out the Lordship of Jesus Christ in an international context.

Each semester, a group of approximately 20 students is selected to participate in this seminar/service experience in Latin America. The academic program, credit for which is awarded by the student's home institution, involves a combination of learning, serving, and observing.

The learning component includes intensive language study at the Spanish Language Institute in San José. Class assignments are based on previous ability in Spanish. Students practice their language skills with local Costa Ricans, including the host families that provide a home away from home for each LASP student. At the same time, students take part in seminars that deal with such issues as Third World development, Latin American history and culture, and the role of the church. Seminar sessions enable students to interact with outside speakers who bring varying perspectives on current issues.

The serving component involves hands-on experience working in a "servant role" in the Third World. In order to get a better understanding of the complexities of Latin society, students are placed in a variety of service activities—among them education, economic development, and health.

In addition to living with Costa Rican families, students take part in a three-week travel component following the language training and seminar sessions. By visiting Latin American countries outside Costa Rica, students witness the rich diversity of cultures in the cities, villages, and countryside of that area.

Students should have the equivalent of one year of college-level Spanish to apply. Additional information on the Latin American Studies Program is available from the academic dean's office at any of the colleges listed in this guide or by writing to:

Latin American Studies Program
Christian College Coalition
329 Eighth Street, NE
Washington, D.C. 20002

LOS ANGELES FILM STUDIES CENTER

The Christian College Coalition is inaugurating a Los Angeles Film Studies Center with opportunities for student involvement beginning January 1991. This Center, which serves as an extension campus for Coalition institutions, incorporates study programs and internship experiences in the Hollywood area for gifted students from member colleges and universities. Its purpose is to enable its graduates to serve in various aspects of the film industry with professional skill and Christian integrity.

The Hollywood Semester, offered in the fall and spring terms for a full semester of academic credit, centers on a liberal arts exposure to the Hollywood film industry. This unique educational opportunity is limited to juniors and seniors and is geared to multidisciplinary exposure to the complex film industry and to ethical and critical considerations of its workings and products.

Its three academic course offerings will be Inside Hollywood: The Work and Workings of the Film Industry (providing exposure to the creative and operational aspects of the film business by taking full advantage of studio tours, location filming, and a variety of guest lecturers), Ethical Challenges in the Entertainment Industry (an examination of common social and professional ethical problems that arise within the film industry, with special emphasis on the central moral themes of the Christian tradition), and Film in Culture: Exploring a Christian Perspective on the Nature and Influence of Film (a survey of major theoretical approaches to film supplemented by a broad understanding of entertainment and culture).

Students interested in the Hollywood Semester are invited to request additional information from the academic dean's office at any of the colleges listed in this guide or by writing to:

Los Angeles Film Studies Center
Christian College Coalition
329 Eighth Street, NE
Washington, D.C. 20002

DIRECTORIES

This section enables the reader to pinpoint colleges listed in the profiles according to their specific offerings in four areas: major fields of study, intercollegiate athletics, and study-abroad and graduate programs.

Majors Directory 104

This directory lists undergraduate major fields of study offered by the colleges in this book. The majors appear in alphabetical order, each followed by an alphabetical list of the colleges that report offering a program in that field and the degree levels (*A* for associate, *B* for bachelor's) available.

Athletics Directory 120

This directory lists the sports in which colleges report offering intercollegiate athletic programs. An *M* or *W* following a college name indicates that the sport is offered for men or women, respectively. An (*s*) following an *M* or *W* indicates that athletic scholarships (or grants-in-aid) are offered by the college for men or women, respectively, in that sport.

Study-Abroad Directory 123

This directory lists the locations in which Coalition colleges offer foreign study opportunities for credit. Programs followed by an *S* are sponsored by the institution listed; those with a *C* are offered through cooperative arrangements with other institutions or associations. Programs range from a term to a year in length.

Graduate Programs Directory . . . 125

This directory lists the graduate programs offered by the colleges in this book. The programs appear in alphabetical order, each followed by an alphabetical list of the colleges that report offering a program in that field and the degree levels (*M* for master's, *D* for doctoral, *P* for professional, and *O* for other advanced degree) available.

MAJORS DIRECTORY

A—associate degree; B—bachelor's degree

Accounting

Anderson University, IN	B
Asbury College, KY	B
Azusa Pacific University, CA	B
Bartlesville Wesleyan College, OK	A,B
Belhaven College, MS	B
Bethel College, IN	B
Bethel College, KS	B
Bethel College, MN	B
Biola University, CA	B
Calvin College, MI	B
Campbellsville College, KY	B
Campbell University, NC	B
Central Wesleyan College, SC	B
Colorado Christian University, CO	B
Dallas Baptist University, TX	B
Dordt College, IA	B
Eastern College, PA	B
Eastern Mennonite College, VA	B
Evangel College, MO	A,B
Fresno Pacific College, CA	B
Geneva College, PA	B
Gordon College, MA	B
Goshen College, IN	B
Grace College, IN	B
Grand Canyon University, AZ	B
Greenville College, IL	B
Houghton College, NY	B
Huntington College, IN	A,B
Indiana Wesleyan University, IN	A,B
John Brown University, AR	B
Judson College, IL	B
King College, TN	B
King's College, NY	B
Lee College, TN	B
LeTourneau University, TX	B
Malone College, OH	B
Messiah College, PA	B
MidAmerica Nazarene College, KS	B
Milligan College, TN	B
Mississippi College, MS	B
Mount Vernon Nazarene College, OH	B
North Park College, IL	B
Northwestern College, IA	B
Northwestern College, MN	A,B
Northwest Nazarene College, ID	B
Olivet Nazarene University, IL	B
Palm Beach Atlantic College, FL	B
Point Loma Nazarene College, CA	B
Redeemer College, ON	B
Roberts Wesleyan College, NY	B
Seattle Pacific University, WA	B
Sioux Falls College, SD	B
Southern California College, CA	B
Southern Nazarene University, OK	B
Sterling College, KS	B
Tabor College, KS	B
Taylor University, IN	B
Trevecca Nazarene College, TN	B
Trinity Christian College, IL	B
Warner Southern College, FL	B
Whitworth College, WA	B
William Jennings Bryan College, TN	B

Actuarial Science

Tabor College, KS	B

Adult and Continuing Education

Bethel College, MN	B
Nyack College, NY	B
Southern Nazarene University, OK	B

Aerospace Engineering

Eastern Nazarene College, MA	B

Agricultural Business

Bethel College, KS	A
Dordt College, IA	A,B
MidAmerica Nazarene College, KS	A,B
Northwestern College, MN	A
Tabor College, KS	B

Agricultural Sciences

Bethel College, KS	A
Dordt College, IA	B
Eastern Mennonite College, VA	B
MidAmerica Nazarene College, KS	B

Aircraft and Missile Maintenance

LeTourneau University, TX	A

American Studies

Anderson University, IN	B
Eastern College, PA	B
Warner Pacific College, OR	B
Whitworth College, WA	B

Anthropology

Bethel College, MN	B
Biola University, CA	B
Judson College, IL	B
North Park College, IL	B
Olivet Nazarene University, IL	B
Seattle Pacific University, WA	B
Southern California College, CA	B

Applied Art

Azusa Pacific University, CA	B
Mississippi College, MS	B
Northwest Nazarene College, ID	A,B
Sioux Falls College, SD	B

Applied Mathematics

Asbury College, KY	B
Campbell University, NC	B
Geneva College, PA	B
Sioux Falls College, SD	B
Southern Nazarene University, OK	B
Tabor College, KS	B
Trinity Western University, BC	B

Archaeology

Simpson College, CA	B
Wheaton College, IL	B

Art Education

Anderson University, IN	B
Asbury College, KY	B
Bethel College, KS	B
Bethel College, MN	B
Biola University, CA	B
Calvin College, MI	B
Campbellsville College, KY	B
Evangel College, MO	B
Goshen College, IN	B
Grace College, IN	B
Grand Canyon University, AZ	B
Greenville College, IL	B
Houghton College, NY	B
Indiana Wesleyan University, IN	B
Mississippi College, MS	B
Mount Vernon Nazarene College, OH	B
North Park College, IL	B
Northwestern College, IA	B
Northwest Nazarene College, ID	B
Olivet Nazarene University, IL	B
Point Loma Nazarene College, CA	B
Roberts Wesleyan College, NY	B
Seattle Pacific University, WA	B
Sioux Falls College, SD	B
Southern Nazarene University, OK	B
Sterling College, KS	B
Taylor University, IN	B
Wheaton College, IL	B
Whitworth College, WA	B

Art/Fine Arts

Anderson University, IN	B
Asbury College, KY	B
Azusa Pacific University, CA	B
Belhaven College, MS	B
Bethel College, IN	B
Bethel College, KS	B
Bethel College, MN	B
Biola University, CA	B
California Baptist College, CA	B
Calvin College, MI	B
Campbellsville College, KY	B
Campbell University, NC	B
Dallas Baptist University, TX	B
Dordt College, IA	B
Eastern Mennonite College, VA	B
Evangel College, MO	B
Goshen College, IN	B
Grace College, IN	B
Grand Canyon University, AZ	B
Greenville College, IL	B
Houghton College, NY	B
Indiana Wesleyan University, IN	A,B
John Brown University, AR	A
Judson College, IL	B
King College, TN	B
Messiah College, PA	B
Mississippi College, MS	B
Mount Vernon Nazarene College, OH	B
North Park College, IL	B
Northwestern College, MN	B
Northwest Nazarene College, ID	A,B
Olivet Nazarene University, IL	B
Point Loma Nazarene College, CA	B
Redeemer College, ON	B
Roberts Wesleyan College, NY	B
Seattle Pacific University, WA	B
Southern Nazarene University, OK	B
Spring Arbor College, MI	B

Sterling College, KS — B
Taylor University, IN — B
Trinity Christian College, IL — B
Trinity Western University, BC — B
Westmont College, CA — B
Wheaton College, IL — B
Whitworth College, WA — B

Art History

Bethel College, MN — B
Calvin College, MI — B
Eastern College, PA — B
Messiah College, PA — B
Wheaton College, IL — B
Whitworth College, WA — B

Arts Administration

Whitworth College, WA — B

Art Therapy

Biola University, CA — B
Goshen College, IN — B

Automotive Technologies

LeTourneau University, TX — A

Aviation Administration

Geneva College, PA — B

Aviation Technology

LeTourneau University, TX — A,B

Behavioral Sciences

Bartlesville Wesleyan College, OK — A,B
California Baptist College, CA — B
Evangel College, MO — B
Grace College, IN — B
Master's College, CA — B
Messiah College, PA — B
Redeemer College, ON — B
Southern Nazarene University, OK — B
Sterling College, KS — B
Trevecca Nazarene College, TN — B
Westmont College, CA — B

Biblical Languages

Asbury College, KY — B
Azusa Pacific University, CA — B
Gordon College, MA — B
Grace College, IN — B
Redeemer College, ON — B
Seattle Pacific University, WA — B
Southern Nazarene University, OK — B
Wheaton College, IL — B

Biblical Studies

Anderson University, IN — B
Asbury College, KY — B
Azusa Pacific University, CA — B
Belhaven College, MS — B
Bethel College, IN — A
Bethel College, KS — B
Bethel College, MN — B
Biola University, CA — B
Campbellsville College, KY — B
Campbell University, NC — B
Central Wesleyan College, SC — B
Colorado Christian University, CO — A,B
Covenant College, GA — A,B
Dallas Baptist University, TX — B
Eastern College, PA — B
Eastern Mennonite College, VA — A,B

Evangel College, MO — B
Fresno Pacific College, CA — A,B
Geneva College, PA — B
George Fox College, OR — B
Gordon College, MA — B
Goshen College, IN — B
Grace College, IN — B
Grand Canyon University, AZ — B
Greenville College, IL — B
Houghton College, NY — A,B
Huntington College, IN — B
Indiana Wesleyan University, IN — A,B
John Brown University, AR — A,B
Judson College, IL — B
King College, TN — B
King's College, NY — B
Lee College, TN — B
LeTourneau University, TX — B
Master's College, CA — B
Messiah College, PA — B
Milligan College, TN — B
Mississippi College, MS — B
Mount Vernon Nazarene College, OH — B
North Park College, IL — B
Northwest Christian College, OR — A,B
Northwestern College, MN — A,B
Nyack College, NY — B
Olivet Nazarene University, IL — B
Point Loma Nazarene College, CA — B
Redeemer College, ON — B
Seattle Pacific University, WA — B
Simpson College, CA — A,B
Southern California College, CA — B
Southern Nazarene University, OK — B
Tabor College, KS — A,B
Taylor University, IN — B
Trinity College, IL — B
Trinity Western University, BC — B
Warner Pacific College, OR — A,B
Warner Southern College, FL — A,B
Wheaton College, IL — B
William Jennings Bryan College, TN — B

Bilingual/Bicultural Education

Goshen College, IN — B

Biochemistry

Asbury College, KY — B
Biola University, CA — B
Olivet Nazarene University, IL — B
Point Loma Nazarene College, CA — B

Biology/Biological Sciences

Anderson University, IN — B
Asbury College, KY — B
Azusa Pacific University, CA — B
Bartlesville Wesleyan College, OK — A,B
Belhaven College, MS — B
Bethel College, IN — A,B
Bethel College, KS — B
Bethel College, MN — B
Biola University, CA — B
California Baptist College, CA — B
Calvin College, MI — B
Campbellsville College, KY — B
Campbell University, NC — B
Central Wesleyan College, SC — B
Colorado Christian University, CO — B
Covenant College, GA — B
Dallas Baptist University, TX — B
Dordt College, IA — B
Eastern College, PA — B
Eastern Mennonite College, VA — B
Eastern Nazarene College, MA — B
Evangel College, MO — B
Fresno Pacific College, CA — A,B
Geneva College, PA — B
George Fox College, OR — B

Gordon College, MA — B
Goshen College, IN — B
Grace College, IN — B
Grand Canyon University, AZ — B
Greenville College, IL — B
Houghton College, NY — B
Huntington College, IN — B
Indiana Wesleyan University, IN — B
John Brown University, AR — B
Judson College, IL — B
King College, TN — B
King's College, AB — B
King's College, NY — B
Lee College, TN — B
LeTourneau University, TX — B
Malone College, OH — B
Master's College, CA — B
MidAmerica Nazarene College, KS — B
Milligan College, TN — B
Mississippi College, MS — B
Mount Vernon Nazarene College, OH — B
North Park College, IL — B
Northwestern College, IA — B
Northwest Nazarene College, ID — B
Olivet Nazarene University, IL — B
Palm Beach Atlantic College, FL — B
Point Loma Nazarene College, CA — B
Redeemer College, ON — B
Roberts Wesleyan College, NY — B
Seattle Pacific University, WA — B
Sioux Falls College, SD — B
Southern California College, CA — B
Southern Nazarene University, OK — B
Spring Arbor College, MI — B
Sterling College, KS — B
Tabor College, KS — B
Taylor University, IN — B
Trevecca Nazarene College, TN — B
Trinity Christian College, IL — B
Trinity College, IL — B
Trinity Western University, BC — B
Warner Pacific College, OR — B
Warner Southern College, FL — B
Westmont College, CA — B
Wheaton College, IL — B
Whitworth College, WA — B
William Jennings Bryan College, TN — B

Biomedical Engineering

Eastern Nazarene College, MA — B

Biomedical Technologies

Campbell University, NC — B

Biophysics

Olivet Nazarene University, IL — B

Botany/Plant Sciences

Olivet Nazarene University, IL — B
Redeemer College, ON — B

Broadcasting

Anderson University, IN — B
Asbury College, KY — B
Biola University, CA — B
Campbell University, NC — B
Evangel College, MO — A,B
Geneva College, PA — B
George Fox College, OR — B
Goshen College, IN — B
John Brown University, AR — A,B
Malone College, OH — B
Mount Vernon Nazarene College, OH — B
Northwestern College, MN — A,B
Northwest Nazarene College, ID — A
Olivet Nazarene University, IL — B
Southern California College, CA — B

Broadcasting (continued)

Trevecca Nazarene College, TN	A,B
Wheaton College, IL	B

Business Administration/ Commerce/Management

Anderson University, IN	B
Asbury College, KY	B
Azusa Pacific University, CA	B
Bartlesville Wesleyan College, OK	A,B
Belhaven College, MS	B
Bethel College, IN	A,B
Bethel College, KS	B
Bethel College, MN	B
Biola University, CA	B
California Baptist College, CA	B
Calvin College, MI	B
Campbellsville College, KY	A,B
Campbell University, NC	B
Central Wesleyan College, SC	B
Colorado Christian University, CO	B
Covenant College, GA	A,B
Dallas Baptist University, TX	B
Dordt College, IA	B
Eastern College, PA	B
Eastern Mennonite College, VA	B
Eastern Nazarene College, MA	B
Evangel College, MO	B
Fresno Pacific College, CA	A,B
Geneva College, PA	A,B
George Fox College, OR	B
Gordon College, MA	B
Goshen College, IN	B
Grace College, IN	B
Grand Canyon University, AZ	B
Greenville College, IL	B
Houghton College, NY	B
Huntington College, IN	A,B
Indiana Wesleyan University, IN	A,B
John Brown University, AR	B
Judson College, IL	B
King College, TN	B
King's College, NY	B
Lee College, TN	B
LeTourneau University, TX	B
Malone College, OH	B
Master's College, CA	B
Messiah College, PA	B
MidAmerica Nazarene College, KS	A,B
Milligan College, TN	B
Mississippi College, MS	B
Montreat-Anderson College, NC	B
Mount Vernon Nazarene College, OH	A,B
North Park College, IL	B
Northwest Christian College, OR	B
Northwestern College, IA	B
Northwestern College, MN	A,B
Northwest Nazarene College, ID	A,B
Nyack College, NY	B
Olivet Nazarene University, IL	B
Palm Beach Atlantic College, FL	B
Point Loma Nazarene College, CA	B
Redeemer College, ON	B
Roberts Wesleyan College, NY	B
Seattle Pacific University, WA	B
Simpson College, CA	B
Sioux Falls College, SD	A,B
Southern California College, CA	B
Southern Nazarene University, OK	A,B
Spring Arbor College, MI	B
Sterling College, KS	B
Tabor College, KS	B
Taylor University, IN	A,B
Trevecca Nazarene College, TN	B
Trinity Christian College, IL	B
Trinity College, IL	B
Trinity Western University, BC	B
Warner Pacific College, OR	B
Warner Southern College, FL	A,B
Whitworth College, WA	B
William Jennings Bryan College, TN	A,B

Business Economics

Biola University, CA	B
Calvin College, MI	B
Campbellsville College, KY	B
Campbell University, NC	B
Dallas Baptist University, TX	B
George Fox College, OR	B
Gordon College, MA	B
Grand Canyon University, AZ	B
Huntington College, IN	B
King College, TN	B
Olivet Nazarene University, IL	B
Southern Nazarene University, OK	B
Spring Arbor College, MI	B
Westmont College, CA	B
Wheaton College, IL	B

Business Education

Anderson University, IN	B
Bartlesville Wesleyan College, OK	B
Bethel College, IN	B
Bethel College, KS	B
Biola University, CA	B
Campbellsville College, KY	B
Dallas Baptist University, TX	B
Dordt College, IA	B
Evangel College, MO	B
Fresno Pacific College, CA	B
Geneva College, PA	B
Goshen College, IN	B
Grand Canyon University, AZ	B
Greenville College, IL	B
Huntington College, IN	B
John Brown University, AR	B
Lee College, TN	B
MidAmerica Nazarene College, KS	B
Mount Vernon Nazarene College, OH	B
Northwestern College, IA	B
Northwest Nazarene College, ID	B
Olivet Nazarene University, IL	B
Point Loma Nazarene College, CA	B
Southern Nazarene University, OK	B
Sterling College, KS	B
Tabor College, KS	B
Trevecca Nazarene College, TN	B
Trinity Christian College, IL	B
William Jennings Bryan College, TN	B

Business Machine Technologies

Biola University, CA	B

Ceramic Art and Design

Bethel College, KS	B

Chemical Engineering

Geneva College, PA	B

Chemical Engineering Technology

Northwest Nazarene College, ID	A

Chemistry

Anderson University, IN	B
Asbury College, KY	B
Azusa Pacific University, CA	B
Bartlesville Wesleyan College, OK	A,B
Belhaven College, MS	B
Bethel College, IN	A,B
Bethel College, KS	B
Bethel College, MN	B
Biola University, CA	B
Calvin College, MI	B
Campbellsville College, KY	B

Campbell University, NC	B
Central Wesleyan College, SC	B
Covenant College, GA	B
Dordt College, IA	B
Eastern College, PA	B
Eastern Mennonite College, VA	B
Eastern Nazarene College, MA	B
Evangel College, MO	B
Geneva College, PA	B
George Fox College, OR	B
Gordon College, MA	B
Goshen College, IN	B
Grand Canyon University, AZ	B
Greenville College, IL	B
Houghton College, NY	B
Huntington College, IN	B
Indiana Wesleyan University, IN	B
John Brown University, AR	B
Judson College, IL	B
King College, TN	B
King's College, NY	B
King's College, AB	B
Lee College, TN	B
LeTourneau University, TX	B
Malone College, OH	B
Messiah College, PA	B
MidAmerica Nazarene College, KS	B
Milligan College, TN	B
Mississippi College, MS	B
Mount Vernon Nazarene College, OH	B
North Park College, IL	B
Northwestern College, IA	B
Northwest Nazarene College, ID	A,B
Olivet Nazarene University, IL	B
Point Loma Nazarene College, CA	B
Roberts Wesleyan College, NY	B
Seattle Pacific University, WA	B
Sioux Falls College, SD	B
Southern California College, CA	B
Southern Nazarene University, OK	B
Spring Arbor College, MI	B
Sterling College, KS	B
Tabor College, KS	B
Taylor University, IN	B
Trevecca Nazarene College, TN	B
Trinity Christian College, IL	B
Trinity College, IL	B
Trinity Western University, BC	B
Westmont College, CA	B
Wheaton College, IL	B
Whitworth College, WA	B

Child Care/Child and Family Studies

Anderson University, IN	B
Bethel College, MN	B
Campbell University, NC	B
Evangel College, MO	A
Goshen College, IN	B
Montreat-Anderson College, NC	B
Olivet Nazarene University, IL	B
Southern Nazarene University, OK	A,B
Sterling College, KS	B
Trevecca Nazarene College, TN	A

Child Psychology/Child Development

Bethel College, MN	B
Fresno Pacific College, CA	A,B
Point Loma Nazarene College, CA	B
Sioux Falls College, SD	A
Southern Nazarene University, OK	B

Civil Engineering

Calvin College, MI	B
Geneva College, PA	B
George Fox College, OR	B

Civil Engineering Technology

Messiah College, PA	B

Classics

Belhaven College, MS	B
Calvin College, MI	B
Redeemer College, ON	B
Wheaton College, IL	B

Clinical Psychology

Messiah College, PA	B
Redeemer College, ON	B

Commercial Art

Bethel College, IN	A,B
Grace College, IN	B
Northwestern College, MN	A,B
Sioux Falls College, SD	B
Southern Nazarene University, OK	A

Communication

Anderson University, IN	B
Azusa Pacific University, CA	B
Bethel College, IN	B
Bethel College, KS	B
Bethel College, MN	B
Biola University, CA	B
California Baptist College, CA	B
Calvin College, MI	B
Campbellsville College, KY	B
Campbell University, NC	B
Colorado Christian University, CO	B
Dallas Baptist University, TX	B
Dordt College, IA	B
Eastern College, PA	B
Eastern Nazarene College, MA	B
Evangel College, MO	A,B
Fresno Pacific College, CA	A,B
Geneva College, PA	B
George Fox College, OR	B
Goshen College, IN	B
Grace College, IN	B
Grand Canyon University, AZ	B
Greenville College, IL	B
Houghton College, NY	B
Huntington College, IN	B
Judson College, IL	B
Lee College, TN	B
Malone College, OH	B
Master's College, CA	B
Messiah College, PA	B
Milligan College, TN	B
Mississippi College, MS	B
Mount Vernon Nazarene College, OH	B
North Park College, IL	B
Northwest Christian College, OR	B
Northwestern College, IA	B
Northwestern College, MN	B
Olivet Nazarene University, IL	B
Point Loma Nazarene College, CA	B
Roberts Wesleyan College, NY	B
Seattle Pacific University, WA	B
Simpson College, CA	B
Sioux Falls College, SD	B
Southern California College, CA	B
Southern Nazarene University, OK	B
Spring Arbor College, MI	B
Sterling College, KS	B
Taylor University, IN	B
Trevecca Nazarene College, TN	B
Trinity College, IL	B
Trinity Western University, BC	B
Warner Southern College, FL	B
Westmont College, CA	B
Wheaton College, IL	B
Whitworth College, WA	B
William Jennings Bryan College, TN	B

Community Services

Eastern Mennonite College, VA	B
North Park College, IL	B

Computer Engineering

Eastern Nazarene College, MA	B
George Fox College, OR	B
LeTourneau University, TX	B

Computer Information Systems

Azusa Pacific University, CA	B
Bartlesville Wesleyan College, OK	A,B
Biola University, CA	B
Campbellsville College, KY	A,B
Campbell University, NC	B
Colorado Christian University, CO	A,B
Eastern Mennonite College, VA	B
Eastern Nazarene College, MA	B
George Fox College, OR	B
Goshen College, IN	B
Indiana Wesleyan University, IN	A,B
Judson College, IL	B
Lee College, TN	B
Messiah College, PA	B
Northwestern College, MN	A,B
Northwest Nazarene College, ID	B
Olivet Nazarene University, IL	B
Point Loma Nazarene College, CA	B
Sioux Falls College, SD	B
Southern Nazarene University, OK	B
Trevecca Nazarene College, TN	A,B
Trinity College, IL	B

Computer Programming

Biola University, CA	B
Eastern Mennonite College, VA	A
Northwest Nazarene College, ID	A
Southern Nazarene University, OK	B

Computer Science

Anderson University, IN	B
Asbury College, KY	B
Azusa Pacific University, CA	B
Bethel College, IN	A,B
Bethel College, KS	B
Bethel College, MN	B
Biola University, CA	B
Calvin College, MI	B
Covenant College, GA	B
Dallas Baptist University, TX	B
Dordt College, IA	B
Eastern Mennonite College, VA	B
Eastern Nazarene College, MA	B
Evangel College, MO	B
Geneva College, PA	B
George Fox College, OR	B
Gordon College, MA	B
Goshen College, IN	B
Grace College, IN	B
Grand Canyon University, AZ	B
Greenville College, IL	B
Houghton College, NY	B
Huntington College, IN	A,B
Judson College, IL	B
King's College, NY	B
LeTourneau University, TX	B
Malone College, OH	B
Messiah College, PA	B
MidAmerica Nazarene College, KS	B
Milligan College, TN	B
Mississippi College, MS	B
Mount Vernon Nazarene College, OH	B
North Park College, IL	B
Northwestern College, IA	B
Northwest Nazarene College, ID	B
Olivet Nazarene University, IL	B
Point Loma Nazarene College, CA	B

Roberts Wesleyan College, NY	B
Seattle Pacific University, WA	B
Sioux Falls College, SD	B
Southern Nazarene University, OK	A,B
Spring Arbor College, MI	B
Sterling College, KS	B
Tabor College, KS	A,B
Taylor University, IN	B
Trevecca Nazarene College, TN	A,B
Trinity Christian College, IL	B
Trinity College, IL	B
Trinity Western University, BC	B
Westmont College, CA	B
Wheaton College, IL	B
Whitworth College, WA	B

Computer Technologies

LeTourneau University, TX	B
Mount Vernon Nazarene College, OH	A

Construction Engineering

John Brown University, AR	B

Construction Management

John Brown University, AR	A,B

Creative Writing

Bethel College, MN	B
Eastern College, PA	B
Houghton College, NY	B
Indiana Wesleyan University, IN	B
Whitworth College, WA	B

Criminal Justice

Anderson University, IN	A,B
Calvin College, MI	B
Campbellsville College, KY	A
Dallas Baptist University, TX	B
Grace College, IN	B
Grand Canyon University, AZ	B
Indiana Wesleyan University, IN	A,B
Mississippi College, MS	B
Mount Vernon Nazarene College, OH	B
Northwestern College, IA	B
Olivet Nazarene University, IL	B
Roberts Wesleyan College, NY	B
Southern Nazarene University, OK	B

Data Processing

Campbellsville College, KY	A
Campbell University, NC	B
Eastern Mennonite College, VA	A
Mississippi College, MS	B
Mount Vernon Nazarene College, OH	A,B
Northwest Nazarene College, ID	A
Southern Nazarene University, OK	B

Deaf Interpreter Training

Dallas Baptist University, TX	B

(Pre)Dentistry Sequence

Anderson University, IN	B
Azusa Pacific University, CA	B
Belhaven College, MS	B
Bethel College, KS	B
Bethel College, MN	B
Calvin College, MI	B
Campbellsville College, KY	B
Campbell University, NC	B
Dallas Baptist University, TX	B
Dordt College, IA	B
Eastern College, PA	B
Eastern Mennonite College, VA	B
Eastern Nazarene College, MA	B

(Pre)Dentistry Sequence (continued)

Evangel College, MO	B
George Fox College, OR	B
Goshen College, IN	B
Grand Canyon University, AZ	B
Greenville College, IL	B
Houghton College, NY	B
Huntington College, IN	B
Indiana Wesleyan University, IN	B
King College, TN	B
LeTourneau University, TX	B
Malone College, OH	B
Milligan College, TN	B
Mississippi College, MS	B
Mount Vernon Nazarene College, OH	B
North Park College, IL	B
Northwestern College, IA	B
Northwest Nazarene College, ID	B
Olivet Nazarene University, IL	B
Palm Beach Atlantic College, FL	B
Point Loma Nazarene College, CA	B
Redeemer College, ON	B
Roberts Wesleyan College, NY	B
Sioux Falls College, SD	B
Southern Nazarene University, OK	B
Sterling College, KS	B
Tabor College, KS	B
Taylor University, IN	B
Trinity Christian College, IL	B
Trinity Western University, BC	B
Westmont College, CA	B
Wheaton College, IL	B
Whitworth College, WA	B

Dietetics

Eastern Mennonite College, VA	B
Goshen College, IN	B
Messiah College, PA	B
Olivet Nazarene University, IL	A,B

Drafting and Design

LeTourneau University, TX	A

Early Childhood Education

Anderson University, IN	A
Bethel College, IN	A
Bethel College, KS	B
Bethel College, MN	B
Campbell University, NC	B
Central Wesleyan College, SC	B
Dallas Baptist University, TX	B
Eastern Mennonite College, VA	B
Eastern Nazarene College, MA	A,B
Evangel College, MO	B
Gordon College, MA	B
Goshen College, IN	B
Greenville College, IL	B
Houghton College, NY	B
John Brown University, AR	B
Malone College, OH	A
Messiah College, PA	B
MidAmerica Nazarene College, KS	A,B
Milligan College, TN	B
Mississippi College, MS	B
Mount Vernon Nazarene College, OH	A,B
North Park College, IL	B
Northwestern College, IA	B
Nyack College, NY	A
Olivet Nazarene University, IL	B
Point Loma Nazarene College, CA	B
Sioux Falls College, SD	A
Southern Nazarene University, OK	B
Spring Arbor College, MI	B
Taylor University, IN	A
Trevecca Nazarene College, TN	B
Warner Southern College, FL	B

Earth Science

Campbell University, NC	B
Olivet Nazarene University, IL	B

Ecology/Environmental Studies

Anderson University, IN	B
Calvin College, MI	B
Seattle Pacific University, WA	B

Economics

Anderson University, IN	B
Bethel College, KS	B
Bethel College, MN	B
Biola University, CA	B
Calvin College, MI	B
Campbellsville College, KY	B
Campbell University, NC	B
Dallas Baptist University, TX	B
Eastern College, PA	B
Geneva College, PA	B
George Fox College, OR	B
Gordon College, MA	B
Goshen College, IN	B
Grand Canyon University, AZ	B
Greenville College, IL	B
Huntington College, IN	B
Indiana Wesleyan University, IN	B
King College, TN	B
Mississippi College, MS	B
North Park College, IL	B
Northwestern College, IA	B
Olivet Nazarene University, IL	B
Point Loma Nazarene College, CA	B
Seattle Pacific University, WA	B
Southern Nazarene University, OK	B
Taylor University, IN	B
Trinity College, IL	B
Westmont College, CA	B
Wheaton College, IL	B

Education

Anderson University, IN	B
Asbury College, KY	B
Azusa Pacific University, CA	B
Bartlesville Wesleyan College, OK	B
Bethel College, IN	B
Bethel College, KS	B
Bethel College, MN	B
Biola University, CA	B
California Baptist College, CA	B
Calvin College, MI	B
Campbell University, NC	B
Central Wesleyan College, SC	B
Dallas Baptist University, TX	B
Dordt College, IA	B
Eastern Mennonite College, VA	A,B
Eastern Nazarene College, MA	B
Evangel College, MO	A,B
Fresno Pacific College, CA	B
Geneva College, PA	B
George Fox College, OR	B
Gordon College, MA	B
Goshen College, IN	B
Greenville College, IL	B
Houghton College, NY	B
Huntington College, IN	B
Indiana Wesleyan University, IN	B
John Brown University, AR	B
Judson College, IL	B
King College, TN	B
Lee College, TN	B
Malone College, OH	B
Master's College, CA	B
Messiah College, PA	B
Mississippi College, MS	B
Mount Vernon Nazarene College, OH	B
North Park College, IL	B
Northwestern College, IA	B

Northwestern College, MN	B
Nyack College, NY	A
Olivet Nazarene University, IL	B
Palm Beach Atlantic College, FL	B
Redeemer College, ON	B
Roberts Wesleyan College, NY	B
Seattle Pacific University, WA	B
Simpson College, CA	B
Sioux Falls College, SD	B
Southern California College, CA	B
Southern Nazarene University, OK	B
Spring Arbor College, MI	B
Sterling College, KS	B
Tabor College, KS	B
Taylor University, IN	B
Trevecca Nazarene College, TN	B
Trinity Christian College, IL	B
Trinity College, IL	B
Trinity Western University, BC	B
Westmont College, CA	B

Educational Administration

Campbell University, NC	B

Educational Media

Seattle Pacific University, WA	B

Electrical Engineering

Calvin College, MI	B
Dordt College, IA	B
Eastern Nazarene College, MA	B
Geneva College, PA	B
George Fox College, OR	B
John Brown University, AR	B
LeTourneau University, TX	B
Seattle Pacific University, WA	B

Electrical Engineering Technology

LeTourneau University, TX	B

Elementary Education

Anderson University, IN	B
Asbury College, KY	B
Bartlesville Wesleyan College, OK	B
Belhaven College, MS	B
Bethel College, IN	B
Bethel College, KS	B
Bethel College, MN	B
Biola University, CA	B
California Baptist College, CA	B
Calvin College, MI	B
Campbellsville College, KY	B
Campbell University, NC	B
Central Wesleyan College, SC	B
Colorado Christian University, CO	B
Covenant College, GA	B
Dallas Baptist University, TX	B
Dordt College, IA	B
Eastern College, PA	B
Eastern Mennonite College, VA	B
Eastern Nazarene College, MA	B
Evangel College, MO	B
Fresno Pacific College, CA	B
Geneva College, PA	B
George Fox College, OR	B
Gordon College, MA	B
Goshen College, IN	B
Grace College, IN	B
Grand Canyon University, AZ	B
Greenville College, IL	B
Houghton College, NY	B
Huntington College, IN	B
Indiana Wesleyan University, IN	B
John Brown University, AR	B
Judson College, IL	B
King College, TN	B

King's College, NY	B
Lee College, TN	B
Malone College, OH	B
Master's College, CA	B
Messiah College, PA	B
MidAmerica Nazarene College, KS	B
Milligan College, TN	B
Mississippi College, MS	B
Mount Vernon Nazarene College, OH	B
North Park College, IL	B
Northwestern College, IA	B
Northwestern College, MN	B
Northwest Nazarene College, ID	B
Nyack College, NY	B
Olivet Nazarene University, IL	B
Palm Beach Atlantic College, FL	B
Redeemer College, ON	B
Roberts Wesleyan College, NY	B
Simpson College, CA	B
Sioux Falls College, SD	B
Southern California College, CA	B
Southern Nazarene University, OK	B
Spring Arbor College, MI	B
Sterling College, KS	B
Tabor College, KS	B
Taylor University, IN	B
Trevecca Nazarene College, TN	B
Trinity Christian College, IL	B
Trinity College, IL	B
Trinity Western University, BC	B
Warner Southern College, FL	B
Westmont College, CA	B
Wheaton College, IL	B
Whitworth College, WA	B
William Jennings Bryan College, TN	B

Engineering (General)

Bethel College, IN	B
Calvin College, MI	B
Dordt College, IA	B
Geneva College, PA	A,B
George Fox College, OR	B
John Brown University, AR	B
LeTourneau University, TX	B
Taylor University, IN	B
Westmont College, CA	B

Engineering and Applied Sciences

Dallas Baptist University, TX	B

Engineering Mechanics

Dordt College, IA	B

Engineering Physics

Eastern Nazarene College, MA	B
Northwest Nazarene College, ID	B
Olivet Nazarene University, IL	B
Point Loma Nazarene College, CA	B
Westmont College, CA	B

Engineering Sciences

George Fox College, OR	B
Olivet Nazarene University, IL	B
Seattle Pacific University, WA	B

(Pre)Engineering Sequence

Anderson University, IN	A
Bethel College, KS	A
Bethel College, MN	A
Campbellsville College, KY	A
Eastern Mennonite College, VA	A
Houghton College, NY	A
Huntington College, IN	A
Indiana Wesleyan University, IN	A
Malone College, OH	A

Mount Vernon Nazarene College, OH	A
Northwestern College, MN	A
Northwest Nazarene College, ID	A
Sioux Falls College, SD	A
Southern Nazarene University, OK	A
Tabor College, KS	A
Trevecca Nazarene College, TN	A

Engineering Technology

John Brown University, AR	A
LeTourneau University, TX	B

English

Anderson University, IN	B
Asbury College, KY	B
Azusa Pacific University, CA	B
Bartlesville Wesleyan College, OK	B
Belhaven College, MS	B
Bethel College, IN	B
Bethel College, KS	B
Bethel College, MN	B
Biola University, CA	B
California Baptist College, CA	B
Calvin College, MI	B
Campbellsville College, KY	B
Campbell University, NC	B
Central Wesleyan College, SC	B
Colorado Christian University, CO	B
Covenant College, GA	B
Dallas Baptist University, TX	B
Dordt College, IA	B
Eastern Mennonite College, VA	B
Eastern Nazarene College, MA	B
Evangel College, MO	B
Fresno Pacific College, CA	A,B
Geneva College, PA	B
George Fox College, OR	B
Gordon College, MA	B
Goshen College, IN	B
Grace College, IN	B
Grand Canyon University, AZ	B
Greenville College, IL	B
Houghton College, NY	B
Huntington College, IN	B
Indiana Wesleyan University, IN	A,B
John Brown University, AR	B
Judson College, IL	B
King College, TN	B
King's College, NY	B
King's College, AB	B
Lee College, TN	B
LeTourneau University, TX	B
Malone College, OH	B
Master's College, CA	B
Messiah College, PA	B
MidAmerica Nazarene College, KS	B
Milligan College, TN	B
Mississippi College, MS	B
Montreat-Anderson College, NC	B
Mount Vernon Nazarene College, OH	B
North Park College, IL	B
Northwestern College, IA	B
Northwestern College, MN	B
Northwest Nazarene College, ID	B
Nyack College, NY	B
Olivet Nazarene University, IL	B
Palm Beach Atlantic College, FL	B
Point Loma Nazarene College, CA	B
Redeemer College, ON	B
Roberts Wesleyan College, NY	B
Seattle Pacific University, WA	B
Simpson College, CA	B
Sioux Falls College, SD	B
Southern California College, CA	B
Southern Nazarene University, OK	B
Spring Arbor College, MI	B
Sterling College, KS	B
Tabor College, KS	B
Taylor University, IN	B
Trevecca Nazarene College, TN	B
Trinity Christian College, IL	B

Trinity College, IL	B
Trinity Western University, BC	B
Warner Pacific College, OR	B
Warner Southern College, FL	B
Westmont College, CA	B
Whitworth College, WA	B
William Jennings Bryan College, TN	B

Environmental Biology

Grand Canyon University, AZ	B
Tabor College, KS	B

Environmental Sciences

Anderson University, IN	B
Bethel College, KS	B
Calvin College, MI	B
Dordt College, IA	B
Seattle Pacific University, WA	B

European Studies

Biola University, CA	B
Calvin College, MI	B
Seattle Pacific University, WA	B

Experimental Psychology

Messiah College, PA	B

Family Services

Goshen College, IN	B
Messiah College, PA	B
Northwest Nazarene College, ID	A
Olivet Nazarene University, IL	B
Southern Nazarene University, OK	B

Fashion Merchandising

Bethel College, KS	B
Campbell University, NC	B
Olivet Nazarene University, IL	B
Southern Nazarene University, OK	A,B

Film Studies

Biola University, CA	B

Finance/Banking

Belhaven College, MS	B
Bethel College, MN	B
Campbell University, NC	B
Dallas Baptist University, TX	B
Grand Canyon University, AZ	B
North Park College, IL	B
Olivet Nazarene University, IL	B
Seattle Pacific University, WA	B
Southern California College, CA	B

Flight Training

LeTourneau University, TX	B
Southern Nazarene University, OK	B
Trinity Western University, BC	B

Food Sciences

Olivet Nazarene University, IL	B

Food Services Management

Campbell University, NC	B
Eastern Mennonite College, VA	B
Olivet Nazarene University, IL	B

French

Anderson University, IN	B
Asbury College, KY	B

French (continued)

Calvin College, MI	
Campbell University, NC	B
Eastern College, PA	B
Eastern Mennonite College, VA	B
Eastern Nazarene College, MA	B
Gordon College, MA	B
Grace College, IN	B
Greenville College, IL	B
Houghton College, NY	B
Messiah College, PA	B
North Park College, IL	B
Northwestern College, IA	B
Redeemer College, ON	B
Spring Arbor College, MI	B
Taylor University, IN	B
Westmont College, CA	B
Wheaton College, IL	B
Whitworth College, WA	B

Geochemistry

Olivet Nazarene University, IL	B

Geography

Messiah College, PA	B
Trinity Western University, BC	B

Geology

Calvin College, MI	B
Olivet Nazarene University, IL	B
Wheaton College, IL	B

Geophysics

Olivet Nazarene University, IL	B

German

Anderson University, IN	B
Bethel College, KS	B
Calvin College, MI	B
Dordt College, IA	B
Eastern Mennonite College, VA	B
Gordon College, MA	B
Goshen College, IN	B
Grace College, IN	B
Messiah College, PA	B
North Park College, IL	B
Wheaton College, IL	B

Germanic Languages and Literature

Calvin College, MI	B

Gerontology

Bethel College, IN	A
Greenville College, IL	B
Roberts Wesleyan College, NY	B
Southern Nazarene University, OK	B

Graphic Arts

Anderson University, IN	B
Northwest Nazarene College, ID	A
Point Loma Nazarene College, CA	B
Roberts Wesleyan College, NY	B

Greek

Belhaven College, MS	B
Biola University, CA	B
Calvin College, MI	B

Central Wesleyan College, SC	B
Grace College, IN	B

Guidance and Counseling

Geneva College, PA	B

Health Education

Bethel College, KS	B
Bethel College, MN	B
Campbellsville College, KY	B
Campbell University, NC	B
John Brown University, AR	B
Lee College, TN	B
Malone College, OH	B
Milligan College, TN	B
Mississippi College, MS	B
Northwest Nazarene College, ID	B
Sioux Falls College, SD	B
Southern Nazarene University, OK	B
Tabor College, KS	B
Trevecca Nazarene College, TN	B
Whitworth College, WA	B

Health Science

Campbell University, NC	B
Covenant College, GA	A
Malone College, OH	B
Mount Vernon Nazarene College, OH	A
Northwest Nazarene College, ID	A
Southern Nazarene University, OK	A

Health Services Administration

Eastern College, PA	B
Milligan College, TN	B

Hispanic Studies

Goshen College, IN	B

History

Anderson University, IN	B
Asbury College, KY	B
Azusa Pacific University, CA	B
Bartlesville Wesleyan College, OK	B
Belhaven College, MS	B
Bethel College, KS	B
Bethel College, MN	B
Biola University, CA	B
California Baptist College, CA	B
Calvin College, MI	B
Campbellsville College, KY	B
Campbell University, NC	B
Central Wesleyan College, SC	B
Colorado Christian University, CO	B
Covenant College, GA	B
Dallas Baptist University, TX	B
Dordt College, IA	B
Eastern College, PA	B
Eastern Mennonite College, VA	B
Eastern Nazarene College, MA	B
Evangel College, MO	B
Fresno Pacific College, CA	A,B
Geneva College, PA	B
George Fox College, OR	B
Gordon College, MA	B
Goshen College, IN	B
Grace College, IN	B
Grand Canyon University, AZ	B
Greenville College, IL	B
Houghton College, NY	B
Huntington College, IN	B
Indiana Wesleyan University, IN	B
John Brown University, AR	B
Judson College, IL	B
King College, TN	B
King's College, NY	B

King's College, AB	B
Lee College, TN	B
LeTourneau University, TX	B
Malone College, OH	B
Master's College, CA	B
Messiah College, PA	B
MidAmerica Nazarene College, KS	B
Milligan College, TN	B
Mississippi College, MS	B
Montreat-Anderson College, NC	B
Mount Vernon Nazarene College, OH	B
North Park College, IL	B
Northwestern College, IA	B
Northwestern College, MN	B
Northwest Nazarene College, ID	B
Nyack College, NY	B
Olivet Nazarene University, IL	B
Palm Beach Atlantic College, FL	B
Point Loma Nazarene College, CA	B
Redeemer College, ON	B
Roberts Wesleyan College, NY	B
Seattle Pacific University, WA	B
Simpson College, CA	B
Sioux Falls College, SD	B
Southern California College, CA	B
Southern Nazarene University, OK	B
Spring Arbor College, MI	B
Sterling College, KS	B
Tabor College, KS	B
Taylor University, IN	B
Trevecca Nazarene College, TN	B
Trinity Christian College, IL	B
Trinity College, IL	B
Trinity Western University, BC	B
Warner Pacific College, OR	B
Westmont College, CA	B
Wheaton College, IL	B
Whitworth College, WA	B
William Jennings Bryan College, TN	B

Home Economics

Bethel College, KS	B
Campbell University, NC	B
George Fox College, OR	B
Master's College, CA	B
Messiah College, PA	B
Mississippi College, MS	B
Mount Vernon Nazarene College, OH	A,B
Northwest Nazarene College, ID	A,B
Olivet Nazarene University, IL	B
Point Loma Nazarene College, CA	B
Seattle Pacific University, WA	B
Southern Nazarene University, OK	B
Sterling College, KS	B

Home Economics Education

Bethel College, KS	B
Campbell University, NC	B
George Fox College, OR	B
Mississippi College, MS	B
Mount Vernon Nazarene College, OH	B
Northwest Nazarene College, ID	B
Olivet Nazarene University, IL	B
Point Loma Nazarene College, CA	B
Seattle Pacific University, WA	B
Southern Nazarene University, OK	B
Sterling College, KS	B

Human Development

MidAmerica Nazarene College, KS	B
Warner Pacific College, OR	B

Humanities

Belhaven College, MS	B
Biola University, CA	B
Calvin College, MI	B
Colorado Christian University, CO	B
Fresno Pacific College, CA	B
Houghton College, NY	B

Messiah College, PA	B
Milligan College, TN	B
Mount Vernon Nazarene College, OH	B
Northwestern College, IA	B
Redeemer College, ON	B
Roberts Wesleyan College, NY	B
Sioux Falls College, SD	A
Southern California College, CA	B
Tabor College, KS	B
Trevecca Nazarene College, TN	B
Trinity College, IL	B
Trinity Western University, BC	B

Human Resources

George Fox College, OR	B
Grand Canyon University, AZ	B
Messiah College, PA	B
MidAmerica Nazarene College, KS	B
Northwestern College, MN	B
Roberts Wesleyan College, NY	B
Southern Nazarene University, OK	B
Trevecca Nazarene College, TN	B

Human Services

Asbury College, KY	B
Colorado Christian University, CO	B
Milligan College, TN	B
Mount Vernon Nazarene College, OH	A
Trinity Western University, BC	B

Industrial Administration

LeTourneau University, TX	B

Industrial Arts

Bethel College, KS	A,B
Trinity Christian College, IL	B

Industrial Engineering

Geneva College, PA	B

Information Science

Southern Nazarene University, OK	B

Interdisciplinary Studies

Bethel College, KS	B
Covenant College, GA	B
Dallas Baptist University, TX	B
George Fox College, OR	B
John Brown University, AR	B
Northwest Christian College, OR	B
Nyack College, NY	B
Olivet Nazarene University, IL	B
Seattle Pacific University, WA	B
Sioux Falls College, SD	A,B
Wheaton College, IL	B

Interior Design

Bethel College, KS	B
Campbell University, NC	B
Mississippi College, MS	B
Southern Nazarene University, OK	A,B

International Business

Grand Canyon University, AZ	B
King College, TN	B
MidAmerica Nazarene College, KS	B
North Park College, IL	B
Whitworth College, WA	B

International Studies

Asbury College, KY	B
Azusa Pacific University, CA	B

Bethel College, KS	B
Bethel College, MN	B
Biola University, CA	B
George Fox College, OR	B
Montreat-Anderson College, NC	B
North Park College, IL	B
Northwest Nazarene College, ID	B
Simpson College, CA	B
Southern Nazarene University, OK	B
Tabor College, KS	B
Warner Southern College, FL	B
Whitworth College, WA	B

Journalism

Anderson University, IN	B
Asbury College, KY	B
Bethel College, IN	A
Biola University, CA	B
Campbell University, NC	B
Dordt College, IA	B
Evangel College, MO	A,B
Geneva College, PA	B
Goshen College, IN	B
John Brown University, AR	A,B
Malone College, OH	B
Messiah College, PA	B
Mississippi College, MS	B
Northwestern College, MN	B
Olivet Nazarene University, IL	B
Point Loma Nazarene College, CA	B
Southern California College, CA	B
Southern Nazarene University, OK	B
Wheaton College, IL	B
Whitworth College, WA	B

Laboratory Technologies

Evangel College, MO	A
Southern Nazarene University, OK	A

Latin

Belhaven College, MS	B
Calvin College, MI	B

Latin American Studies

Geneva College, PA	B

Law Enforcement/Police Sciences

Indiana Wesleyan University, IN	A
Mississippi College, MS	B

(Pre)Law Sequence

Anderson University, IN	B
Azusa Pacific University, CA	B
Bethel College, KS	B
Bethel College, MN	B
Calvin College, MI	B
Campbellsville College, KY	B
Campbell University, NC	B
Covenant College, GA	B
Dallas Baptist University, TX	B
Eastern Mennonite College, VA	B
Eastern Nazarene College, MA	B
Evangel College, MO	B
Fresno Pacific College, CA	B
Geneva College, PA	B
George Fox College, OR	B
Gordon College, MA	B
Goshen College, IN	B
Grace College, IN	B
Grand Canyon University, AZ	B
Greenville College, IL	B
Houghton College, NY	B
Huntington College, IN	B
Indiana Wesleyan University, IN	B

Judson College, IL	B
King College, TN	B
LeTourneau University, TX	B
Malone College, OH	B
Messiah College, PA	B
Mississippi College, MS	B
Mount Vernon Nazarene College, OH	B
North Park College, IL	B
Northwestern College, IA	B
Northwest Nazarene College, ID	B
Olivet Nazarene University, IL	B
Palm Beach Atlantic College, FL	B
Point Loma Nazarene College, CA	B
Redeemer College, ON	B
Southern California College, CA	B
Southern Nazarene University, OK	B
Sterling College, KS	B
Tabor College, KS	B
Taylor University, IN	B
Trevecca Nazarene College, TN	B
Trinity Western University, BC	B
Westmont College, CA	B
Wheaton College, IL	B
Whitworth College, WA	B

Legal Secretarial Studies

Northwestern College, MN	A
Tabor College, KS	B

Liberal Arts/General Studies

Azusa Pacific University, CA	A,B
Bartlesville Wesleyan College, OK	A
Belhaven College, MS	B
Bethel College, IN	A,B
Bethel College, KS	A,B
Bethel College, MN	A
Biola University, CA	B
California Baptist College, CA	B
Calvin College, MI	B
Campbell University, NC	A
Colorado Christian University, CO	A,B
Dallas Baptist University, TX	B
Eastern Mennonite College, VA	A,B
Eastern Nazarene College, MA	A
Fresno Pacific College, CA	A,B
George Fox College, OR	B
Goshen College, IN	B
Grand Canyon University, AZ	B
Greenville College, IL	B
Indiana Wesleyan University, IN	A,B
John Brown University, AR	A
King's College, NY	A
Malone College, OH	B
Master's College, CA	B
Messiah College, PA	B
MidAmerica Nazarene College, KS	A
Montreat-Anderson College, NC	A,B
Mount Vernon Nazarene College, OH	A
Northwest Christian College, OR	A
Northwestern College, MN	A
Nyack College, NY	A
Olivet Nazarene University, IL	B
Point Loma Nazarene College, CA	B
Redeemer College, ON	B
Seattle Pacific University, WA	B
Simpson College, CA	B
Southern Nazarene University, OK	B
Spring Arbor College, MI	A
Sterling College, KS	B
Trevecca Nazarene College, TN	A
Trinity College, IL	B
Trinity Western University, BC	B
Warner Pacific College, OR	B
Westmont College, CA	B

Linguistics

Gordon College, MA	B
Judson College, IL	B
Seattle Pacific University, WA	B
Trinity Western University, BC	B

Literature

Bethel College, MN	B
Biola University, CA	B
Calvin College, MI	B
Eastern College, PA	B
Fresno Pacific College, CA	B
George Fox College, OR	B
Gordon College, MA	B
Grand Canyon University, AZ	B
Houghton College, NY	B
Judson College, IL	B
Mount Vernon Nazarene College, OH	B
North Park College, IL	B
Northwestern College, IA	B
Northwestern College, MN	B
Olivet Nazarene University, IL	B
Point Loma Nazarene College, CA	B
Redeemer College, ON	B
Southern Nazarene University, OK	B
Westmont College, CA	B
Wheaton College, IL	B
Whitworth College, WA	B

Management Information Systems

Bethel College, MN	B
Dordt College, IA	B
Fresno Pacific College, CA	B
Geneva College, PA	B
Sioux Falls College, SD	B
Southern Nazarene University, OK	B

Manufacturing Engineering

Eastern Nazarene College, MA	B

Marine Biology

Seattle Pacific University, WA	B

Marketing/Retailing/ Merchandising

Anderson University, IN	B
Azusa Pacific University, CA	B
Belhaven College, MS	B
Biola University, CA	B
Dallas Baptist University, TX	B
Grand Canyon University, AZ	B
Greenville College, IL	B
LeTourneau University, TX	B
Messiah College, PA	B
Mississippi College, MS	B
North Park College, IL	B
Northwestern College, MN	B
Olivet Nazarene University, IL	B
Seattle Pacific University, WA	B
Southern California College, CA	B
Southern Nazarene University, OK	A,B

Mathematics

Anderson University, IN	B
Asbury College, KY	B
Azusa Pacific University, CA	B
Bartlesville Wesleyan College, OK	B
Belhaven College, MS	B
Bethel College, IN	B
Bethel College, KS	B
Bethel College, MN	B
Biola University, CA	B
Calvin College, MI	B
Campbellsville College, KY	B
Campbell University, NC	B
Central Wesleyan College, SC	B
Dallas Baptist University, TX	B
Dordt College, IA	B
Eastern College, PA	B
Eastern Mennonite College, VA	B
Eastern Nazarene College, MA	B

Evangel College, MO	B
Fresno Pacific College, CA	A,B
Geneva College, PA	B
George Fox College, OR	B
Gordon College, MA	B
Goshen College, IN	B
Grace College, IN	B
Grand Canyon University, AZ	B
Greenville College, IL	B
Houghton College, NY	B
Huntington College, IN	B
Indiana Wesleyan University, IN	B
John Brown University, AR	B
Judson College, IL	B
King College, TN	B
King's College, NY	B
Lee College, TN	B
LeTourneau University, TX	B
Malone College, OH	B
Master's College, CA	B
Messiah College, PA	B
MidAmerica Nazarene College, KS	B
Milligan College, TN	B
Mississippi College, MS	B
Mount Vernon Nazarene College, OH	B
North Park College, IL	B
Northwestern College, IA	B
Northwestern College, MN	B
Northwest Nazarene College, ID	B
Olivet Nazarene University, IL	B
Palm Beach Atlantic College, FL	B
Point Loma Nazarene College, CA	B
Redeemer College, ON	B
Roberts Wesleyan College, NY	B
Seattle Pacific University, WA	B
Sioux Falls College, SD	B
Southern California College, CA	B
Southern Nazarene University, OK	B
Spring Arbor College, MI	B
Sterling College, KS	B
Tabor College, KS	B
Taylor University, IN	B
Trevecca Nazarene College, TN	B
Trinity Christian College, IL	B
Trinity College, IL	B
Trinity Western University, BC	B
Warner Pacific College, OR	A,B
Westmont College, CA	B
Wheaton College, IL	B
Whitworth College, WA	B
William Jennings Bryan College, TN	B

Mechanical Engineering

Calvin College, MI	B
Eastern Nazarene College, MA	B
Geneva College, PA	B
John Brown University, AR	B
LeTourneau University, TX	B

Mechanical Engineering Technology

LeTourneau University, TX	B

Medical Assistant Technologies

Trevecca Nazarene College, TN	A

Medical Laboratory Technology

Indiana Wesleyan University, IN	A
Southern Nazarene University, OK	A

Medical Secretarial Studies

Geneva College, PA	A,B
Tabor College, KS	B
Trevecca Nazarene College, TN	A

Medical Technology

Anderson University, IN	B
Asbury College, KY	B
Bethel College, KS	B
Calvin College, MI	B
Campbellsville College, KY	B
Campbell University, NC	B
Central Wesleyan College, SC	B
Dordt College, IA	B
Eastern College, PA	B
Eastern Mennonite College, VA	B
Evangel College, MO	B
Geneva College, PA	B
Greenville College, IL	B
Houghton College, NY	B
Huntington College, IN	B
Indiana Wesleyan University, IN	B
John Brown University, AR	B
King College, TN	B
King's College, NY	B
Lee College, TN	B
LeTourneau University, TX	B
Malone College, OH	B
Messiah College, PA	B
Milligan College, TN	B
Mississippi College, MS	B
Mount Vernon Nazarene College, OH	B
North Park College, IL	B
Northwestern College, IA	B
Northwest Nazarene College, ID	B
Olivet Nazarene University, IL	B
Roberts Wesleyan College, NY	B
Sioux Falls College, SD	B
Southern Nazarene University, OK	B
Tabor College, KS	B
Trevecca Nazarene College, TN	B
Trinity Christian College, IL	B

(Pre)Medicine Sequence

Anderson University, IN	B
Asbury College, KY	B
Azusa Pacific University, CA	B
Belhaven College, MS	B
Bethel College, KS	B
Bethel College, MN	B
Biola University, CA	B
Calvin College, MI	B
Campbellsville College, KY	B
Campbell University, NC	B
Covenant College, GA	B
Dallas Baptist University, TX	B
Dordt College, IA	B
Eastern College, PA	B
Eastern Mennonite College, VA	B
Eastern Nazarene College, MA	B
Evangel College, MO	B
Fresno Pacific College, CA	B
Geneva College, PA	B
George Fox College, OR	B
Gordon College, MA	B
Goshen College, IN	B
Grace College, IN	B
Grand Canyon University, AZ	B
Greenville College, IL	B
Houghton College, NY	B
Huntington College, IN	B
Indiana Wesleyan University, IN	B
Judson College, IL	B
King College, TN	B
LeTourneau University, TX	B
Malone College, OH	B
Messiah College, PA	B
Milligan College, TN	B
Mississippi College, MS	B
Mount Vernon Nazarene College, OH	B
North Park College, IL	B
Northwestern College, IA	B
Northwest Nazarene College, ID	B
Olivet Nazarene University, IL	B
Palm Beach Atlantic College, FL	B
Point Loma Nazarene College, CA	B
Redeemer College, ON	B

Sioux Falls College, SD	B
Southern California College, CA	B
Southern Nazarene University, OK	B
Sterling College, KS	B
Tabor College, KS	B
Taylor University, IN	B
Trevecca Nazarene College, TN	B
Trinity Christian College, IL	B
Trinity Western University, BC	B
Westmont College, CA	B
Wheaton College, IL	B
Whitworth College, WA	B

Mental Health/ Rehabilitation Counseling

Evangel College, MO	A,B
Indiana Wesleyan University, IN	A

Military Science

Campbell University, NC	B

Ministries

Asbury College, KY	B
Azusa Pacific University, CA	B
Belhaven College, MS	B
Bethel College, IN	B
Biola University, CA	B
Campbellsville College, KY	B
Central Wesleyan College, SC	B
Colorado Christian University, CO	B
Dallas Baptist University, TX	B
Eastern College, PA	B
Eastern Mennonite College, VA	B
Fresno Pacific College, CA	B
Geneva College, PA	B
George Fox College, OR	B
Gordon College, MA	B
Grand Canyon University, AZ	B
Greenville College, IL	B
Houghton College, NY	B
Huntington College, IN	B
Indiana Wesleyan University, IN	A,B
Malone College, OH	B
Master's College, CA	B
Milligan College, TN	B
Montreat-Anderson College, NC	B
Northwest Christian College, OR	B
Northwestern College, MN	B
Northwest Nazarene College, ID	B
Nyack College, NY	B
Olivet Nazarene University, IL	A,B
Roberts Wesleyan College, NY	B
Seattle Pacific University, WA	B
Simpson College, CA	B
Southern California College, CA	B
Southern Nazarene University, OK	B
Spring Arbor College, MI	B
Tabor College, KS	B
Trevecca Nazarene College, TN	A,B
Trinity College, IL	B
Warner Pacific College, OR	A,B
Warner Southern College, FL	A,B
Westmont College, CA	B

Modern Languages

Azusa Pacific University, CA	B
Biola University, CA	B
Eastern Mennonite College, VA	B
Greenville College, IL	B
King's College, NY	B
Lee College, TN	B
Messiah College, PA	B
MidAmerica Nazarene College, KS	B
Mississippi College, MS	B
Olivet Nazarene University, IL	B
Point Loma Nazarene College, CA	B
Redeemer College, ON	B
Southern Nazarene University, OK	B

Taylor University, IN	B
Westmont College, CA	B
Wheaton College, IL	B

Museum Studies

Anderson University, IN	B

Music

Anderson University, IN	B
Asbury College, KY	B
Azusa Pacific University, CA	B
Belhaven College, MS	B
Bethel College, IN	A,B
Bethel College, KS	B
Bethel College, MN	B
Biola University, CA	B
California Baptist College, CA	B
Calvin College, MI	B
Campbellsville College, KY	B
Campbell University, NC	B
Central Wesleyan College, SC	B
Colorado Christian University, CO	B
Covenant College, GA	B
Dallas Baptist University, TX	B
Dordt College, IA	B
Eastern Mennonite College, VA	B
Eastern Nazarene College, MA	B
Evangel College, MO	B
Fresno Pacific College, CA	A,B
Geneva College, PA	B
George Fox College, OR	B
Gordon College, MA	B
Goshen College, IN	B
Grace College, IN	B
Grand Canyon University, AZ	B
Greenville College, IL	B
Houghton College, NY	B
Huntington College, IN	B
Indiana Wesleyan University, IN	A,B
John Brown University, AR	A,B
Judson College, IL	B
King College, TN	B
King's College, NY	B
King's College, AB	B
Lee College, TN	B
Malone College, OH	B
Master's College, CA	B
Messiah College, PA	B
MidAmerica Nazarene College, KS	B
Milligan College, TN	B
Mississippi College, MS	B
Mount Vernon Nazarene College, OH	B
North Park College, IL	B
Northwestern College, IA	B
Northwestern College, MN	A,B
Northwest Nazarene College, ID	B
Nyack College, NY	B
Olivet Nazarene University, IL	B
Palm Beach Atlantic College, FL	B
Point Loma Nazarene College, CA	B
Redeemer College, ON	B
Roberts Wesleyan College, NY	A,B
Seattle Pacific University, WA	B
Simpson College, CA	B
Sioux Falls College, SD	B
Southern California College, CA	B
Southern Nazarene University, OK	B
Spring Arbor College, MI	B
Sterling College, KS	B
Tabor College, KS	B
Taylor University, IN	B
Trevecca Nazarene College, TN	B
Trinity Christian College, IL	B
Trinity College, IL	B
Trinity Western University, BC	B
Warner Pacific College, OR	B
Warner Southern College, FL	A,B
Westmont College, CA	B
Wheaton College, IL	B
Whitworth College, WA	B
William Jennings Bryan College, TN	B

Music Business

Geneva College, PA	B
Grand Canyon University, AZ	B
Indiana Wesleyan University, IN	B
North Park College, IL	B
Point Loma Nazarene College, CA	B
Sioux Falls College, SD	B
Sterling College, KS	B
Trevecca Nazarene College, TN	B
Wheaton College, IL	B

Music Education

Anderson University, IN	B
Asbury College, KY	B
Azusa Pacific University, CA	B
Bethel College, IN	B
Bethel College, KS	B
Bethel College, MN	B
Biola University, CA	B
Calvin College, MI	B
Campbellsville College, KY	B
Campbell University, NC	B
Central Wesleyan College, SC	B
Colorado Christian University, CO	B
Covenant College, GA	B
Dallas Baptist University, TX	B
Dordt College, IA	B
Eastern Mennonite College, VA	B
Eastern Nazarene College, MA	B
Evangel College, MO	B
Geneva College, PA	B
George Fox College, OR	B
Gordon College, MA	B
Goshen College, IN	B
Grace College, IN	B
Grand Canyon University, AZ	B
Greenville College, IL	B
Houghton College, NY	B
Huntington College, IN	B
Indiana Wesleyan University, IN	B
John Brown University, AR	B
King's College, NY	B
Lee College, TN	B
Malone College, OH	B
Messiah College, PA	B
MidAmerica Nazarene College, KS	B
Milligan College, TN	B
Mississippi College, MS	B
Mount Vernon Nazarene College, OH	B
North Park College, IL	B
Northwestern College, IA	B
Northwestern College, MN	B
Northwest Nazarene College, ID	B
Nyack College, NY	B
Olivet Nazarene University, IL	B
Point Loma Nazarene College, CA	B
Roberts Wesleyan College, NY	B
Seattle Pacific University, WA	B
Sioux Falls College, SD	B
Southern California College, CA	B
Southern Nazarene University, OK	B
Spring Arbor College, MI	B
Sterling College, KS	B
Tabor College, KS	B
Taylor University, IN	B
Trevecca Nazarene College, TN	B
Trinity Christian College, IL	B
Trinity College, IL	B
Warner Pacific College, OR	B
Warner Southern College, FL	B
Wheaton College, IL	B
Whitworth College, WA	B
William Jennings Bryan College, TN	B

Music History

Wheaton College, IL	B

Natural Resource Management

Huntington College, IN — B
Mount Vernon Nazarene College, OH — A

Natural Sciences

Bartlesville Wesleyan College, OK — B
Bethel College, KS — B
Bethel College, MN — B
Campbellsville College, KY — B
Campbell University, NC — B
Covenant College, GA — B
Dordt College, IA — B
Fresno Pacific College, CA — A,B
Goshen College, IN — B
Houghton College, NY — B
Lee College, TN — B
LeTourneau University, TX — B
Master's College, CA — B
North Park College, IL — B
Northwestern College, IA — B
Olivet Nazarene University, IL — B
Redeemer College, ON — B
Roberts Wesleyan College, NY — A
Southern Nazarene University, OK — B
Sterling College, KS — B
Tabor College, KS — B
Taylor University, IN — B
Trevecca Nazarene College, TN — B
Trinity Western University, BC — B
Westmont College, CA — B

Nursing

Anderson University, IN — A,B
Azusa Pacific University, CA — B
Bethel College, IN — B
Bethel College, KS — B
Bethel College, MN — B
Biola University, CA — B
Calvin College, MI — B
Central Wesleyan College, SC — B
Dallas Baptist University, TX — B
Eastern College, PA — B
Eastern Mennonite College, VA — B
Goshen College, IN — B
Grace College, IN — A
Grand Canyon University, AZ — B
Indiana Wesleyan University, IN — B
Judson College, IL — B
King's College, NY — B
Malone College, OH — B
Messiah College, PA — B
MidAmerica Nazarene College, KS — B
Mississippi College, MS — B
North Park College, IL — B
Nyack College, NY — A
Olivet Nazarene University, IL — B
Point Loma Nazarene College, CA — B
Roberts Wesleyan College, NY — B
Seattle Pacific University, WA — B
Southern Nazarene University, OK — B
Trinity Christian College, IL — B
Whitworth College, WA — B

Nutrition

Eastern Mennonite College, VA — B
Goshen College, IN — B
Mississippi College, MS — B
Seattle Pacific University, WA — B
Sterling College, KS — B

Occupational Therapy

Mississippi College, MS — B
Southern Nazarene University, OK — A

Painting/Drawing

Bethel College, KS — B
Biola University, CA — B

Judson College, IL — B
Trinity Christian College, IL — B

Paralegal Studies

Dallas Baptist University, TX — B
Eastern Mennonite College, VA — A
Milligan College, TN — A,B
Mississippi College, MS — B

Pastoral Studies

Azusa Pacific University, CA — B
Biola University, CA — B
Campbellsville College, KY — B
Campbell University, NC — B
Central Wesleyan College, SC — B
Colorado Christian University, CO — B
Eastern Mennonite College, VA — B
Eastern Nazarene College, MA — B
Geneva College, PA — B
Greenville College, IL — B
Houghton College, NY — B
Indiana Wesleyan University, IN — A,B
Messiah College, PA — B
Northwest Christian College, OR — B
Northwestern College, MN — B
Northwest Nazarene College, ID — B
Nyack College, NY — B
Olivet Nazarene University, IL — B
Point Loma Nazarene College, CA — B
Simpson College, CA — B
Southern California College, CA — B
Southern Nazarene University, OK — B
Trevecca Nazarene College, TN — B
Warner Pacific College, OR — B
Warner Southern College, FL — B

Peace Studies

Bethel College, KS — B
Eastern Mennonite College, VA — B
Whitworth College, WA — B

Pharmacy/Pharmaceutical Sciences

Southern Nazarene University, OK — A

Philosophy

Anderson University, IN — B
Asbury College, KY — B
Azusa Pacific University, CA — B
Bethel College, KS — B
Bethel College, MN — B
Biola University, CA — B
Calvin College, MI — B
Dordt College, IA — B
Eastern College, PA — B
Eastern Mennonite College, VA — B
Geneva College, PA — B
Gordon College, MA — B
Greenville College, IL — B
Houghton College, NY — B
Huntington College, IN — B
Indiana Wesleyan University, IN — B
Judson College, IL — B
King's College, AB — B
Mount Vernon Nazarene College, OH — B
North Park College, IL — B
Northwestern College, IA — B
Northwest Nazarene College, ID — B
Nyack College, NY — B
Olivet Nazarene University, IL — B
Point Loma Nazarene College, CA — B
Redeemer College, ON — B
Seattle Pacific University, WA — B
Southern Nazarene University, OK — B
Spring Arbor College, MI — B
Sterling College, KS — B

Tabor College, KS — B
Taylor University, IN — B
Trevecca Nazarene College, TN — B
Trinity Christian College, IL — B
Trinity College, IL — B
Trinity Western University, BC — B
Westmont College, CA — B
Wheaton College, IL — B
Whitworth College, WA — B

Physical Education

Anderson University, IN — B
Asbury College, KY — B
Azusa Pacific University, CA — B
Bartlesville Wesleyan College, OK — B
Belhaven College, MS — B
Bethel College, KS — B
Bethel College, MN — B
Biola University, CA — B
California Baptist College, CA — B
Calvin College, MI — B
Campbellsville College, KY — B
Campbell University, NC — B
Central Wesleyan College, SC — B
Dallas Baptist University, TX — B
Dordt College, IA — B
Eastern College, PA — B
Eastern Mennonite College, VA — B
Eastern Nazarene College, MA — B
Evangel College, MO — B
Fresno Pacific College, CA — A,B
George Fox College, OR — B
Goshen College, IN — B
Grace College, IN — B
Grand Canyon University, AZ — B
Greenville College, IL — B
Houghton College, NY — B
Huntington College, IN — B
Indiana Wesleyan University, IN — B
John Brown University, AR — B
Judson College, IL — B
King's College, NY — B
Lee College, TN — B
LeTourneau University, TX — B
Malone College, OH — B
Master's College, CA — B
Messiah College, PA — B
MidAmerica Nazarene College, KS — B
Milligan College, TN — B
Mississippi College, MS — B
Mount Vernon Nazarene College, OH — B
North Park College, IL — B
Northwestern College, IA — B
Northwestern College, MN — B
Northwest Nazarene College, ID — B
Olivet Nazarene University, IL — B
Point Loma Nazarene College, CA — B
Redeemer College, ON — B
Seattle Pacific University, WA — B
Sioux Falls College, SD — B
Southern California College, CA — B
Southern Nazarene University, OK — B
Spring Arbor College, MI — B
Sterling College, KS — B
Tabor College, KS — B
Taylor University, IN — B
Trevecca Nazarene College, TN — B
Trinity Christian College, IL — B
Trinity College, IL — B
Trinity Western University, BC — B
Warner Pacific College, OR — B
Warner Southern College, FL — B
Westmont College, CA — B
Wheaton College, IL — B
Whitworth College, WA — B

Physical Fitness/Human Movement

Gordon College, MA — B
John Brown University, AR — B

North Park College, IL — B
Point Loma Nazarene College, CA — B
Seattle Pacific University, WA — B
Sioux Falls College, SD — B
Trevecca Nazarene College, TN — B

Physical Sciences

Biola University, CA — B
California Baptist College, CA — B
Calvin College, MI — B
Eastern College, PA — B
Goshen College, IN — B
Houghton College, NY — B
Indiana Wesleyan University, IN — B
Judson College, IL — B
Olivet Nazarene University, IL — A,B
Roberts Wesleyan College, NY — A
Westmont College, CA — B

Physical Therapy

Mississippi College, MS — B
Olivet Nazarene University, IL — B
Southern Nazarene University, OK — A
Trevecca Nazarene College, TN — A

Physician's Assistant Studies

Trevecca Nazarene College, TN — B

Physics

Anderson University, IN — B
Azusa Pacific University, CA — B
Bethel College, KS — B
Bethel College, MN — B
Biola University, CA — B
Calvin College, MI — B
Dordt College, IA — B
Eastern Nazarene College, MA — B
Geneva College, PA — B
Gordon College, MA — B
Goshen College, IN — B
Greenville College, IL — B
Houghton College, NY — B
King College, TN — B
Messiah College, PA — B
MidAmerica Nazarene College, KS — B
Mississippi College, MS — B
North Park College, IL — B
Northwestern College, IA — B
Northwest Nazarene College, ID — B
Point Loma Nazarene College, CA — B
Roberts Wesleyan College, NY — B
Seattle Pacific University, WA — B
Southern Nazarene University, OK — B
Spring Arbor College, MI — B
Taylor University, IN — B
Westmont College, CA — B
Wheaton College, IL — B
Whitworth College, WA — B

Piano/Organ

Anderson University, IN — B
Belhaven College, MS — B
Bethel College, IN — A,B
Biola University, CA — B
Campbellsville College, KY — B
Campbell University, NC — B
Covenant College, GA — B
Dallas Baptist University, TX — B
Grace College, IN — B
Grand Canyon University, AZ — B
Houghton College, NY — B
Huntington College, IN — B
Indiana Wesleyan University, IN — B
John Brown University, AR — A
Lee College, TN — B
Mississippi College, MS — B
Nyack College, NY — B
Olivet Nazarene University, IL — B

Point Loma Nazarene College, CA — B
Roberts Wesleyan College, NY — A,B
Southern Nazarene University, OK — B
Spring Arbor College, MI — B
Sterling College, KS — B
Tabor College, KS — B
Trinity Christian College, IL — B
Wheaton College, IL — B

Political Science/Government

Anderson University, IN — B
Azusa Pacific University, CA — B
Bartlesville Wesleyan College, OK — B
Bethel College, KS — B
Bethel College, MN — B
California Baptist College, CA — B
Calvin College, MI — B
Campbellsville College, KY — B
Campbell University, NC — B
Dallas Baptist University, TX — B
Dordt College, IA — B
Eastern College, PA — B
Evangel College, MO — B
Fresno Pacific College, CA — A,B
Geneva College, PA — B
Gordon College, MA — B
Goshen College, IN — B
Greenville College, IL — B
Indiana Wesleyan University, IN — B
King College, TN — B
Master's College, CA — B
Mississippi College, MS — B
North Park College, IL — B
Northwestern College, IA — B
Point Loma Nazarene College, CA — B
Redeemer College, ON — B
Seattle Pacific University, WA — B
Southern California College, CA — B
Southern Nazarene University, OK — B
Sterling College, KS — B
Taylor University, IN — B
Westmont College, CA — B
Wheaton College, IL — B
Whitworth College, WA — B

Psychology

Anderson University, IN — B
Asbury College, KY — B
Azusa Pacific University, CA — A,B
Belhaven College, MS — B
Bethel College, IN — B
Bethel College, KS — B
Bethel College, MN — B
Biola University, CA — B
California Baptist College, CA — B
Calvin College, MI — B
Campbellsville College, KY — B
Campbell University, NC — B
Central Wesleyan College, SC — B
Colorado Christian University, CO — B
Covenant College, GA — B
Dallas Baptist University, TX — B
Dordt College, IA — B
Eastern College, PA — B
Eastern Mennonite College, VA — B
Eastern Nazarene College, MA — B
Evangel College, MO — B
Fresno Pacific College, CA — A,B
Geneva College, PA — B
George Fox College, OR — B
Gordon College, MA — B
Goshen College, IN — B
Grace College, IN — B
Grand Canyon University, AZ — B
Greenville College, IL — B
Houghton College, NY — B
Huntington College, IN — B
Indiana Wesleyan University, IN — B
John Brown University, AR — B
Judson College, IL — B

King College, TN — B
King's College, NY — B
King's College, AB — B
Lee College, TN — B
Malone College, OH — B
Messiah College, PA — B
MidAmerica Nazarene College, KS — B
Milligan College, TN — B
Mississippi College, MS — B
Mount Vernon Nazarene College, OH — B
North Park College, IL — B
Northwestern College, IA — B
Northwestern College, MN — B
Northwest Nazarene College, ID — B
Nyack College, NY — B
Olivet Nazarene University, IL — B
Palm Beach Atlantic College, FL — B
Point Loma Nazarene College, CA — B
Redeemer College, ON — B
Roberts Wesleyan College, NY — B
Seattle Pacific University, WA — B
Simpson College, CA — A,B
Sioux Falls College, SD — B
Southern California College, CA — B
Southern Nazarene University, OK — B
Spring Arbor College, MI — B
Sterling College, KS — B
Tabor College, KS — B
Taylor University, IN — B
Trevecca Nazarene College, TN — B
Trinity Christian College, IL — B
Trinity College, IL — B
Trinity Western University, BC — B
Warner Pacific College, OR — B
Warner Southern College, FL — B
Westmont College, CA — B
Wheaton College, IL — B
Whitworth College, WA — B
William Jennings Bryan College, TN — B

Public Administration

California Baptist College, CA — B
Evangel College, MO — B
LeTourneau University, TX — B
Mississippi College, MS — B

Public Affairs and Policy Studies

Anderson University, IN — B

Public Relations

Anderson University, IN — B
Bethel College, KS — B
Biola University, CA — B
Campbell University, NC — B
John Brown University, AR — A,B
Sioux Falls College, SD — B

Publishing

Bethel College, KS — B

Radio and Television Studies

Biola University, CA — B
Campbell University, NC — B
Evangel College, MO — B
Geneva College, PA — B
John Brown University, AR — B
Messiah College, PA — B
Northwestern College, MN — A,B
Olivet Nazarene University, IL — B
Sioux Falls College, SD — B
Southern California College, CA — B
Trevecca Nazarene College, TN — A,B

Radiological Sciences

Malone College, OH	B

Reading Education

Seattle Pacific University, WA	B
Southern Nazarene University, OK	B

Recreational Facilities Management

Indiana Wesleyan University, IN	B
Sioux Falls College, SD	B

Recreation and Leisure Services

Anderson University, IN	B
Asbury College, KY	B
Azusa Pacific University, CA	B
Bethel College, IN	B
California Baptist College, CA	B
Calvin College, MI	B
Campbellsville College, KY	B
Eastern Mennonite College, VA	B
Evangel College, MO	B
Gordon College, MA	B
Greenville College, IL	B
Houghton College, NY	B
Huntington College, IN	B
Indiana Wesleyan University, IN	A
Messiah College, PA	B
MidAmerica Nazarene College, KS	B
Montreat-Anderson College, NC	B
Northwestern College, IA	B
Northwest Nazarene College, ID	B
Seattle Pacific University, WA	B
Southern Nazarene University, OK	B
Spring Arbor College, MI	B
Taylor University, IN	B

Religious Education

Biola University, CA	B
Calvin College, MI	B
Campbellsville College, KY	B
Campbell University, NC	B
Dallas Baptist University, TX	B
Eastern Nazarene College, MA	A,B
Houghton College, NY	A,B
Indiana Wesleyan University, IN	A,B
King's College, NY	B
Lee College, TN	B
Malone College, OH	B
Messiah College, PA	B
MidAmerica Nazarene College, KS	A,B
Milligan College, TN	B
Mississippi College, MS	B
Mount Vernon Nazarene College, OH	B
Northwestern College, MN	B
Northwest Nazarene College, ID	A,B
Nyack College, NY	B
Olivet Nazarene University, IL	B
Point Loma Nazarene College, CA	B
Seattle Pacific University, WA	B
Simpson College, CA	B
Southern California College, CA	B
Southern Nazarene University, OK	B
Sterling College, KS	B
Taylor University, IN	B
Trevecca Nazarene College, TN	B
Trinity Christian College, IL	B
Warner Pacific College, OR	A,B
Warner Southern College, FL	A,B
Wheaton College, IL	B
William Jennings Bryan College, TN	B

Religious Studies

Anderson University, IN	B
Azusa Pacific University, CA	B
Bethel College, IN	B
Bethel College, KS	B
Biola University, CA	B
California Baptist College, CA	B
Calvin College, MI	B
Campbellsville College, KY	B
Central Wesleyan College, SC	B
Dallas Baptist University, TX	B
Dordt College, IA	B
Eastern College, PA	B
Eastern Mennonite College, VA	B
Eastern Nazarene College, MA	B
Fresno Pacific College, CA	B
George Fox College, OR	B
Gordon College, MA	B
Goshen College, IN	B
Grand Canyon University, AZ	B
Greenville College, IL	B
Houghton College, NY	B
Huntington College, IN	B
Indiana Wesleyan University, IN	B
John Brown University, AR	B
Judson College, IL	B
King College, TN	B
King's College, NY	B
Messiah College, PA	B
MidAmerica Nazarene College, KS	A,B
Mississippi College, MS	B
Montreat-Anderson College, NC	B
Mount Vernon Nazarene College, OH	B
North Park College, IL	B
Northwest Christian College, OR	A,B
Northwestern College, IA	B
Northwest Nazarene College, ID	B
Nyack College, NY	B
Olivet Nazarene University, IL	B
Palm Beach Atlantic College, FL	B
Point Loma Nazarene College, CA	B
Redeemer College, ON	B
Roberts Wesleyan College, NY	B
Seattle Pacific University, WA	B
Sioux Falls College, SD	A,B
Southern California College, CA	B
Southern Nazarene University, OK	B
Spring Arbor College, MI	B
Sterling College, KS	B
Tabor College, KS	A,B
Taylor University, IN	B
Trevecca Nazarene College, TN	A,B
Trinity Christian College, IL	B
Trinity Western University, BC	B
Warner Pacific College, OR	B
Warner Southern College, FL	A,B
Westmont College, CA	B
Wheaton College, IL	B
Whitworth College, WA	B

Retail Management

Mississippi College, MS	B

Romance Languages

Belhaven College, MS	B
MidAmerica Nazarene College, KS	B
Olivet Nazarene University, IL	B
Redeemer College, ON	B

Russian

Seattle Pacific University, WA	B

Sacred Music

Anderson University, IN	B
Bethel College, IN	A,B
Bethel College, MN	B
Calvin College, MI	B
Campbellsville College, KY	B
Campbell University, NC	B
Central Wesleyan College, SC	B
Colorado Christian University, CO	B
Dallas Baptist University, TX	B

Grace College, IN	B
Grand Canyon University, AZ	B
Greenville College, IL	B
Houghton College, NY	B
Indiana Wesleyan University, IN	B
Malone College, OH	B
MidAmerica Nazarene College, KS	A,B
Milligan College, TN	B
Mississippi College, MS	B
Mount Vernon Nazarene College, OH	A,B
North Park College, IL	B
Northwest Christian College, OR	B
Nyack College, NY	B
Olivet Nazarene University, IL	B
Point Loma Nazarene College, CA	B
Seattle Pacific University, WA	B
Simpson College, CA	B
Southern Nazarene University, OK	B
Spring Arbor College, MI	B
Taylor University, IN	B
Trevecca Nazarene College, TN	B

Scandinavian Languages/ Studies

North Park College, IL	B

Science

Bartlesville Wesleyan College, OK	B
Bethel College, IN	B
Bethel College, KS	B
Calvin College, MI	B
Eastern Nazarene College, MA	B
Geneva College, PA	B
George Fox College, OR	B
Houghton College, NY	B
Huntington College, IN	B
Indiana Wesleyan University, IN	A,B
Judson College, IL	B
King College, TN	B
Malone College, OH	B
Montreat-Anderson College, NC	A
North Park College, IL	B
Northwestern College, MN	A
Olivet Nazarene University, IL	B
Palm Beach Atlantic College, FL	B
Redeemer College, ON	B
Roberts Wesleyan College, NY	B
Southern California College, CA	B
Southern Nazarene University, OK	B
Tabor College, KS	B
Trinity Western University, BC	B
Warner Pacific College, OR	B

Science Education

Bartlesville Wesleyan College, OK	B
Bethel College, IN	B
Bethel College, KS	B
Bethel College, MN	B
Calvin College, MI	B
Campbellsville College, KY	B
Campbell University, NC	B
Dallas Baptist University, TX	B
Eastern Mennonite College, VA	B
Evangel College, MO	B
George Fox College, OR	B
Goshen College, IN	B
Grace College, IN	B
Grand Canyon University, AZ	B
Houghton College, NY	B
Huntington College, IN	B
Indiana Wesleyan University, IN	B
Malone College, OH	B
Mississippi College, MS	B
Mount Vernon Nazarene College, OH	B
Northwest Nazarene College, ID	B
Olivet Nazarene University, IL	B
Tabor College, KS	B
Taylor University, IN	B
Trevecca Nazarene College, TN	B
Trinity Christian College, IL	B

Warner Pacific College, OR	B
Warner Southern College, FL	B
Wheaton College, IL	B
William Jennings Bryan College, TN	B

Secondary Education

Anderson University, IN	B
Azusa Pacific University, CA	B
Bartlesville Wesleyan College, OK	B
Bethel College, IN	B
Bethel College, KS	B
Bethel College, MN	B
California Baptist College, CA	B
Calvin College, MI	B
Campbellsville College, KY	B
Campbell University, NC	B
Dallas Baptist University, TX	B
Dordt College, IA	B
Eastern College, PA	B
Eastern Mennonite College, VA	B
Evangel College, MO	B
Fresno Pacific College, CA	B
Geneva College, PA	B
George Fox College, OR	B
Gordon College, MA	B
Goshen College, IN	B
Grand Canyon University, AZ	B
Greenville College, IL	B
Houghton College, NY	B
Huntington College, IN	B
Indiana Wesleyan University, IN	B
John Brown University, AR	B
King's College, NY	B
Lee College, TN	B
Malone College, OH	B
Master's College, CA	B
Messiah College, PA	B
MidAmerica Nazarene College, KS	B
Milligan College, TN	B
Mount Vernon Nazarene College, OH	B
North Park College, IL	B
Northwestern College, IA	B
Northwestern College, MN	B
Northwest Nazarene College, ID	B
Olivet Nazarene University, IL	B
Redeemer College, ON	B
Roberts Wesleyan College, NY	B
Seattle Pacific University, WA	B
Simpson College, CA	B
Sioux Falls College, SD	B
Southern California College, CA	B
Southern Nazarene University, OK	B
Spring Arbor College, MI	B
Sterling College, KS	B
Tabor College, KS	B
Taylor University, IN	B
Trevecca Nazarene College, TN	B
Trinity Christian College, IL	B
Trinity Western University, BC	B
Warner Pacific College, OR	B
Warner Southern College, FL	B
Westmont College, CA	B
Wheaton College, IL	B
Whitworth College, WA	B

Secretarial Studies/Office Management

Anderson University, IN	A
Bartlesville Wesleyan College, OK	A
Bethel College, IN	A
Campbellsville College, KY	A,B
Dordt College, IA	A
Evangel College, MO	A,B
Geneva College, PA	A,B
Grace College, IN	A
Huntington College, IN	A
Indiana Wesleyan University, IN	A
John Brown University, AR	A,B
Lee College, TN	B
Milligan College, TN	A,B
Mississippi College, MS	B

Mount Vernon Nazarene College, OH	A,B
Northwestern College, IA	A
Northwestern College, MN	A,B
Northwest Nazarene College, ID	A,B
Olivet Nazarene University, IL	A,B
Point Loma Nazarene College, CA	B
Southern Nazarene University, OK	A,B
Tabor College, KS	A,B
Trevecca Nazarene College, TN	A,B
Warner Southern College, FL	A

Social Science

Azusa Pacific University, CA	B
Bethel College, IN	A,B
Bethel College, MN	B
Biola University, CA	B
California Baptist College, CA	B
Calvin College, MI	B
Campbellsville College, KY	B
Campbell University, NC	B
Central Wesleyan College, SC	B
Dordt College, IA	B
Eastern Nazarene College, MA	B
Evangel College, MO	A,B
Fresno Pacific College, CA	B
Gordon College, MA	B
Grand Canyon University, AZ	B
Houghton College, NY	B
Indiana Wesleyan University, IN	A,B
John Brown University, AR	B
Judson College, IL	B
King's College, AB	B
Lee College, TN	B
Messiah College, PA	B
Mississippi College, MS	B
Mount Vernon Nazarene College, OH	B
North Park College, IL	B
Northwestern College, MN	B
Northwest Nazarene College, ID	B
Nyack College, NY	B
Olivet Nazarene University, IL	B
Point Loma Nazarene College, CA	B
Roberts Wesleyan College, NY	B
Seattle Pacific University, WA	B
Sioux Falls College, SD	A,B
Southern California College, CA	B
Southern Nazarene University, OK	B
Spring Arbor College, MI	B
Tabor College, KS	B
Taylor University, IN	B
Trevecca Nazarene College, TN	B
Trinity College, IL	B
Trinity Western University, BC	B
Warner Pacific College, OR	A,B
Warner Southern College, FL	B
Westmont College, CA	B

Social Work

Anderson University, IN	B
Azusa Pacific University, CA	B
Bethel College, KS	B
Bethel College, MN	B
Calvin College, MI	B
Campbell University, NC	B
Dordt College, IA	B
Eastern College, PA	B
Eastern Mennonite College, VA	B
Eastern Nazarene College, MA	B
Evangel College, MO	B
George Fox College, OR	B
Gordon College, MA	B
Goshen College, IN	B
Greenville College, IL	B
Indiana Wesleyan University, IN	B
Malone College, OH	B
Messiah College, PA	B
Milligan College, TN	B
Mississippi College, MS	B
Mount Vernon Nazarene College, OH	B
Northwestern College, IA	B
Northwest Nazarene College, ID	A,B
Olivet Nazarene University, IL	A,B

Roberts Wesleyan College, NY	B
Sioux Falls College, SD	B
Spring Arbor College, MI	B
Tabor College, KS	B
Taylor University, IN	B
Trevecca Nazarene College, TN	B
Warner Pacific College, OR	B

Sociology

Anderson University, IN	B
Asbury College, KY	B
Azusa Pacific University, CA	B
Bethel College, IN	B
Bethel College, MN	B
Biola University, CA	B
California Baptist College, CA	B
Calvin College, MI	B
Campbellsville College, KY	B
Covenant College, GA	B
Dallas Baptist University, TX	B
Dordt College, IA	B
Eastern College, PA	B
Eastern Mennonite College, VA	B
Eastern Nazarene College, MA	B
Evangel College, MO	B
Fresno Pacific College, CA	A,B
Geneva College, PA	B
George Fox College, OR	B
Gordon College, MA	B
Goshen College, IN	B
Grace College, IN	B
Grand Canyon University, AZ	B
Greenville College, IL	B
Houghton College, NY	B
Huntington College, IN	B
Indiana Wesleyan University, IN	B
Judson College, IL	B
King's College, NY	B
Lee College, TN	B
Messiah College, PA	B
Milligan College, TN	B
Mississippi College, MS	B
Mount Vernon Nazarene College, OH	B
North Park College, IL	B
Northwestern College, IA	B
Olivet Nazarene University, IL	A,B
Point Loma Nazarene College, CA	B
Redeemer College, ON	B
Roberts Wesleyan College, NY	B
Seattle Pacific University, WA	B
Sioux Falls College, SD	B
Southern California College, CA	B
Southern Nazarene University, OK	B
Spring Arbor College, MI	B
Sterling College, KS	B
Tabor College, KS	B
Taylor University, IN	B
Trinity Christian College, IL	B
Trinity College, IL	B
Warner Pacific College, OR	B
Warner Southern College, FL	B
Westmont College, CA	B
Wheaton College, IL	B
Whitworth College, WA	B

Spanish

Anderson University, IN	B
Asbury College, KY	B
Bethel College, MN	B
Biola University, CA	B
California Baptist College, CA	B
Calvin College, MI	B
Campbell University, NC	B
Dordt College, IA	B
Eastern College, PA	B
Eastern Mennonite College, VA	B
Eastern Nazarene College, MA	B
Evangel College, MO	B
Fresno Pacific College, CA	B
Geneva College, PA	B
Gordon College, MA	B
Goshen College, IN	B

Sociology (continued)

Grace College, IN	B
Greenville College, IL	B
Houghton College, NY	B
Indiana Wesleyan University, IN	B
Messiah College, PA	B
MidAmerica Nazarene College, KS	B
Mount Vernon Nazarene College, OH	B
North Park College, IL	B
Northwestern College, IA	B
Point Loma Nazarene College, CA	B
Southern Nazarene University, OK	B
Spring Arbor College, MI	B
Taylor University, IN	B
Westmont College, CA	B
Wheaton College, IL	B
Whitworth College, WA	B

Special Education

Bethel College, KS	B
Calvin College, MI	B
Central Wesleyan College, SC	B
Eastern Mennonite College, VA	B
Evangel College, MO	B
Gordon College, MA	B
Grand Canyon University, AZ	B
Greenville College, IL	B
Huntington College, IN	B
John Brown University, AR	B
Malone College, OH	B
Milligan College, TN	B
Mississippi College, MS	B
Northwestern College, IA	B
Northwest Nazarene College, ID	B
Seattle Pacific University, WA	B
Sterling College, KS	B
Tabor College, KS	B
Trevecca Nazarene College, TN	B

Speech Pathology and Audiology

Biola University, CA	B
Geneva College, PA	B
Mississippi College, MS	B
Northwest Nazarene College, ID	B

Speech/Rhetoric/Public Address/Debate

Anderson University, IN	B
Asbury College, KY	B
Bethel College, KS	B
Bethel College, MN	B
Calvin College, MI	B
Evangel College, MO	B
Geneva College, PA	B
Grace College, IN	B
Grand Canyon University, AZ	B
Greenville College, IL	B
Judson College, IL	B
Messiah College, PA	B
MidAmerica Nazarene College, KS	B
North Park College, IL	B
Northwestern College, MN	B
Northwest Nazarene College, ID	B
Olivet Nazarene University, IL	B
Palm Beach Atlantic College, FL	B
Sioux Falls College, SD	B
Southern California College, CA	B
Southern Nazarene University, OK	B
Spring Arbor College, MI	B
Sterling College, KS	B
Taylor University, IN	B
Trevecca Nazarene College, TN	B
Warner Southern College, FL	B
Wheaton College, IL	B
Whitworth College, WA	B

Speech Therapy

Biola University, CA	B
Point Loma Nazarene College, CA	B

Sports Administration

Campbell University, NC	B
Houghton College, NY	B
LeTourneau University, TX	B
Northwestern College, MN	B
Spring Arbor College, MI	B

Sports Medicine

Anderson University, IN	B
Azusa Pacific University, CA	B
George Fox College, OR	B
Malone College, OH	B
Messiah College, PA	B
North Park College, IL	B

Stringed Instruments

Belhaven College, MS	B
Covenant College, GA	B
Houghton College, NY	B
Messiah College, PA	B
Olivet Nazarene University, IL	B
Point Loma Nazarene College, CA	B
Wheaton College, IL	B

Studio Art

Bethel College, MN	B
Campbell University, NC	B
Eastern College, PA	B
Grand Canyon University, AZ	B
Indiana Wesleyan University, IN	B
Point Loma Nazarene College, CA	B
Roberts Wesleyan College, NY	B
Wheaton College, IL	B
Whitworth College, WA	B

Systems Engineering

Eastern Nazarene College, MA	B

Systems Science

Taylor University, IN	A

Teacher Aide Studies

Eastern Mennonite College, VA	A
Olivet Nazarene University, IL	A

Teaching English as a Second Language

Eastern Mennonite College, VA	B
Goshen College, IN	B

Telecommunications

Calvin College, MI	B
George Fox College, OR	B

Textiles and Clothing

Olivet Nazarene University, IL	B
Seattle Pacific University, WA	B

Theater Arts/Drama

Anderson University, IN	B
Bethel College, KS	B
Bethel College, MN	B
Biola University, CA	B
California Baptist College, CA	B

Campbell University, NC	B
Colorado Christian University, CO	B
Dordt College, IA	B
Goshen College, IN	B
Grand Canyon University, AZ	B
Greenville College, IL	B
Judson College, IL	B
King College, TN	B
Malone College, OH	B
Mount Vernon Nazarene College, OH	B
Northwestern College, IA	B
Northwestern College, MN	B
Point Loma Nazarene College, CA	B
Redeemer College, ON	B
Seattle Pacific University, WA	B
Sioux Falls College, SD	A,B
Southern California College, CA	B
Sterling College, KS	B
Taylor University, IN	B
Trevecca Nazarene College, TN	B
Trinity Western University, BC	B
Westmont College, CA	B
Wheaton College, IL	B
Whitworth College, WA	B

Theology

Azusa Pacific University, CA	B
Bartlesville Wesleyan College, OK	B
Bethel College, KS	B
Bethel College, MN	B
Biola University, CA	B
Calvin College, MI	B
Campbell University, NC	B
Central Wesleyan College, SC	B
Dordt College, IA	B
Eastern Mennonite College, VA	B
Gordon College, MA	B
Grand Canyon University, AZ	B
Greenville College, IL	B
Huntington College, IN	B
Indiana Wesleyan University, IN	B
Lee College, TN	B
Master's College, CA	B
Messiah College, PA	B
North Park College, IL	B
Northwest Christian College, OR	B
Northwestern College, IA	B
Northwestern College, MN	B
Olivet Nazarene University, IL	B
Point Loma Nazarene College, CA	B
Redeemer College, ON	B
Southern Nazarene University, OK	B
Taylor University, IN	B
Trevecca Nazarene College, TN	B
Trinity Christian College, IL	B
Warner Pacific College, OR	B
Warner Southern College, FL	B

Urban Studies

North Park College, IL	B
Seattle Pacific University, WA	B

(Pre)Veterinary Medicine Sequence

Anderson University, IN	B
Azusa Pacific University, CA	B
Belhaven College, MS	B
Bethel College, MN	B
Calvin College, MI	B
Campbellsville College, KY	B
Campbell University, NC	B
Dallas Baptist University, TX	B
Dordt College, IA	B
Eastern Mennonite College, VA	B
Eastern Nazarene College, MA	B
Evangel College, MO	B
George Fox College, OR	B
Gordon College, MA	B
Goshen College, IN	B
Grand Canyon University, AZ	B

Greenville College, IL	B
Houghton College, NY	B
Huntington College, IN	B
Indiana Wesleyan University, IN	B
King College, TN	B
LeTourneau University, TX	B
Malone College, OH	B
Messiah College, PA	B
Milligan College, TN	B
Mount Vernon Nazarene College, OH	B
North Park College, IL	B
Northwestern College, IA	B
Northwest Nazarene College, ID	B
Olivet Nazarene University, IL	B
Point Loma Nazarene College, CA	B
Redeemer College, ON	B
Sioux Falls College, SD	B
Southern California College, CA	B
Southern Nazarene University, OK	B
Sterling College, KS	B
Taylor University, IN	B
Trinity Christian College, IL	B
Trinity Western University, BC	B
Westmont College, CA	B
Whitworth College, WA	B

Voice

Anderson University, IN	B
Azusa Pacific University, CA	B

Belhaven College, MS	B
Bethel College, IN	B
Calvin College, MI	B
Campbellsville College, KY	B
Campbell University, NC	B
Covenant College, GA	B
Dallas Baptist University, TX	B
Grand Canyon University, AZ	B
Houghton College, NY	B
Huntington College, IN	B
Indiana Wesleyan University, IN	B
John Brown University, AR	B
Judson College, IL	B
Lee College, TN	B
Messiah College, PA	B
North Park College, IL	B
Nyack College, NY	B
Olivet Nazarene University, IL	B
Point Loma Nazarene College, CA	B
Roberts Wesleyan College, NY	A,B
Southern Nazarene University, OK	B
Spring Arbor College, MI	B
Sterling College, KS	B
Tabor College, KS	B
Taylor University, IN	B
Wheaton College, IL	B

Welding Engineering

LeTourneau University, TX	B

Welding Technology

LeTourneau University, TX	B

Western Civilization and Culture

Trinity Christian College, IL	B

Wind and Percussion Instruments

Covenant College, GA	B
Grand Canyon University, AZ	B
Houghton College, NY	B
Indiana Wesleyan University, IN	B
Olivet Nazarene University, IL	B
Point Loma Nazarene College, CA	B
Spring Arbor College, MI	B
Wheaton College, IL	B

Zoology

Olivet Nazarene University, IL	B
Southern Nazarene University, OK	B

ATHLETICS DIRECTORY

M—for men; W—for women;
(s) scholarship offered

Badminton

Redeemer College, ON	M,W

Baseball/Softball

Anderson University, IN	M,W
Asbury College, KY	M,W
Azusa Pacific University, CA	M(s),W(s)
Bartlesville Wesleyan College, OK	W
Belhaven College, MS	M(s)
Bethel College, IN	M(s),W(s)
Bethel College, MN	M
Biola University, CA	M(s)
California Baptist College, CA	M(s),W(s)
Calvin College, MI	M,W
Campbellsville College, KY	M(s),W(s)
Campbell University, NC	M(s),W(s)
Central Wesleyan College, SC	M(s),W(s)
Dallas Baptist University, TX	M(s)
Dordt College, IA	M,W
Eastern College, PA	M(s),W(s)
Eastern Mennonite College, VA	M,W
Eastern Nazarene College, MA	M,W
Evangel College, MO	M(s),W(s)
Geneva College, PA	M(s),W(s)
George Fox College, OR	M(s),W(s)
Gordon College, MA	M,W
Goshen College, IN	M
Grace College, IN	M(s),W(s)
Grand Canyon University, AZ	M(s)
Greenville College, IL	M,W
Huntington College, IN	M(s),W(s)
Indiana Wesleyan University, IN	M(s),W(s)
Judson College, IL	M(s),W(s)
King College, TN	M(s)
King's College, NY	M(s),W(s)
Lee College, TN	W(s)
LeTourneau University, TX	M
Malone College, OH	M(s)
Master's College, CA	M(s)
Messiah College, PA	M
MidAmerica Nazarene College, KS	M(s),W(s)
Milligan College, TN	M(s),W(s)
Mississippi College, MS	M(s),W
Montreat-Anderson College, NC	M(s),W(s)
Mount Vernon Nazarene College, OH	M(s),W(s)
North Park College, IL	M,W
Northwestern College, IA	M(s),W(s)
Northwestern College, MN	M,W
Northwest Nazarene College, ID	M(s)
Nyack College, NY	M(s),W(s)
Olivet Nazarene University, IL	M(s),W(s)
Palm Beach Atlantic College, FL	M,W
Point Loma Nazarene College, CA	M(s)
Roberts Wesleyan College, NY	M,W(s)
Southern California College, CA	M(s),W(s)
Spring Arbor College, MI	M(s),W(s)
Sterling College, KS	M(s),W(s)
Tabor College, KS	M(s),W(s)
Taylor University, IN	M,W
Trevecca Nazarene College, TN	M(s)
Trinity Christian College, IL	M,W
Trinity College, IL	M(s),W(s)
Warner Pacific College, OR	M,W
Warner Southern College, FL	M,W
Westmont College, CA	M(s)
Wheaton College, IL	M,W
Whitworth College, WA	M

Basketball

Anderson University, IN	M,W
Azusa Pacific University, CA	M(s),W(s)
Bartlesville Wesleyan College, OK	M(s),W(s)
Belhaven College, MS	M(s),W(s)
Bethel College, IN	M(s),W(s)
Bethel College, KS	M(s),W(s)
Bethel College, MN	M,W
Biola University, CA	M(s),W(s)
California Baptist College, CA	M(s),W(s)
Calvin College, MI	M,W
Campbellsville College, KY	M(s),W(s)
Campbell University, NC	M(s),W(s)
Central Wesleyan College, SC	M(s),W(s)
Colorado Christian University, CO	M(s),W(s)
Covenant College, GA	M(s),W(s)
Dallas Baptist University, TX	M(s)
Dordt College, IA	M,W
Eastern College, PA	M(s),W(s)
Eastern Mennonite College, VA	M,W
Eastern Nazarene College, MA	M,W
Evangel College, MO	M(s),W(s)
Fresno Pacific College, CA	M(s),W(s)
Geneva College, PA	M(s),W(s)
George Fox College, OR	M(s),W(s)
Gordon College, MA	M,W
Goshen College, IN	M,W
Grace College, IN	M(s),W(s)
Grand Canyon University, AZ	M(s),W(s)
Greenville College, IL	M,W
Houghton College, NY	M(s),W(s)
Huntington College, IN	M(s),W(s)
Indiana Wesleyan University, IN	M(s),W(s)
John Brown University, AR	M(s),W(s)
Judson College, IL	M(s),W(s)
King College, TN	M(s),W(s)
King's College, NY	M(s),W(s)
King's College, AB	M,W
Lee College, TN	M(s),W(s)
LeTourneau University, TX	M
Malone College, OH	M(s),W(s)
Master's College, CA	M(s),W(s)
Messiah College, PA	M,W
MidAmerica Nazarene College, KS	M(s),W(s)
Milligan College, TN	M(s),W(s)
Mississippi College, MS	M(s),W(s)
Montreat-Anderson College, NC	M(s),W(s)
Mount Vernon Nazarene College, OH	M(s),W(s)
North Park College, IL	M,W
Northwest Christian College, OR	M
Northwestern College, IA	M(s),W(s)
Northwestern College, MN	M,W
Northwest Nazarene College, ID	M(s),W(s)

Nyack College, NY	M(s),W(s)
Olivet Nazarene University, IL	M(s),W(s)
Palm Beach Atlantic College, FL	M
Point Loma Nazarene College, CA	M(s),W(s)
Roberts Wesleyan College, NY	M(s),W(s)
Seattle Pacific University, WA	M(s),W(s)
Simpson College, CA	M(s),W(s)
Sioux Falls College, SD	M(s),W(s)
Southern California College, CA	M(s),W(s)
Southern Nazarene University, OK	M(s),W(s)
Spring Arbor College, MI	M(s),W(s)
Sterling College, KS	M(s),W(s)
Tabor College, KS	M(s),W(s)
Taylor University, IN	M,W
Trevecca Nazarene College, TN	M(s)
Trinity Christian College, IL	M,W
Trinity College, IL	M(s),W(s)
Trinity Western University, BC	M,W
Warner Pacific College, OR	M(s),W(s)
Warner Southern College, FL	M,W
Westmont College, CA	M(s)
Wheaton College, IL	M,W
Whitworth College, WA	M,W
William Jennings Bryan College, TN	M(s),W(s)

Crew

Seattle Pacific University, WA	M,W

Cross-Country Running

Anderson University, IN	M,W
Asbury College, KY	M,W
Azusa Pacific University, CA	M(s),W(s)
Bethel College, MN	M,W
Biola University, CA	M(s),W(s)
Calvin College, MI	M,W
Campbell University, NC	M(s),W(s)
Covenant College, GA	M,W
Eastern College, PA	M(s),W(s)
Eastern Mennonite College, VA	M,W
Eastern Nazarene College, MA	M,W
Evangel College, MO	M(s),W(s)
Fresno Pacific College, CA	M(s),W(s)
Geneva College, PA	M(s),W
George Fox College, OR	M(s),W(s)
Gordon College, MA	M,W
Goshen College, IN	M,W
Grand Canyon University, AZ	M(s),W(s)
Greenville College, IL	M,W
Houghton College, NY	M,W
Huntington College, IN	M(s),W(s)
Indiana Wesleyan University, IN	M(s)
John Brown University, AR	M(s),W(s)
King's College, NY	M(s),W(s)
LeTourneau University, TX	M,W
Malone College, OH	M(s),W(s)
Master's College, CA	M(s),W(s)
Messiah College, PA	M,W
MidAmerica Nazarene College, KS	M(s),W(s)
Mississippi College, MS	M(s)
North Park College, IL	M,W
Northwestern College, IA	M(s),W(s)
Northwestern College, MN	M,W

Olivet Nazarene University, IL	M(s),W(s)
Point Loma Nazarene College, CA	M(s),W(s)
Redeemer College, ON	M,W
Roberts Wesleyan College, NY	M(s),W(s)
Seattle Pacific University, WA	M(s),W(s)
Southern California College, CA	M(s),W(s)
Spring Arbor College, MI	M(s),W(s)
Sterling College, KS	M(s),W(s)
Tabor College, KS	M,W
Taylor University, IN	M,W
Westmont College, CA	M(s),W(s)
Wheaton College, IL	M,W
Whitworth College, WA	M,W

Equestrian Sports

Anderson University, IN	M,W

Field Hockey

Calvin College, MI	W
Eastern College, PA	W(s)
Eastern Mennonite College, VA	W
Gordon College, MA	W
Goshen College, IN	W
Houghton College, NY	W(s)
Indiana Wesleyan University, IN	W(s)
Messiah College, PA	W

Football

Anderson University, IN	M
Azusa Pacific University, CA	M(s)
Bethel College, KS	M(s)
Bethel College, MN	M
Campbellsville College, KY	M
Colorado Christian University, CO	M
Evangel College, MO	M(s)
Geneva College, PA	M(s)
Greenville College, IL	M
MidAmerica Nazarene College, KS	M(s)
Mississippi College, MS	M(s)
North Park College, IL	M
Northwestern College, IA	M(s)
Northwestern College, MN	M
Olivet Nazarene University, IL	M(s)
Sioux Falls College, SD	M(s)
Sterling College, KS	M(s)
Tabor College, KS	M(s)
Taylor University, IN	M
Trinity College, IL	M(s)
Wheaton College, IL	M
Whitworth College, WA	M

Golf

Anderson University, IN	M
Bartlesville Wesleyan College, OK	M
Bethel College, IN	M(s)
Bethel College, MN	M
Calvin College, MI	M
Campbellsville College, KY	M(s)
Campbell University, NC	M(s),W(s)
Central Wesleyan College, SC	M(s)
Colorado Christian University, CO	M
Dordt College, IA	M,W
Goshen College, IN	M
Grace College, IN	M(s)
Grand Canyon University, AZ	M(s)
Greenville College, IL	M
Huntington College, IN	M(s),W(s)
Indiana Wesleyan University, IN	M(s)
Lee College, TN	M(s)
Malone College, OH	M(s)
Messiah College, PA	M

Milligan College, TN	M(s)
Mississippi College, MS	M(s)
Mount Vernon Nazarene College, OH	M(s)
North Park College, IL	M
Northwestern College, IA	M(s),W(s)
Olivet Nazarene University, IL	M
Point Loma Nazarene College, CA	M(s)
Spring Arbor College, MI	M(s)
Taylor University, IN	M
Trinity Christian College, IL	M,W
Trinity College, IL	M(s)
Wheaton College, IL	M

Gymnastics

Seattle Pacific University, WA	W(s)

Ice Hockey

Bethel College, MN	M

Lacrosse

Eastern College, PA	W(s)
Gordon College, MA	M

Rugby

Trinity Western University, BC	M

Soccer

Anderson University, IN	M
Asbury College, KY	M
Azusa Pacific University, CA	M(s),W
Bartlesville Wesleyan College, OK	M(s)
Belhaven College, MS	M(s)
Bethel College, IN	M(s)
Bethel College, KS	M(s)
Bethel College, MN	M
Biola University, CA	M(s)
California Baptist College, CA	M(s)
Calvin College, MI	M,W
Campbell University, NC	M(s)
Central Wesleyan College, SC	M(s)
Colorado Christian University, CO	M(s),W(s)
Covenant College, GA	M(s)
Dordt College, IA	M
Eastern College, PA	M(s)
Eastern Mennonite College, VA	M
Eastern Nazarene College, MA	M
Fresno Pacific College, CA	M(s)
Geneva College, PA	M(s),W(s)
George Fox College, OR	M(s)
Gordon College, MA	M,W
Goshen College, IN	M
Grace College, IN	M(s)
Grand Canyon University, AZ	M(s)
Greenville College, IL	M
Houghton College, NY	M(s),W(s)
Huntington College, IN	M(s)
Indiana Wesleyan University, IN	M(s)
John Brown University, AR	M(s)
Judson College, IL	M(s)
King College, TN	M(s)
King's College, NY	M(s),W(s)
Lee College, TN	M(s)
LeTourneau University, TX	M
Malone College, OH	M(s)
Master's College, CA	M(s)
Messiah College, PA	M,W
Milligan College, TN	M(s)
Montreat-Anderson College, NC	M(s)
Mount Vernon Nazarene College, OH	M(s)
North Park College, IL	M,W

Northwestern College, MN	M
Northwest Nazarene College, ID	M(s)
Nyack College, NY	M(s)
Olivet Nazarene University, IL	M
Palm Beach Atlantic College, FL	M
Point Loma Nazarene College, CA	M(s)
Redeemer College, ON	M,W
Roberts Wesleyan College, NY	M(s),W(s)
Seattle Pacific University, WA	M(s)
Simpson College, CA	M(s)
Southern California College, CA	M(s)
Southern Nazarene University, OK	M(s)
Spring Arbor College, MI	M(s),W(s)
Sterling College, KS	M(s)
Tabor College, KS	M(s)
Taylor University, IN	M
Trinity Christian College, IL	M
Trinity College, IL	M(s),W
Trinity Western University, BC	M
Warner Pacific College, OR	M(s)
Westmont College, CA	M(s),W(s)
Wheaton College, IL	M,W
Whitworth College, WA	M,W
William Jennings Bryan College, TN	M(s)

Swimming and Diving

Asbury College, KY	M,W
Calvin College, MI	M,W
Campbellsville College, KY	M(s),W(s)
Dordt College, IA	M,W
John Brown University, AR	M(s),W(s)
Wheaton College, IL	M,W
Whitworth College, WA	M,W

Tennis

Anderson University, IN	M,W
Asbury College, KY	M,W
Azusa Pacific University, CA	M(s)
Bartlesville Wesleyan College, OK	M
Belhaven College, MS	M(s)
Bethel College, IN	M(s),W(s)
Bethel College, KS	M(s),W(s)
Bethel College, MN	M,W
Biola University, CA	W(s)
California Baptist College, CA	M(s)
Calvin College, MI	M,W
Campbellsville College, KY	M(s),W(s)
Campbell University, NC	M(s),W(s)
Colorado Christian University, CO	M(s),W(s)
Dordt College, IA	M,W
Eastern College, PA	M,W
Eastern Mennonite College, VA	M,W
Eastern Nazarene College, MA	M,W
Geneva College, PA	M(s),W(s)
Gordon College, MA	M,W
Goshen College, IN	M,W
Grace College, IN	M(s)
Grand Canyon University, AZ	M(s)
Greenville College, IL	M,W
Huntington College, IN	M(s),W(s)
Indiana Wesleyan University, IN	M(s)
John Brown University, AR	M(s),W(s)
Judson College, IL	M(s),W
King College, TN	M
Lee College, TN	M(s)
Malone College, OH	M(s),W(s)
Milligan College, TN	M(s),W(s)
Mississippi College, MS	M(s),W(s)
Montreat-Anderson College, NC	M

Tennis (continued)

Mount Vernon Nazarene College, OH	M(s),W(s)
North Park College, IL	M,W
Northwestern College, IA	M(s),W(s)
Nyack College, NY	M,W
Olivet Nazarene University, IL	M,W
Point Loma Nazarene College, CA	M(s),W(s)
Seattle Pacific University, WA	M,W
Sioux Falls College, SD	M(s),W(s)
Southern California College, CA	M
Spring Arbor College, MI	M(s),W(s)
Sterling College, KS	M(s),W(s)
Tabor College, KS	M(s),W(s)
Taylor University, IN	M,W
Trevecca Nazarene College, TN	M(s),W(s)
Trinity College, IL	M(s),W(s)
Westmont College, CA	M(s),W(s)
Wheaton College, IL	M,W
Whitworth College, WA	M,W

Track and Field

Anderson University, IN	M,W
Azusa Pacific University, CA	M(s),W(s)
Bethel College, KS	M(s),W(s)
Bethel College, MN	M,W
Biola University, CA	M(s),W(s)
Calvin College, MI	M,W
Campbell University, NC	M(s),W(s)
Dordt College, IA	M,W
Eastern Mennonite College, VA	M,W
Evangel College, MO	M(s),W(s)
Fresno Pacific College, CA	M(s),W(s)
Geneva College, PA	M(s),W
George Fox College, OR	M(s),W(s)
Goshen College, IN	M,W
Greenville College, IL	M,W
Houghton College, NY	M(s),W(s)
Huntington College, IN	M(s),W(s)
Indiana Wesleyan University, IN	M(s),W(s)
John Brown University, AR	M(s),W(s)
King's College, NY	M(s),W(s)
Malone College, OH	M(s),W(s)
Messiah College, PA	M,W
MidAmerica Nazarene College, KS	M(s),W(s)
Mississippi College, MS	M(s)
North Park College, IL	M,W
Northwestern College, IA	M(s),W(s)
Northwestern College, MN	M,W
Northwest Nazarene College, ID	M(s),W(s)

Point Loma Nazarene College, CA	M(s),W(s)
Roberts Wesleyan College, NY	M(s),W(s)
Seattle Pacific University, WA	M,W
Sioux Falls College, SD	M(s),W(s)
Spring Arbor College, MI	M(s),W(s)
Sterling College, KS	M(s),W(s)
Tabor College, KS	M(s),W(s)
Taylor University, IN	M,W
Trinity Christian College, IL	M,W
Westmont College, CA	M(s),W(s)
Wheaton College, IL	M,W
Whitworth College, WA	M,W

Volleyball

Anderson University, IN	W
Asbury College, KY	W
Azusa Pacific University, CA	W(s)
Bartlesville Wesleyan College, OK	W
Bethel College, IN	W(s)
Bethel College, KS	W(s)
Bethel College, MN	W
Biola University, CA	W(s)
California Baptist College, CA	W(s)
Calvin College, MI	W
Campbell University, NC	W(s)
Central Wesleyan College, SC	W(s)
Colorado Christian University, CO	W(s)
Covenant College, GA	W
Dallas Baptist University, TX	W(s)
Dordt College, IA	W
Eastern College, PA	W(s)
Eastern Mennonite College, VA	W
Eastern Nazarene College, MA	W
Evangel College, MO	W(s)
Fresno Pacific College, CA	W
Geneva College, PA	M,W(s)
George Fox College, OR	W(s)
Gordon College, MA	W
Goshen College, IN	W
Grace College, IN	W(s)
Grand Canyon University, AZ	W(s)
Greenville College, IL	W
Houghton College, NY	W(s)
Huntington College, IN	W(s)
Indiana Wesleyan University, IN	W(s)
John Brown University, AR	W(s)
Judson College, IL	M,W(s)
King College, TN	W(s)
King's College, AB	M,W
King's College, NY	W(s)
Lee College, TN	W
LeTourneau University, TX	W
Malone College, OH	W(s)

Master's College, CA	W(s)
Messiah College, PA	W
MidAmerica Nazarene College, KS	W(s)
Milligan College, TN	W(s)
Mississippi College, MS	W(s)
Montreat-Anderson College, NC	W(s)
Mount Vernon Nazarene College, OH	W(s)
North Park College, IL	M,W
Northwestern College, IA	W(s)
Northwestern College, MN	W
Northwest Nazarene College, ID	W(s)
Nyack College, NY	W
Olivet Nazarene University, IL	W
Palm Beach Atlantic College, FL	W
Point Loma Nazarene College, CA	W(s)
Redeemer College, ON	M,W
Seattle Pacific University, WA	W(s)
Simpson College, CA	M(s),W(s)
Sioux Falls College, SD	W(s)
Southern California College, CA	W(s)
Southern Nazarene University, OK	W(s)
Spring Arbor College, MI	W(s)
Sterling College, KS	W(s)
Tabor College, KS	W(s)
Taylor University, IN	W
Trevecca Nazarene College, TN	W(s)
Trinity Christian College, IL	W
Trinity College, IL	M,W(s)
Trinity Western University, BC	M,W
Warner Pacific College, OR	W(s)
Warner Southern College, FL	W
Westmont College, CA	W(s)
Wheaton College, IL	W
Whitworth College, WA	W
William Jennings Bryan College, TN	W(s)

Wrestling

Campbell University, NC	M(s)
Messiah College, PA	M
Northwestern College, IA	M(s)
Northwestern College, MN	M
Olivet Nazarene University, IL	M(s)
Trinity College, IL	M
Wheaton College, IL	M

STUDY-ABROAD DIRECTORY

S—sponsored by institution; C—cooperatively offered

Africa

Bethel College, MN	C
Calvin College, MI	S
Gordon College, MA	S,C
Greenville College, IL	C
Houghton College, NY	C
Messiah College, PA	S
Wheaton College, IL	C
Whitworth College, WA	C

Amsterdam

Bethel College, MN	S

Australia

Bethel College, MN	C
Taylor University, IN	S

Austria

Bethel College, MN	C
Wheaton College, IL	S

Belize

Gordon College, MA	S
Goshen College, IN	S
Spring Arbor College, MI	S
Whitworth College, WA	S

Bolivia/Peru

George Fox College, OR	S

British Isles

Eastern Mennonite College, WA	S
Whitworth College, WA	S

Central America

Calvin College, MI	C
Eastern Mennonite College, VA	S
George Fox College, OR	S
Grand Canyon University, AZ	C
Greenville College, IL	C
Houghton College, NY	S
Spring Arbor College, MI	S
Whitworth College, WA	S

Costa Rica

Azusa Pacific University, CA	C
Bethel College, MN	C
Eastern Mennonite College, VA	S
Seattle Pacific University, WA	S
Southern California College, CA	S
Southern Nazarene University, OK	S
Westmont College, CA	C
Whitworth College, WA	S

Dominican Republic/Haiti

Azusa Pacific University, CA	C
Goshen College, IN	S

Greenville College, IL	S
Judson College, IL	S
King's College, NY	S,C
Roberts Wesleyan College, NY	S
Spring Arbor College, MI	S
Taylor University, IN	S

East Asia

Azusa Pacific University, CA	C
Wheaton College, IL	S
Whitworth College, WA	S

Eastern Europe

Bethel College, MN	C

East Germany

Bethel College, KS	S
Goshen College, IN	S

Ecuador

Bethel College, MN	S

Egypt

Bethel College, MN	S,C

England

Asbury College, KY	S
Azusa Pacific University, CA	C
Bethel College, KS	S
Bethel College, MN	S,C
Biola University, CA	S
Calvin College, MI	S,C
Eastern College, PA	S
Fresno Pacific College, CA	C
Geneva College, PA	S
George Fox College, OR	S
Gordon College, MA	S
Greenville College, IL	S
Indiana Wesleyan University, IN	S
King College, TN	S
King's College, NY	S,C
Lee College, TN	S
Messiah College, PA	C
Milligan College, TN	S
Mississippi College, MS	C
Montreat-Anderson College, NC	C
Northwest Christian College, OR	S
Nyack College, NY	S
Roberts Wesleyan College, NY	S,C
Taylor University, IN	S
Westmont College, CA	S
Wheaton College, IL	S
Whitworth College, WA	S,C

Europe

Bethel College, MN	C
Biola University, CA	S
Campbellsville College, KY	S
George Fox College, OR	S
Gordon College, MA	S
Grand Canyon University, AZ	S
Greenville College, IL	S
Houghton College, NY	C
Indiana Wesleyan University, IN	S

Judson College, IL	S
King College, TN	S
Lee College, TN	S
Seattle Pacific University, WA	S
Spring Arbor College, MI	S
Taylor University, IN	S,C
Westmont College, CA	S
Wheaton College, IL	S
Whitworth College, WA	S

France

Asbury College, KY	S
Azusa Pacific University, CA	C
Bethel College, KS	C
Bethel College, MN	C
Calvin College, MI	C
Covenant College, GA	C
Fresno Pacific College, CA	C
Goshen College, IN	C
Grace College, IN	S
Greenville College, IL	S
Houghton College, NY	C
King College, TN	S
King's College, NY	S,C
Messiah College, PA	C
Northwestern College, IA	C
Redeemer College, ON	C
Roberts Wesleyan College, NY	S
Taylor University, IN	S
Wheaton College, IL	S
Whitworth College, WA	S,C

Greece

King College, TN	S
Taylor University, IN	S
Whitworth College, WA	S

Guadeloupe

Goshen College, IN	S

Guatemala

Bethel College, MN	C
Fresno Pacific College, CA	S
Malone College, OH	S
Spring Arbor College, MI	S

Honduras

Goshen College, IN	S
Whitworth College, WA	S

Hong Kong

Biola University, CA	S
Gordon College, MA	C
Malone College, OH	C

Israel

Asbury College, KY	C
Azusa Pacific University, CA	C
Bethel College, IN	C
Bethel College, MN	C
Biola University, CA	C
Campbellsville College, KY	S
Covenant College, GA	C
Fresno Pacific College, CA	C

Israel (continued)

Gordon College, MA	C
Grace College, IN	C
Greenville College, IL	S
Houghton College, NY	C
Huntington College, IN	C
Indiana Wesleyan University, IN	C
John Brown University, AR	C
Judson College, IL	C
King College, TN	C
King's College, NY	C
Malone College, OH	C
Master's College, CA	C
Messiah College, PA	C
Mount Vernon Nazarene College, OH	S
North Park College, IL	S
Northwest Christian College, OR	S
Northwestern College, MN	C
Northwest Nazarene College, OR	C
Point Loma Nazarene College, CA	C
Roberts Wesleyan College, NY	C
Seattle Pacific University, WA	C
Simpson College, CA	C
Sioux Falls College, SD	S,C
Southern California College, CA	S,C
Spring Arbor College, MI	C
Sterling College, KS	C
Taylor University, IN	S,C
Westmont College, CA	S,C
Wheaton College, IL	S,C
Whitworth College, WA	S,C
William Jennings Bryan College, TN	C

Jamaica

Bethel College, MN	S
Huntington College, IN	S

Japan

Azusa Pacific University, CA	C
Bethel College, KS	C
Bethel College, MN	S
Eastern College, PA	S
Eastern Mennonite College, VA	S
Grand Canyon University, AZ	S
Houghton College, NY	C
Roberts Wesleyan College, NY	C
Seattle Pacific University, WA	C
Sioux Falls College, SD	S
Whitworth College, WA	C

Kenya

Bethel College, MN	C
Malone College, OH	C

Korea

King College, TN	S
Whitworth College, WA	S,C

Malaysia

Taylor University, IN	S

Mexico

Bethel College, KS	S
Bethel College, MN	C

Biola University, CA	S
Dordt College, IA	S
Fresno Pacific College, CA	S
Geneva College, PA	S
George Fox College, OR	S
Grand Canyon University, AZ	S
Greenville College, IL	S
North Park College, IL	S
Northwestern College, IA	C
Sioux Falls College, SD	S
Whitworth College, WA	S,C

Middle East

Bethel College, KS	S
Eastern Mennonite College, VA	S
George Fox College, OR	S
King College, TN	S

The Netherlands

Bethel College, MN	C
Calvin College, MI	S,C
Dordt College, IA	C
George Fox College, OR	S
Redeemer College, ON	C
Wheaton College, IL	S

New Zealand

Bethel College, MN	C

Paraguay

Bethel College, KS	S

People's Republic of China

Bethel College, KS	C
California Baptist College, CA	S
Eastern Mennonite College, VA	S
Fresno Pacific College, CA	C
Goshen College, IN	S
Grand Canyon University, AZ	S
Sioux Falls College, SD	S
Taylor University, IN	S
Warner Pacific College, OR	C
Whitworth College, WA	C

The Philippines

Bethel College, MN	S

Scandinavia

Bethel College, MN	C

Soviet Union

Bethel College, KS	S
California Baptist College, CA	C
George Fox College, OR	S
Grand Canyon University, AZ	S
Mississippi College, MS	C
Roberts Wesleyan College, NY	S
Warner Pacific College, OR	S

Spain

Azusa Pacific University, CA	C
Bethel College, KS	C

Bethel College, MN	C
Calvin College, MI	S
Covenant College, GA	C
Dordt College, IA	C
Fresno Pacific College, CA	C
Goshen College, IN	C
Grace College, IN	S
Greenville College, IL	S
Houghton College, NY	C
King's College, NY	S,C
Messiah College, PA	C
Seattle Pacific University, WA	S
Trinity Christian College, IL	S

Sweden

North Park College, IL	S

Taiwan

Bethel College, MN	C
Seattle Pacific University, WA	S

Thailand

Whitworth College, WA	C

Tunisia

Bethel College, MN	S

Turkey

Whitworth College, WA	C

Virgin Islands

Bethel College, MN	S

Wales

Bethel College, MN	C
Calvin College, MI	C
Redeemer College, ON	C

West Germany

Azusa Pacific University, CA	C
Bethel College, KS	S
Bethel College, MN	S
Biola University, CA	S
Calvin College, MI	S,C
Covenant College, GA	C
Dordt College, IA	C
Eastern Mennonite College, VA	S
Fresno Pacific College, CA	C
Goshen College, IN	C
Grace College, IN	S
King's College, NY	S,C
Messiah College, PA	C
Mississippi College, MS	C
Wheaton College, IL	S
Whitworth College, WA	S,C

GRADUATE PROGRAMS DIRECTORY

M—master's degree; D—doctoral degree; P—professional degree; O—other advanced degree

Art Education
Calvin College	M
Mississippi College	M,O

Art/Fine Arts
Mississippi College	M

Bilingual and Bicultural Education
Fresno Pacific College	M
Point Loma Nazarene College	M

Biology and Biomedical Sciences
Mississippi College	M

Business Administration and Management
Azusa Pacific University	M,O
Campbell University	M
Dallas Baptist University	M
Eastern College	M
Indiana Wesleyan University	M
Mississippi College	M
Seattle Pacific University	M
Southern Nazarene University	M

Clinical Psychology
Wheaton College	M

Communication
Wheaton College	M

Computer Education
Azusa Pacific University	M

Computer Science
Azusa Pacific University	M

Counseling Psychology
Azusa Pacific University	M
California Baptist College	M
Eastern Nazarene College	M

Counselor Education
Campbell University	M
Fresno Pacific College	M
Mississippi College	M,O
Point Loma Nazarene College	M
Whitworth College	M

Curriculum and Instruction
Campbell University	M,O
Eastern Nazarene College	M
Fresno Pacific College	M
Point Loma Nazarene College	M,O
Seattle Pacific University	M
Simpson College	M
Southern Nazarene University	M
Trevecca Nazarene College	M

Early Childhood Education
Campbell University	O
Dallas Baptist University	M
Eastern Nazarene College	M
Mississippi College	M
Southern Nazarene University	M

Economics
Eastern College	M

Education
Azusa Pacific University	M,D
Biola University	M
Calvin College	M
Campbell University	M,D,O
Dallas Baptist University	M
Eastern Nazarene College	M
Fresno Pacific College	M
Grand Canyon University	M
Mississippi College	M,O
Northwest Nazarene College	M
Point Loma Nazarene College	M,O
Seattle Pacific University	M
Simpson College	M
Sioux Falls College	M
Southern Nazarene University	M
Trevecca Nazarene College	M
Whitworth College	M

Educational Administration
Azusa Pacific University	M,D
Calvin College	M
Campbell University	M,D,O
Fresno Pacific College	M
Mississippi College	M,O
Point Loma Nazarene College	M,O
Seattle Pacific University	M
Whitworth College	M

Education of the Gifted
Whitworth College	M

Education of the Multiply Handicapped
Fresno Pacific College	M

Elementary Education
Campbell University	M
Dallas Baptist University	M
Eastern Nazarene College	M
Mississippi College	M,O
Northwestern College	M
Sioux Falls College	M
Southern Nazarene University	M
Trevecca Nazarene College	M

English
Mississippi College	M,O

English Education
Calvin College	M
Campbell University	M
Dallas Baptist University	M
Mississippi College	O
Southern Nazarene University	M

Finance and Banking
Eastern College	M

Health Education
Whitworth College	M

Health Services Management and Hospital Administration
Eastern College	M
Mississippi College	M

History
Mississippi College	M,O

Home Economics and Human Development
Mississippi College	M

Human Resources Management and Personnel
Eastern College	M

Interdisciplinary Programs in the Humanities and Social Sciences
Mississippi College	M,O
Wheaton College	M

International Business
Azusa Pacific University	M

Journalism
Wheaton College	M

Law
Campbell University	P
Mississippi College	P

Management Information Systems
Seattle Pacific University	M

Marketing

Eastern College   M

Mass and Organizational Communication

Mississippi College   M

Mathematics Education

Campbell University	M
Dallas Baptist University	M
Fresno Pacific College	M
Mississippi College	M,O

Medical Technology

Mississippi College   M

Middle School Education

Campbell University   M

Missions and Missiology

Biola University	M,D
Nyack College	M
Simpson College	M
Wheaton College	M

Music

Azusa Pacific University	M
Mississippi College	M
Seattle Pacific University	M
Warner Pacific College	M

Music Education

Calvin College	M
Mississippi College	M

Nursing

Azusa Pacific University	M
Indiana Wesleyan University	M

Pastoral Ministry and Counseling

Azusa Pacific University	M
Bethel College	M
Eastern Nazarene College	M
Indiana Wesleyan University	M
Warner Pacific College	M

Pharmacy

Campbell University   P

Philosophy

Point Loma Nazarene College   M

Physical Education and Human Movement Studies

Azusa Pacific University	M
Campbell University	M
Seattle Pacific University	M

Physical Therapy

Mississippi College   M

Psychology

Biola University	M,D
Geneva College	M

Public and Community Health

Indiana Wesleyan University   M

Public Health Nursing

Indiana Wesleyan University   M

Radio, Television, and Film

Wheaton College   M

Reading

Calvin College	M
Dallas Baptist University	M
Eastern Nazarene College	M
Fresno Pacific College	M
Seattle Pacific University	M
Sioux Falls College	M
Southern Nazarene University	M
Whitworth College	M

Religion

Azusa Pacific University	M
Dallas Baptist University	M
Eastern Nazarene College	M
Huntington College	M
Northwest Christian College	M
Northwest Nazarene College	M
Nyack College	M
Point Loma Nazarene College	M
Seattle Pacific University	M
Simpson College	M
Southern California College	M
Southern Nazarene University	M
Trevecca Nazarene College	M
Warner Pacific College	M

Religious Education

Calvin College	M
Wheaton College	M

Science Education

Calvin College	M
Campbell University	M

(unlabeled)

Fresno Pacific College	M
Mississippi College	M

Secondary Education

Campbell University	M
Eastern Nazarene College	M
Mississippi College	M,O

Social Sciences Education

Calvin College	M
Campbell University	M
Mississippi College	O

Sociology

Mississippi College   M

Special Education

Azuda Pacific University	M
Calvin College	M
Eastern Nazarene College	M
Fresno Pacific College	M
Point Loma Nazarene College	M
Whitworth College	M

Speech and Interpersonal Communication

Southern Nazarene University   M

Speech-Language Pathology and Audiology

Mississippi College   M

Sports Administration

Seattle Pacific University   M

Teaching English as a Second Language

Azusa Pacific University   M,O

Theology

Anderson University	M,P
Azusa Pacific University	M,P
Biola University	M,D,P
Calvin College	M
Huntington College	M
Master's College	P
Nyack College	M,P
Seattle Pacific University	M
Simpson College	M
Southern Nazarene University	M
Wheaton College	M,O

GEOGRAPHICAL INDEX OF COLLEGES AND UNIVERSITIES